plume
ANTHOLOGY OF
poetry
5

edited by Daniel Lawless

MADHAT PRESS
ASHEVILLE, NORTH CAROLINA

MadHat Press
MadHat Incorporated
PO Box 8364, Asheville, NC 28814

The Library of Congress has assigned
this edition a Control Number of
2017930592

ISBN 978-1-941196-43-4 (paperback)

Book layout and design by F. J. Bergmann
Cover design by Marc Vincenz

PlumePoetry.com
MadHat-Press.com

Il semble que la joie de lire soit le reflet de la joie d'écrire comme si le lecteur était le fantôme de l'écrivain.

—Gaston Bachelard, *La poétique de l'espace*

"*Plume*'s apparent lack of a narrow editorial policy (except a fondness for interesting poems) makes for lots of strange bedfellows, but what was the last time that was a bad idea?"
~ *Billy Collins*

"Of all the things that might claim one's attention, and they are in the multitudes! *Plume* is well worth making time for since it isn't just another magazine. Its difference? Wonderful work, on the edge, room for play and dash, new forms, a great discerning editor in Danny Lawless!"
~ *Tess Gallagher*

"*Plume* is one of the most exciting, eclectic gatherings of writers on the web. Editor Daniel Lawless has a knack for putting together voices that create surprising neighborhoods of words, related in complex ways that only gradually reveal themselves. It's one of very few webzines that I always read."
~ *Chase Twichell*

"*Plume* is rapidly becoming one of the best places in America to read poetry, online and in print, thanks to the untiring efforts of Danny Lawless. It's where to find dazzling work by new and established writers, and, thanks to the new technology, it is available instantly to readers by the millions. *Plume* proves once more that poetry is essential to our lives, and that 'Men die every day for want of what is found in it.'"
~ *Grace Schulman*

"*Plume* continues to publish amazing poets in beautiful formats—both online and in-print. The magazine has an exciting vision, embracing a broad gamut of poetries, including collaborations. The work has a consistently intriguing quality about the joys and unsettling aspects of being alive."
~ *Denise Duhamel*

"*Plume* is a new force in the poetry world, bringing together, in its online zine and in this anthology, a unique, eclectic and impressive group of poets."
- Rae Armantrout

"I've never seen a literary magazine become so important so quickly. I have no idea how Daniel Lawless does it, but I dare anyone to find another journal that contains 1) the high quality of the individual poems, 2) the wide range of voices and styles, and 3) the large number of leading voices in contemporary American poetry. I would love to see all these poets in the same room, but I'll take them here, all in the same book."
- Jim Daniels

"I usually hate to read poems on the computer but *Plume* has changed my mind. It is attractive, well-edited, and possesses the compelling virtue of being concise—not too many poems, not too few. Since I always end up wanting to print out one or two, I'm grateful for Danny Lawless's equally exciting, good-looking, and well-chosen, *Plume* anthologies."
- Lawrence Raab

"*Plume* is a gathering place where strangers become old friends. Each issue is a celebration of images and words that touch the heart and bind us together as community."
- Lawrence Matsuda

"The first word I remember using to describe Danny Lawless's online *Plume* was the word elegant. And now I discover that the word derives from a Latin verb for *to select*. *Plume* endeavors to select and showcase— yes, elegantly—the best poems of the twenty-first century. *Plume* not only encourages, it honors poetry."
- Ron Smith

"*Plume* is a gem—in the rare-and-wondrous-find sense. Each issue is a hand-plucked, precisely curated composition, tended with great care, full of mystery, and delivering batches of the freshest, most provocative, and necessary writing around. Danny Lawless's vision is exquisite."
~ *Lia Purpura*

"Though I've been known to shy away from online publications, I'm an avid reader of *Plume*, a beautifully designed monthly periodical featuring an international selection of works by some of today's best poets. Hard to beat that."
~ *William Trowbridge*

"Plume (Noun): An anthology or journal of fine writing edited with passion and immaculate attention to detail.
"Plume (Verb): To erupt with energy, enthusiasm and poetic spirit. To dazzle.
"Derivative of Plume: Plumelike (Adjective): As fine as down and as lively as peacock feathers.
"Origins of *Plume*: American, but with an internationalist bent, some time during the 2000s."
~ *John Kinsella*

Daniel Lawless has a gift for publishing poets who not only represent the breadth and depth at which the art is practiced today, but who together make—how to say it?—a feisty crowd, their proximity in the pages of *Plume* creating all sorts of surprising angles of vision. There's nothing rote in Daniel's editorial choices, nothing of what Emerson called "a foolish consistency." His assemblages of poems, images, and editorial musings have a hand-crafted, one-of-a-kind feel. That's why there's ever cause for celebration when another *Plume*, whether online or in print, makes its way into the world.
~ *Clare Rossini*

"*Plume* magazine is an anomaly of taste: any literary dwelling that can shelter under one roof a family of poets as distantly related as Rae Armantrout, James Richardson, Kim Addonizio, Jorie Graham, Linda Pastan, G.C. Waldrep, Grace Schulman, Carl Phillips, Sharon Olds, Billy Collins, and more, must be both capacious and *odd*. What in the world unites these writers, one thinks? And then one reads an issue of *Plume* with the dawning recognition what they have in common is Danny Lawless, the founder and editor of this superb new journal. Lawless has the audacity to choose the poets he loves, and believes are writing *good* poetry, no matter on what wildly disparate branch of the family tree he finds them. And then he gets these poets to send him poems. *Plume* establishes its place on the literary scene somewhere above fashion, apart from all questions of Hipster vs. ... whatever. The work within its pages has the unpredictable, idiosyncratic strength of things that haunt, and may endure."
- *Jeffrey Skinner*

"Always astonishing and diverse in content, *Plume* is one of our most elite and essential online journals and a roving museum of contemporary poetry curated by Daniel Lawless. 'Glancing blow' after glancing blow, it makes me hungry, ad infinitum, for the strange and beautiful—and the annual anthology is a sumptuous feast of enduring American poetry."
- *Mark Irwin*

"Like a bird landing in the absent shadow of a bird,
Plume has gorgeously and unabashedly
taken up residence inside an inner vane, an ache
in contemporary poetry, and sunk its hooklets in.
Now many of us cannot exist without it,
so drab and songless does a world without *Plume* seem to seem...."
- *Robin Behn*

"Like *Antaeus* and *Ironwood,* two of the greatest American poetry magazines of the past fifty years, *Plume* is eclectic in the most purposeful and pleasurable of ways. In a very short amount of time, Danny Lawless has made it a 'must-read' like no other. *Plume* is one of my favorite sources for new poetry—online or in print. Thoughtful, entertaining, capacious, with no use for aesthetic axe-grinding, its highly-enriched oxygen will add energy to your life!"
~ *David Rivard*

"Among the new magazines of recent years in print and on-line formats, one—*PLUME*—stands above all the rest and offers us both venues.What a delight it is to read the work of newcomers beside the poems of poets I've followed for years! The eclecticism of the editor's taste never ceases to amaze me. I just used the print anthology in my Advanced Poetry Writing Workshop at Tulane and the students echoed my enthusiasm.
~ *Peter Cooley*

THE PLUME ANTHOLOGY OF POETRY is a wild and lovely gathering of poems and poets. Lawless has pulled together a time and place in a selection of some of the most interesting work being done.
~ *Laura Kasischke*

Elegant *Plume* appeared with the flourish of a cyberquill pen in 2011 and quickly became the place where superlative poets showcase their brightest work. Editor Danny Lawless displays his adoration for electric, emotional and, dare I say, meaningful poetry—and for poets themselves—with all the vigor of a steward of this art. Once a year the revered, sparky, sagacious *Plume* comes into print, subtly changing our cultural foundations. Hold it, read it, and applaud!
~ *Molly Peacock*

Reading *Plume* is like having a conversation with your best friend, your best self, and all the people who love the world in its beauty and craziness.
~ *Barbara Hamby*

Preface
Chard deNiord

This year's edition of the *Plume Anthology*, the fifth in as many years, contains a teeming collection of poems by an equally diverse omnibus of poets and translators. The aesthetic spectrum of strong voices in this volume testifies to the expansive vision of its editor, Daniel Lawless, who has for the last five years created an invaluable, poetic "news" service with his online poetry journal, *Plume*, and yearly hard-copy anthology.

Walt Whitman wrote prophetically of the poet in his preface to *Leaves of Grass*, "He is the arbiter of the diverse, and he is the key." Whitman wisely leaves this sentence in limbo, just as he does his advice to poets in his poem "Poets to Come" which he concludes with these challenging lines, "Leaving it to you to prove and define it, / Expecting the main things from you." But how to choose an adequate selection of poems from today's unwieldy abundance of contemporary poetry that captures the "main things"—poems that define the *Zeitgeist* of our age as *the news that stays news*, to quote Ezra Pound? How to provide a literary forum large enough to showcase those poets who witness either privately or publically to the agons of our time—extinction, terrorism, genocide, "fake news," climate change, rampant despotism, religious intolerance—in memorable language? How to sustain the integrity of the lyrical and narrative "I" in a time when the world cries out for disinterested witnessing?

While there may be no single answer to these questions, Daniel Lawless has accepted Whitman's challenge to edit as an "arbiter of the diverse." With a catholic but fine-tuned ear for what Emily Dickinson called "adequate" verse; that is, superb poetry, Lawless has assembled another motley collection of riveting, poignant, and timely poems in his latest *Plume* anthology that range in their topics from modern relationships to urban desolation, to end-time lists, to eschatological landscapes, to the loose shoelaces of America, to the assumptions of two by twos, to fate writ large on a forehead, to "fuck me, fuck me not," to atavistic nostalgia, to Mandelstam's widow, to roadside shrines, to a mysterious woman dancing before a mirror, to a dead-bird theory of everything, to "mom's red convertible," to the elegiac scent of vermouth, to serving the "mandatory minimum … in the "white project," these poems. These selections reflect an overdue inclusivity in American poetry anthology-making that enlightens because of their eclectic array rather than in spite of it. Lawless has, since the inception of *Plume*, set out to mine the accomplished "new" with unslaked interest in just that, what he has described specifically as "the fineness of language, the huge absences to which it points and partakes of, and the urgency and permanence of its state of departure—the coattails forever—just now—disappearing around the corner."

As in the previous four *Plume* anthologies, the 2016 edition provides a bounty of vital new poems concatenating in an ironic chorus of diverse voices that nonetheless harmonize in their common human witness to what Philip Levine called "the news of the world."

Introduction

Brevity, I promise, will be my watchword here, readers—for I know what treasures await you.

A moment, though, to pick up the thread of the previous two introductions, wherein I addressed the past—the "origin myth"—of the Plume anthologies, and the at-that-time present; here I will try to imagine what the future might hold in store. To that end, I thought I'd change things up this time: a self-interview.

DL: *Hello, Daniel. Nice to meet you. Or do you prefer Dan, or Danny?*

DL: Nice to meet you, Daniel. Daniel's fine, or Danny. Not really a "Dan" guy. I can't say why—never met a "Dan" I liked, actually. Very solid name, though, outgoing, confident: *Dan Lawless. How the hell are you?* So, naturally, gives me the creeps a little. Sorry, Dans of the world.

DL: *OK, then. Danny it is, then. Or Daniel?*

DL: Really, either is fine. Your choice.

DL: *Let's go with Danny.*

DL: Hang on. I think … let's go with Daniel, if you don't mind. Kind of stuffy, though, isn't it? Look good on a lanyard, fourth down on the Insurance Committee …

DL: *Right. Daniel. So, Daniel …*

DL: Or maybe Danny is better. Danny Lawless—in ye olde punk days no one believed it was my real name. My dad, not a sentimental man by any means, called me Danny Boy sometimes, well once or twice, and I remember I loved it for some reason. Great song, too, of course. What did Ben Johnson say? "There's a woundy luck in names."

DL: *So, Danny?*

DL: Danny. Definitely Danny.

DL: *All right, Danny, now that that's cleared up …* Plume *has been a* *remarkable success, you know. Lots of people tell me they've never seen anything like it. Can you identify some elements that have contributed to this phenomenon?*

DL: Milk spatters in my baptismal cup, a gold ring around the clouds ...

DL: *Pardon?*

DL: Sorry. It's a quote from an Aragon poem. The poet gives "surreal" answers to the interviewer's questions. Bad joke.

DL: *Oh ...*

DL: No, no. Quite all right. But, I think I covered that ground in the last two introductions.

DL: *OK. The future of Plume? Given the history of literary journals, particularly online ones, let's start with an existential question. Do you think there is a future for Plume?*

DL: I hope so, I really do. I mean, it's a pain in the ass sometimes, getting the issues out every month—editing, layout, all that—setting up readings, writing those Editor's Notes I seriously doubt anyone reads—I mean, do we really need one more story extracted from my childhood?—the newsletter, finding cover art. But, I do have help for some of those things—a truly marvelous staff. Best of all, however, I get to read, every day, such superb work, mind-blowingly good, often. Poets who shouldn't even think of sending somewhere like *Plume*— let's face it, not a "big" name by any stretch—let alone gratis—do, in fact, send their poems to us. Why, I don't know. I've stopped asking, afraid it'll jinx it.... I'm with Simic—"Don't wake up the damn cards."

DL: *That's very modest of you. Is that honestly how you feel?*

DL: Word. No one says that anymore though, do they? Yes, that is honestly how I feel.

DL: *I take it then that you believe Plume will be around for a while?*

DL: I do. I talked to a poet the other day, he's in his nineties, very refined gentleman as far as I know, read everything, gorgeous poems, and he said he absolutely hates when people ask him if he is retired. It was pretty funny, I didn't expect his answer at all, as I say he didn't seem the type, but he shot back his answer or rather the answer he'd like to give, "Like, what the fuck else am I going to do? Play golf?" That's how it is with *Plume*. And that's the thing about the arts, writing especially, you can do it until you drop dead, and many have.

DL: *So you don't see handing over the reins at some point?*

DL: Maybe the day to day stuff, if I get completely knackered or arthritic or go blind or fall prey to some other illness—which is certainly a possibility—but reading the work, arranging each issue so it makes some kind of sense, to me at least, the same with the anthologies, no, I think that will continue.

DL: *Surely there will be changes, though? Over the last five years we've seen* Plume *alter its web design, add new material. I'm thinking of the Featured Selection, the Book Reviews, the Essays and Comment column, none of which were present in the first issues. Can we expect this expansion to continue, if we can call it that?*

DL: You'd think so, wouldn't you? But the truth is, we're running out of space, and I don't want to stray too far from our original format. Our readers seem to like the not too big-not too small element: twelve poems—sometimes I sneak in a few more with Two Poems by so and so—that Editor's Note, an interesting photograph (I hope), and now the three new additions.

DL: *I agree. It's what drew me to* Plume …

DL: On the other hand—excuse me for interrupting—I *am* interested in incorporating more audio-visual material—I have a line on, I met this guy, a poet and archivist, recently, and he has an amazing collection of interviews with poets—Creeley, Bly, everybody. I'm trying to figure out how to approach him to see if he'd let us run them in *Plume*. Then I'd have to figure out the technical side, where I'm worse than useless, and as I said, find a place for them on the homepage. If we do get the OK from him, which is not certain by any means, I imagine we'll change the website to accommodate them. They're fascinating, and it's something I believe our readers would find fascinating.

DL: *Was this something you've thought about for some time, something you've had in the works, as it were?*

DL: Ha! No. Complete accident. Like most things with *Plume*.

DL: *Anything other "accidents" you can foresee? Although I guess they wouldn't be accidents then.*

DL: Right. No, not in terms of design, unless that new website becomes necessary. Content, maybe. I'd like to, well, I'd love to be much more diverse. As of now, we're fairly monochrome, and that's on me. I came into poetry reading the Europeans, the French, obviously, and the Germans, mostly, but also the Poles, the Romanians, the Scandinavians, you could guess the names. What I didn't read much of were people of color, neither American nor from anywhere else. Very few of the poets from Japan or Vietnam, say, or the South Pacific. Some South Americans. I don't know why. I had this sensibility, I guess, an affinity for the Old World—god, it sounds so stupid now that I say it out loud. But there it is: myopic, isn't it? I could go on about this for hours, and have here and there in other interviews, but in end, it's my responsibility—no, that's not the word -- it's I who have deprived myself, and so our readers, of the immense pleasures of reading any number of poets who in any light are the equals if not the superiors of many of the poets who regularly appear in our pages. I definitely need to do a much better job of seeking out these poets and getting them published in *Plume*. I've started—some poets I know have been a tremendous help with this—but we have a long way to go. I think that's one change you'll see in future—*Plume*, reaching out to poets of color and getting their work to our readers, and it won't be an "accident." I think we're doing well, gender-representation-wise, and I don't think we're locked in to any particular school or approach. In fact, I'm pretty sure of that, and I take some pride in that—we "have no aesthetic axe to grind," as one of our blurbs has it. I like very much that there will be poems people hate and people love side by side in the issues. That tension, that discomfort, is a good thing, in my book. Charles Bernstein, G. C. Waldrep, Jane Hirshfield, so-called new formalists like Molly Peacock and Phillis Levin, maybe a translation of Andre du Bouchet or Hsia Yü—always looking for more translated work, which we run with the originals—a prose poem by Rachel Carreau or Lydia Davis—that's a nice line-up. And fairly typical for us.

DL: *So we can expect more work from people of color and more work in translation in the future. And possibly an audio-visual presence. What else?*

DL: I'd like to have a more balanced presentation of emerging poets. We do well in publishing very established poets, and mid-career poets, but lag somewhat in offering work from young ones. And there are so many! Again, this is an area in which I, as editor, need to step up. And I will—I think it will be greatly to the journal's benefit.

DL: *Have you considered running advertisements or holding contests? Or the big one—charging reading fees? A contentious issue at the moment. I don't know what your funding is like.*

DL: For the first few years *Plume* was self-funded—but that might be misleading. I'm not a millionaire, more like a thousandaire. On the other hand, it doesn't require a lot of money to publish an online journal, really. For the past two years, my college, Saint Petersburg College, has been very generous in supporting our efforts, for which I am deeply grateful. Now, this will, or may, change when I retire in a couple of years, who knows? When I go, *Plume* goes with me. I can only hope that we will stay connected to the college in some way and that they will continue to throw some funding our way. We'll see. But for now, no ads, no contests, no reading fees. They just don't sit right with me, aside from the aesthetic challenges—I'm speaking of ads—and they involve a lot of work, a lot of administration, and I just don't have the time for them. Regarding the reading fees, I know this is silly, but I read every submission—no first or second readers—and I guess I'd feel obliged in some way—the same as at yard sales, which I never attend anymore, because when I go I feel I have to buy something so that I won't be hurting the seller's feelings. I know the analogy isn't perfect, but what I'm trying to say is in there somewhere. Finally, I'm trying to give my own work more attention, as well.

DL: *Will there ever be a Danny Lawless poem in* Plume*?*

DL: No.

DL: *What are you most excited about, as you look to the years ahead, apart from the things you have just mentioned?*

DL: Plume Editions. How's that for a short, declarative answer? In conjunction with MadHat Press, we've published two books so far this year—the Tess Gallagher/Lawrence Matsuda collaboration *Boogie-Woogie CrissCross*, and Nin Andrews' *Our Lady of the Orgasm*. And we have on the way W. S. Di Piero's *The Man on the Water*, Christopher Buckley's *Chaos Theory*, and *Plume—The Interviews*, which Nancy Mitchell and I co-edited, taking pieces from the Featured Selections. Others in the pipeline. Terrific poets, *huge*, to use the current term. Very exciting. Oh, and the readings—we just came back from Asheville, and we were recently in Cambridge again. We have an astonishing roster lined up for AWP in Washington, DC, and after that I imagine we'll go to the West Coast, L.A. or Seattle, and maybe back to Paris, or to London or perhaps Dublin in the Spring.

DL: *Last—and I can't believe I forgot to ask about this—can you say a few words about this anthology,* Plume Poetry 5*? After all, this interview is to form the introduction of the print anthology, if I have it right!*

DL: You're right, that was to be the subject, wasn't it? Let's see. I think that almost all of what we've talked about so far applies equally to the anthologies. Of course, it's larger this time—about 400 pages as of now. Absolutely stellar poets writing at the top of their game. After an uneven start, Marc Vincenz has stabilized the cover art—I love it for all sorts of reasons. Now we have a "brand," and each succeeding cover will retain the current design elements with only the changing colors to mark each year's volume. He does the layout, too. I'm not quite sure who will be writing the preface this time; we'll cross that bridge soon, however. Daniel Tobin's was masterful last year, and before that Terese Svoboda's. But all of the important aspects of *Plume*—its eclecticism, the quality of work—all new work, by the way, not recycled from the online issues— remain very much the same in the print format. After its debut at AWP in February, we'll begin touring a bit in support of the book, as I said.

DL: *Just quickly—why the dual iterations of* Plume, *digital and print?*

DL: I think people like both—the instant availability of the online version and its relative smallness; I know many of our readers connect with us on their phones, reading a poem or essay here or there on the subway, walking down the street, in a waiting room, what have you. But they also enjoy the physical presence of the print anthologies— they tell me this all the time. And I get it; I do, too. Old school. Yet it—print—retains its charms, its advantages, as all readers know. Just look at the success of the indie bookstores. And the printing expenses have come down, so it's not a budget-killer as it once was, probably. A big expense is mailing out contributor's copies, especially overseas. But, c'mon, these poets have handed over, without charge, their best work, which often represents hours and hours of labor—I'm not complaining. It is the very least we can do.

DL: *Well, it's been a pleasure, Danny. Any last words—I don't like the sound of that!—I mean, any parting remarks, words of wisdom from the editor?*

DL: Yes, a pleasure! Parting remarks? None come to mind. A lot of thank-you's, though—to the poets, first—I wish I could name each and every one, here, and extend my most profound gratitude to them. And our readers, of course! And not just the ones who we publish, but those who think enough of our little adventure to want to join us, sending their poems through Submittable, so faithfully. I'd say 50–60% of the poems I see there are from poets with a book or sometimes several books under their belt, lists of awards and prestigious publications. It's hard, saying "no," believe me. But I think our loss is someone else's gain—other journals will snap them up and eventually readers will see them. Then there is our staff—Marc Vincenz, Nancy Mitchell, Helene Cardona, Robert Archmbeau, Adam Tavel, Steve Elder, Bryan Duffy. I came across the word "cracker-jack" today, somewhere, and it fits here: they are a constant wonder. So gifted. Tireless. Professional in the best way. Jason Cook, who inspired the whole shebang and designed our first website. Scott at MassiveAnt, our tech guru. My wife, Donna, who now does the layout for the online issues. A team effort, as corny s that sounds.

DL: *Not corny at all … well, a little corny.*

DL: A lot corny, but who cares? All true, I swear.

DL: *Thank you for your time, and good luck to you and to* Plume, *whatever it becomes.*

DL: Thank you.

Daniel Lawless
Editor, *Plume*
December 2016

Contents

The palm reader
~ Ekiwah Adler-Beléndez

These blithe lines
across your open upturned hand—seem

to do absolutely nothing.

But watch how the small marks
that ring the summit of your five fingers
trickle down through even thinner rivulets of wrinkles
to turn into the widening noiseless
streams of your palm.

Certain lines
plummet way past the edges of your bones
and converge in a whirlpool of nearly endless space
where their flowing—remains invisible.

Yet as you wait
you can hear and see them this time
rushing out of you
and past you again

these lines from your hand
that I type and sound out now
through the channel of your half-opened mouth
and spiraling fingertips.

Calendars Do Not Hold Fortunes
~ Kelli Russell Agodon

One day you're old and thankful. One day
you're buying a guitar and searching
for your favorite pen and notebook. One day,
you scream at another driver. One day you open
the jewelry box to find the ring
you thought you lost. One day
the ring is God. One day
a knock on the door—a delivery,
a lost dog is found. One day a friend asks
how she can help. One day *A Streetcar
Named Desire*, a glass of wine, and a breakdown.
One day you're leaning too close
to the stranger on your left. One day
you drop your keys in a parking lot and pray
for the best. One day the biopsy is cancerous, one day,
but not today.

Murmur of A Modern-Day Relationship
~ Kelli Russell Agodon

If it's not broken it doesn't belong to us.

We are boundless when we stargaze at the ocean,
looking for falling stars in the seaglass.

What shall we trouble about?

The gin fizz of the whitecaps or the vodka
sundowner behind the mountains?

We are comparing nature to cocktails,
trying to relax on the edge
of a thirsty ocean.

If it's not broken it doesn't belong
to my body, your body. We set a blanket
on the sand and tried to undress.

It takes a long time to remember the ocean
is inside of us when we are falling, under

stars landing in the shallow
tidepools. There is no answer in the waves

yet all that endless grousing,
constantly drowning our faulty hearts.

Caffè Dolce
~Sandra Alcosser

I think I shall end by not feeling lonesome
Van Gogh wrote to his brother Theo

And here at the Mall could it be the same—
Mother waiting under an ancient clock face

She dips a chocolate biscotti
Into the latté of a Stranger Sea—

People treat me like I am a piece
Of them—which is what I want to be

In case anyone should ever ask—she lies
On a cot at night to memorize her life

Story—Van Gogh painted his walls fresh-butter yellow
Painted *friendship* starboard on a beached blue boat

He wanted to flame us each with haloes
For the wilderness we wear like hope

Enlaced
~ Sandra Alcosser

Unable to eat—unable to take
the Host—Saint Juliana begs to kiss Jesus
And so on linen a wafer is placed
that blazes a cross upon her breast

Love is migration—a pilgrim weighted
by sores by cleaving and empty space
and when love walks in the shadow of death
how voluptuous it becomes—the taste
of flesh tatted with pain—Heloise unwed
to Abelard—chose concubine
over empress—whore above wife
and lovers became nun and castrate

dropped face-to-face in the same
grave—by kissing a soul enlaced

Studio
~ Meena Alexander

for Cecilia Edefalk

I was on an island where few birds call.
Old trees swirled in the wind.

The door to my studio tore off
Stones struck clouds, church bells echoed

—Earthly unsettlement.
Forced to go on, what did I do?

I pulled down a wall,
Set up another with pasteboard,

Tacked a strip of mirror all along the floor
Till white plaster was afloat, gravity unhinged.

The lights I had set up fell to one side
I stepped through the mirror to touch her—

She was that sort of being, what was the word
You gave me—*sakshi*, yes, that.

No one would see her seeing, I thought
Without themselves being altered in some way

So in the end she could have a chance
Of being saved from all the body remembers.

I took the face, making it very precise,
Filling in the eyes with several strokes

Reddening under the lids—fire turned to blood,
Each element as the Gnostics tell us

Resolved into its own roots.
The neck of course is simple and straight.

She is in a white dress as usual,
A child whose mother

Takes pleasure in dressing her well.
In the end my hands were pocked

And bruised with paint
And when I lifted them off the canvas

I felt something warm,
Very like torn skin fluttering off.

Mystic Teashop
~ Meena Alexander

You come to me and I am full of noises,
That curl in the crevices of ribcage, hollows of wrist
You stroke me, tiny syllables thrum.

In winter light I quiver and twitch.
Walking with me to a teashop on 32nd street
You think—Here's a woman quite beside her self

Shall we take tea at a table set by the Muses—
Erato who fled in a taxi, abandoning
A room of starched linen, glass vessels, fretted gold

And cold Melpomene whose petticoat is sodden,
Whose lips have sipped all the tea in India and China
And still cries out for more.

Field
~ Pamela Alexander

Crows amid the stubble, kernels
like coins. Counting-house.

Around the fenceposts, late fall blooms.
Butterfly tongues unroll like black
party horns, soprano above
the continuo of bees. Fewer
of these flower tenders
each year. Fewer
flowers.
       Same amount
of light: field
on field.

The third time we passed the cornfield he said
Yes the birds have found it now.

The flowers bees board
capsize. Cool sugar
on mouth parts. Pollen stippling
black feet, striped fur.

Crow feathers
flash blue, bronze.

The first time we passed it he said
You'll see this field full of birds.

All of them, and fence and bee,
made of sunlight, a given. We
thicken and pulse with it.

And then none.
Black and gold. Been and gone.

Hammock full of leaves.

Truck bed full of snow.

Skull I found in the desert,
full of bees.

Backs of Shopping Centers
~ Dick Allen

There's little to say for them, these places
of cracked asphalt,
trash bins and dumpsters,
back doors propped open by old concrete blocks,

except how gun-metal gray they are,
and littered with cigarette butts,
lunch break cellophane bags
blown into wire fences.

Shall you declare your love against
splashed paint, scattered graffiti,
or on an unswept loading dock
drop to your knees, staring into nothing?

At night, the feral cats
slip through their darknesses;
the moon illuminates these hidden parking lots,
a friend of my daughter's blew his brains out here.

The Road, the Barn, the Hill
~ Dick Allen

What we don't tell you, the poet said, is that often
we write about one thing to not
write about another. Often
I'll write about a road or barn to not

write about my failing health, how steadily
it fails, how it's sometimes like floating
down steadily
and other times instead of floating,

it's like plunging downward in a broken grain elevator,
with buttons I keep pushing to make it stop,
inwardly yelling as the elevator
(up there, I could see forever) won't stop,

and that's why, on most fearsome days,
a poet may describe a road that curves beside a hill
and a barn upon that hill—day after day
the certain solid shapes of road and barn and hill,

words focusing upon the light
flooding the hill and cast upon the road,
with nothing other on that hill than light
upon the barn just there beside the road.

Dead Doll
~ Nathalie Anderson

1.

Too thin-skinned always, the sort
best kept to a shelf, yet always
he was skying, he was always
avalanching himself. So first

as if frost bit, of the one hand gone
the fingers; then, fist first, the other
as if frost-beaten, ice-shivered,
the whole arm from the arm-hole gone

as if wholly eaten; and the left foot
crushed off; of the foot left uncrushed
the Achilles heel gone flimsy; and
on the last limb a piercing—

curved elegance, a Bodhi-leaf
whimsy curled to the arm and
tattooed through, a piercing third-eye
gaze into nothing—but otherwise

unchanged for nearly sixty years,
that baby face not aging a day, lips
pinked and pursed, cheeks and chin plumped in
full as his sister's, and the same rolled hair.

2.

Well, that's all done. This last fall's
cold-cocked him, knocked him cock-eyed, crack-
pated. His jaunty hat's turned skull-cap, blows
and bowls about, pawn for every cat's paw. Clothes

make the man, they say—and unmake:
his sister bends at the hip, sits tight beneath her dirndl
wherever you leave her. Stuck from the start
in stiff lederhosen, he could always ever only

stand and fall, stand and fall. One of a passel
smuggled post-war through the checkpoints
by my kindly Aunt Corinne: plumed aristo,
oak-foot Dutch girl, tammed and wild-haired Scot—

all of them shock-eyed, all of them shaky, all of them
standing nevertheless their new ground, and him
the lone rover. Now for sure he's Euro-trash: crack-up,
casualty, cavity, chasm. That's what jaunty gets you.

3.

Were I Isis, I'd be picking up the pieces, lifting
his face, backing that jigsaw with muslin,
getting precise with tweezer and glue-stick. But no,
I'm not that girl. Stay put, don't go anywhere,

I tell his sister: these sixty-some-odd years I've
been bossing her around. She doesn't move a muscle,
doesn't turn a hair—but lately, when I glance her way,
she's standing, balanced, digging in the baby-doll toes

you can see through the boot black, the child
she still is shaping her face to her brother's, pursing
the baby-doll lips as though wondering where
he's gone. I think she's thinking she's been good too long.

Spun
~ Rae Armantrout

As sadder than ever
may represent
the new
among today's
offerings.

      *

As representation
is magical
spun straw.

      *

After what passes for thought,
she leans forward, extracts
a honey-flavored cough drop
from its yellow packaging.

Funnel
~ Rae Armantrout

Target a high
value audience low

in the purchasing
funnel.

              Coke

has always been about
inclusion

The Quick Brown Fox Jumped Over The Lazy Dog
~ Simon Armitage

Ever since you closed the door behind you I've been a
regular visitor to a website called Less Than 100 Grams.
Dedicated to collectable ephemera of a throwaway
nature and presented in the style of an old magazine
or periodical, its twelve published issues thus far showcase
bottle tops, vintage erasers, model animals (including
a grumpy-looking rhinoceros and a plastic cow), old
postage stamps, toothbrushes, guitar picks (what I would
have called plectrums), neckties, antique bookmarks,
matchbox labels, Polaroid photographs and airline
luggage tags. Issue thirteen features deformed plastic
soldiers in the shape of letters, manipulated and arranged
so as to spell out the phrase The Quick Brown Fox Jumped
Over The Lazy Dog, but the page appears only partially
constructed, leaving the impression that the creator of
Less That 100 Grams has become disheartened at the lack
of interest in the world of miniatures, and abandoned the
whole project to go in search of a big-money contract
with a multinational corporation within an expanding
economy. Or has eloped with a giant. In response, I've
found myself making my own Less Than 100 Grams list,
which as of this evening goes something like this: banknotes
of the world, dead leaves, earrings, beermats, fingerprints,
apostle teaspoons, butterflies of the Algarve, one-night
stands, sunglasses, grass-smoke, *déjà vus*, Yuri Gagarin
in zero gravity, an hour in a waiting room, echoes, boiled
sweets of the seventies, fishing stories, house keys, angel
turds, teeth, naked flames, kestrel feathers, pencil shavings,
promises, where I stand in your affections as expressed
in metric weight, owl pellets, lipsticks, paper cuts, clouds.

For My Lover, Upon my Impending Death
~ Juliana Baggott

Motorous heart, quit me not.
My body—as murmurious rumor mill—
You know what you know and spill
What you spill. Fuck me. Fuck me not.
Blood of little feathered pulse
Quickening on my wrist. Split me open.
Split me not. My tongue desires
Bitter pills. Poison me now.
Poison me not. Deathy sleep. Sleepy
Death. It doesn't matter which
Because the death-watch beetles
Tick. Tick for me. Tock me not.
I love you now. I'll love you not.
Forever was never, ever time spent well.

To Walt Whitman
~ Angela Ball

"Walt Whitman Promoted a Paleo Diet"
—*The New York Times*

Walt I know which way
your beard Is pointing
tonight—toward meat!
Dripping joints of every
description, legs, sides,
stomachs—a manly diet.
But Walt for every atom
of you as good belongs
to me! Atoms of
blueberries, blackberries,
kumquats, arugula,
tangerines. Of bread,
effulgent at dawn and
rumbling (if you listen)
the oven's songs. No wonder
you speak of "The sound
of the belch'd words
of my voice." That is indigestion!
Walt I know I am just a "tripper
and asker," a "puller and hauler,"
but is it really too late
to change your mind? I call
to the thousand responses
of your heart. Death, strong
and delicious word,
is not so appealing in the form
of bloody flesh on a plate!

This gentle call is for you, my love,
for you. It comes from the 29th
bather. Surely you must know
who is here.

No Selfies for Mary
~ J. T Barbarese

In the mausoleum shadow, eye-mopping mother, O Mary,
married to the carpenter, living in alienation in an unfurnished studio,
    cable wheels for chairs, wine crates for bookshelves, bare floors
    and tools underfoot,
no fun, this life, whether kid-encumbered or (now) kid-less and lonely,
no husband around when your only child is executed, carpenter Joe, a
    typical Joe, too busy to show up in the Stations or on the holy cards,
O full of grace and all-loving what never loved back,
for his love was for the forest and not the trees, it was global, not local,
tell me

whose Kleenex, Mar', whose tissues, whose bright black pumps,
whose missal, whose limo, whose purse, whose dress, whose compact,
whose mother when you become that macabre Other, a Virgin Mother,
whose black death suit, whom sue and who to press the suit?

Behold the phone-pointers, hangers-on fanning themselves with mass
    cards, behold the pants suits and pinstripes,
funeral director hand-rubbing and converging, handing out maps to
    Holy Cross,
relatives queuing for the final rose-chuck, four pall bearers, two
    cousins and two strangers with beefy shoulders, bursting out of
    their suits, lifting shovels,
a fist of earth on each shiny tongue,
behold the drivers whispering *Where are his* [expletive] *friends, where's
his old man,*
smell the mix of diesel and honeysuckle, stale aromatics trapped in
    the limos, and remember the sexual odor of newly cut grass,
that kid, somebody's nephew, with earbuds leaning on the new headstone,
that hammer-knife parked in the distance, the driver having a smoke,
    chin in his palm

Pater Noster
~ J. T Barbarese

—after Prévert

Our Father That art in Heaven
Stay there
Who are the power and the glory etcetera
We're fine
You and your so-called heaven
We don't need your help
Once you've seen Paris or New York or even Vegas
Heaven is ho-hum
Once you have lived in a body, had mumps, extractions
Credits and debits
Good and bad
No need for fatwas and bulls and your Ten Negations
Paradise is so Disney
The Fall was the best thing ever next to
Leaning on the rail of the boardwalk
Eating popcorn taking pictures sweating
Her beside me
We are wild fallen and miserable
We have fallen into ourselves
The one I see
Green eyes long limbs good mouth
Imperfect?
We are sleeping in on Sunday
Don't make any noise

Ouija Blink
~ Amy Beeder

Once again your fingers on that over-fingered lacquer
hazard murmur over borders of corruption, ash
& corpse. *The dead should lie back down, they make me*

decipher in the black script's arc some hatch or hide:
I never ever spelled in haste between the yes & no
between the moon & sun. A passage, peek or peep

You know that it is only hands, the dead don't speak

(How The Dead Speak)

in ether canticles, in gas, a motor's shudder. The sickle's
track on grass, the chiffarobe that weeps clear sap,
the tiny saint emerging from a pinto bean, in dreams:

quickly packing—yes, again,—that satchel while a taxi
idles just below. Your books. Inkwells all light-filled,
sequined gowns & statuettes. You'll never make that plane.

The Needs
~ Robin Behn

Anyway, the needs. The many needy needs
here at the Conference of Needs where we are
revving up the day with our dead friend's favorite coffee cup
wrapped, Gumby handle-arm glued
back to its hip, packed, unpacked, and now fill up
from the big carafe.
Next resident of earth in line's
pills are downed with Joe, then
the next one circles, landing
on the fruit, and, next, a long-gray soul whose
antique Tinwoodsman armor shines, coalesces, already
having eaten or not planning to, hovering like a rare vaccine
next to the one with the phone above her heart,
then, last in line at the buffet, her hearing aids
snugged in her pocket like snails under a leaf,
the one who searches for some fact, the paper in front
of her face a verbose gravestone, hers.

Brochure: The "Gathering."
Single, Couple, Fox Trot Only rates
As we were saying, Needs. We mostly
stumble on with them on leashes getting petted or
our heart is dog meat and they chew themselves
or pump themselves up, or they are *met*—intense petting
behind the ears, on the soul, on under-belly, heart—
commencing at the proper time and constantly since then.

We go on through our seven days.
Lapels, deep V-necks, swanky glasses.
In between the nametags and the coffee and
MetLife, optional slots—

World Peace, Planet Gardening,
Hurricanes That Soften Us…

Lunch already! Sandwiches! With bread, or slathered with air, or both
in the grand ballroom of the afternoon
sessions of whatever we signed up for back at home.

Brochure: breakouts, rounds, peps, slides.
No head count, so no way to know who's in whose room
though foxtrot's soon. The gray one's
posing by the lake, working on
the "Statue of Today" she has been working on.
Wheat is safely undulating
distant picturesques. Your friend would have liked this
smart paintable place and flirted with the profs.
Your need limps on. Why have you come. You miss
the keynote nap, fast-forward to C major hopes,
a thimbleful of liquids, notes,
a little practice time. Everything's a band name the
bandnamegenerator dot com says
is taken and suggests instead:
Riders of the Gray Confetti Statue $25.
Her band, you think, would not have disbanded
with a name like that. You snap it on your wrist,
a good-for-you-pain like spine-curdling bells
at Koan Camp last year where The Air was Air and
Here was Here.

Brochure: Supper served lakeside
so all the dogs can come.
You lost your dog. It jumped. It died.
Who knew dog life was hard
as hers? She'd gone

all-state, all-statue, all—the double-
grave already all ready ...

But you've constructed, here, a kind
of skateboard with a rope
her whole need would have fit on (once, in a restaurant,
you saw four women wheel their fifth friend's torso in
on a gurney, belly down, head raised,
she talked, ordered, chewed) and yours too.
To pull it sort of suits you, meets your need, this day.
Seeing as how you've paid.

You Betcha
~ Charles Bernstein

For Mary Ann Caws

What's the up side & down in betting God's imaginary? Of course, better lay off betting. But you can't, you're hooked. The stakes are high: truth & freedom if heads, delusion and tyranny if tails. If you win, you win everything, the world is yours and with it God. If you lose, you lose nothing but haunting premonitions, speculations disguised as command, & illusions of comfort (not nothing—nothing much). But, then, without doubt, God's a matter of mind.

Bone Cockerel:
Norman Cross Prisoner of War Camp, England
~ Linda Bierds

c. 1800, bones on wooden armature. Carver unknown.

Any year, in any tilting hemisphere,
any set of bones, split and polished, gathered
from the cooking pots ... But I am—
this hour—here, he wrote, my art a single shape lifted
from whatever squealed or snarled or lowed across
war's holding pen. Just touch and feathered bones hatched
into a bird, a set of wings, a textured silence throughout
a cape and blade, a blackened eye that looked
at soot and grain and linseed oil. I,
the prisoner wrote, I am here. My days are aimed
as light is aimed, shaft by shaft across a turning armature.

*

As light is aimed, shaft by shaft across a turning armature,
the prisoner wrote, I am here. My days are aimed
at soot and grain and linseed oil. I:
a cape and blade, a blackened eye that looked
into a bird, a set of wings, a textured silence throughout
war's holding pen. Just touch and feathered bones hatched
from whatever squealed or snarled or lowed across
this hour. Here, he wrote: my art, a single shape lifted
from the cooking pots ... But I am
any set of bones, split and polished, gathered
any year, in any tilting hemisphere.

Burnt Offerings
~ Michelle Bitting

No older than ten and sucking Fresca
from blue aluminum in a wooded L.A. canyon,
I wandered the quiet street alone, past
the mysterious burnt down house.
Back and forth I crossed it,
fascinated by the scarred, macabre frame,
the pitch incinerated beams
and tattered doorways
like sagging ladies in soiled negligees,
scorched bricks and toppled remains of a fireplace
that felt ironic under the circumstances.
Nearby, a tree grew, bloated and gnarled,
billowed with umber fungus.
And this sidewalk grotesquery, the unseemly
blight consuming trunk and root-base
fed my obsession, the way the saucer-hewn sponges
that infiltrated bark armor,
splitting open the Oak's rough living skin
matched the peculiar handiwork
of whatever made fire touch down in the first place,
eating up family walls and lintels,
lace curtains, shoe racks and teddy bears,
the still smoking inferno that reeked of damp, acrid
charcoal and sickly sweet ruins
crazy nature had left behind. Accidents will happen,
although hardly without invitation,
the material world craving it, the soul leaping
blood-first to its purging. To denude, to undress,
to wear a lampshade for a crown
and become a flame dancing on altars reflecting
wine's redness reaching aloft to mingle music

with the spheres. Things you know but can't say, urped.
The unburied life. This is what I sensed
but only silently. The silt that builds up, daring forces
to bear down, naturally. Like ships locked in require ghosts
and significant dredging to exit the bay, bucket by bucket.
So beautiful to behold their unharnessing then.
Muck sailed through on a map scaled to freedom,
this heaven where I knew I might someday find myself.

From *Transfers*
~ Chantal Bizzini, translated by J. Bradford Anderson

inspired by Steve Reich's *Different Trains*

1. AMERICA—BEFORE THE WAR

The sun's moved to Jersey, the sun's behind Hoboken.

Covers are clicking on typewriters, rolltop desks are closing; elevators go up empty, come down jammed. It's ebbtide in the downtown district, flood in Flatbush, Woodlawn, Dyckman Street, Sheepshead Bay, New Lots Avenue, Canarsie.

Pink sheets, green sheets, gray sheets, FULL MARKET REPORTS, FINALS ON HAVRE DE GRACE. Print squirms among the shopworn officeworn sagging faces, sore fingertips, aching insteps, strongarm men cram into subway expresses. SENATORS 8, GIANTS 2, DIVA RECOVERS PEARLS, $800,000 ROBBERY.

It's ebbtide on Wall Street, floodtide in the Bronx.

The sun's gone down in Jersey.

—John Dos Passos, *Manhattan Transfer*, III. Nine Days' Wonder

Always this guy, at work, in front of me;
he doesn't look at the rain, cross-hatching
the windowpane, fogging up the landscape,
the countryside, tonight ...
is it a face, this reflection superimposed on the black windowpane?
is it a real landscape, unspooling like this,
like film
that consumes itself and leaves in clouds of ink?

In the projection room, black and white
suite of flecked images, dark, striped
now out of sync,
The Man Who Laughs,

the child,
the snow, his bare feet,
his frozen laugh,
even in suffering, and pain,
the machine gets carried away,
reel rustles, melts, strains, twists,
the screen is devoured by the light,
the film is on fire ...

To the South, to the West; he retraces the path of his childhood,
in other times from New York to Chicago,
a destiny given over to wheels;
against the tide of those who fled to the south,
or who marched into the west;
and the *hobos*, what loss determined their flight
how did they grasp
the destiny-train
and its steady beat?

En route, abandoned paths scatter,
and the screams are no longer from animals,
hunted down in the desert or the mountains,
but from the wind, its power multiplied by speed.

The animals hid, far
from the paths, far from the rails that lead
to human settlements
—some captured, killed, eaten,
or brought up well in captivity, tortured, mutilated—
where beings meet up with each other, work, multiply,
in misery and repetition.

However, on the tapestry, pacified prairie dotted with flowers,
the animals smile:
unicorn and rabbits, birds ...

There is a direction: what do these
city names mean
for the one who says them:

—*Chicago, New York*

when the voice
and memory rings with them?
What is their echo now?
… measure these waves
…
On your knees, this book, tracings,
lives woven together, maps crossed out, folded, used up
in this back and forth
crossing the countryside
—but on both sides of these paths
everything that escapes the rectilinear tracings
from forest, to mountain
to source lives;
what life takes refuge there still?

This river's current no longer beats this new industrial
land, it yields neither life nor rapture,
nor does it allow you to give in to the voyage
to the delta, and then the gulf.
…
On your daily path (what does daily mean?),
what variation in the repetition?
Different trains lead through storms,

seeing them pass does not lead to understanding …
on the spot, whistles of progress,
the rails, and this syncopated beat …
Directions: from one point to another,
carried away by the expansiveness,
could you then consider…?
pursuing happiness, maybe …
how does the sun shine
today, or
is it raining?
… tomorrow …
but you,
are you the same person twice?

The rail,
is already laid, cut through the forests, through stone,
through the earth and through the lives of men;
and we go forward into this dissolution,
this end,
in the wide streets, between buildings
more or less dense according to the reflections
on glass or metal
or the passage of clouds;

… storming the heights, but always in the changeable light
and the breeze,
from the sea,
on this pacified island
that receives and gives, where the least contradiction
is not, at Bryant Square,
the twisting of its branches on the black and white stripes
of buildings,
or these cranes, from afar, which climb even higher

and, from their movement, unfurl the sky, parks, their shadows,
and the churches open to the passing street shining
in the dark.
The yellow cabs, glide, slowly,
and the crowd goes on foot,
among the brightened shop windows.

Here are tiny Japanese presents,
these new fruits, sweeter, artificial
that melt between the lips like the kiss
of flowers
and these armfuls, in the basement, in the restaurant's
shadow,
and the entwining of branches
arranged,

but all of this is nothing but memories from before,
(remember, this paper mask)
—before the acceleration, the danger—
that travel and change places: words, letters, post cards, photographs,
here is a new year where
progress has taken us ...
Crystal Palace and Chrysler Building ...
we are long past carelessness ...
and we climb,
—Empire State Building,
all the way up, to see
the shipwrecked crowd, below,
or we visit the museum
where the model blinks, a big toy:
you can walk around this miniature city,
time passes and night alternates with day, it brightens,
then darkens, trembling with electric life;

Refugees in these margins
of the world
or homeless,
blind,
we come hard against the walls,
—oh bitter shore,
which had in its mouth the taste of a promise, in
the other tongue.

Where must you be to still see
the succession of suns and nights?
Shipwrecked,
shipwrecked in New Orleans, shipwrecked
in New York,
shipwrecked in the heart of the crowd
and not only on the island set apart from maritime routes,
a shipwreck in each of us;
porous walls, fabrics,
weather vanes sensitive to screams, to the radiance of
beacons,
men,
animals
now made mad ...

a kangaroo stands up, the eye
grown large and the jaw open, frozen
by the beam in the night
that stopped it ...

—2009

magus
~ Danielle Blau

Our father had in his repertoire
some really funny tricks. While mom

left to ready dessert, he'd regard us
from the distance of his

tipped-back chair, sing
Pick a hand—and whichever

one we'd choose
would bloom a wild black

cloud of ducks. When they made
my sister cry once, dad twirled

his sibylline mustache
and asked *Did you know mallards*

nipped children's eyelids? Neither did I.

Like I said, these
powerful tricks could fill you with

true despair; there may be nothing
our dad can't do, because

a heedful set
—mother and sister and me—

you never will catch us
outdoors with no keys in our

pockets, so comes all the more
as a shock, how he

got us—our father—to lose him
completely, like magic, forget

him clean out of our world.

And, look, how it
breaks on deep-

fried pork rinds, on grease-smeared
fuchsia lips, now, at the deli—this

light: some dies
snail-like, retreats into an object's

private folds; some snarls back *Yes,*
a thing here (if you really

think it matters) for your
checklist of tragedies. But wait—that's

off: the Corner Tick Tock
Market-Lotto, a woman stopping

for cheese fries on her way home
from the club—

what, in all,
in any of these, could

be so unbearably grim? Only distortion
of surface, of tint—it's just a trick

of light, played by dad, wherever he is.

From his limitless life-
feats, though, could be the greatest

and most dismal's been
to strike each

trace, for him, of human
sympathy in us, so

we—who'd hardly managed
to cope with the natural

decline of our angelfish—can
with ease disregard

from the distance, as object
unnatural, our father: we've been

tricked into this—and with him
only, for all I know, a strange lonely

man, just a baffled old tragedy.

Fable
~ Sally Bliumis-Dunn

He would learn that same night
that her wearing all white
had little to do with purity,

though he had imagined an Emily D. kind of thing
when he saw her, alone in a library carrel,
arms curved around her book like wings.

He asked her out and she agreed;
they perched on the stools at the local bar,
and she claimed she wasn't hungry

though she swooped to snatch
his pizza crusts.
And after all their pleasant cooing,

for it was clear they were both attracted,
he was a little unnerved
by her sudden flutter

at his simple mention of the beach.
Though I hear they are still a pair today
and she in fact hates poetry,

and that he wonders why
he dreams of her flying,
gull wings tilting at the wind.

Fable
~ Sally Bliumis-Dunn

She feels a sense of contentment
when the slugs appear
on the terrace after the rain,

as though a safety net
had fallen away from the world
and allowed them to emerge,

stark and vulnerable
even unattractive.
So different from her sense

of what permanently lay buried.
First, her father, then her only son.
In their great ugliness

these glistery smudges shone
like harbingers of redemption
along the terrace stone,

with slow-moving antennae
on their faces,
if you can call them faces,

searching the summer air.

Corpus Memoria
~ Bruce Bond

> *Reason is alone.*
> —Emanuel Levinas

The great frame and fluted carving of the altar
hide the source, or one source among the many,

the long tones of the chapel organ passing through
an unseen hand, through the flesh a spirit comes from,

what it leaves, what dissolves in expectation
of the unseen ear, as the widow takes her place.

Another passage, another question drawn from the well.
Between the world and the world as understood,

a little music. Between the eye and the iris,
a space to breathe, as music breathes, and singers

whose unseen parts teach our instruments to phrase.
We are all taking cues from the bodies of strangers,

funereal conventions, the dark instinctual pit
or loft where someone lays his palms on the keys

like withered flowers. Sometimes you say more
that way: saying nothing in the shape of something.

Sometimes you send a card next day, and you know
between the widow and the widow as understood,

there is an emptiness the size of a cathedral.
The slightest kindness grows large in a place like this.

Before the place consumes it. The quiet in a voice
says yes, me too, and it, like music, is never true

or false. All those years you thought language would
say what you wanted. And it did, as silence did,

and music that is nowhere and everywhere
that hides in us. Between the singer and the sung,

the emptiness blown back to where it came from.
It was ours once, and we understand so little

still of the body's ghost currency of exchange.
Take this special breed of laughter among friends

at something less than funny, this convivial spilling
of lonely joy whose sources are anonymous:

yours and not yours. Like a life made weird
with gratitude in the wake of some close call.

What are hands if not the widows of the hands
they were. Too large for a child. Too small for all

they do not hold. Between the past and the passing,
the lost faces you wore, wore out, and discarded,

and still the unseen face, the paradigm, continues,
the tune that is one tune and therefore no one thing.

The lamp in memory's slide show has no portrait
and so might be the source of each. Or one source.

Graves of light open and close, and close again,
remembered, and sometimes music undoes the clasp

on a book you wrote and never read, and sometimes
bodies play their part. The organist understands

his memory might fail. You can spook yourself,
he thinks, lost in future measures. Hearts kick.

Minds go blank. And the fingering continues
over the keys, down a path whose darkness surprises

what it threatens to expose. Then a stumble.
The part that says, hey, I am only flesh.

It calms you into thinking, there it was, and now
it's over. Now the hand is all the light you know.

The Room, the Garden
~ Yves Bonnefoy, translated by Hoyt Rogers

I

This room, closed
Since before time began. Furniture, sleep
Speak to each other softly. Light
Holds out its hand through the panes. The vase
Waking on the table is a pallid blue.

Painter, you alone, you who remember,
Can enter this room today.
You know who smoothed, in the eternal,
The rumpled sheets, decking them
With fabrics whose pictures fade.

Enter,
Silence breathes to you—the silence that you are.
Enter with this vinous red, this yellow-ochre,
This blue of other years.
Make them take light by the hand,
And guide it…. They show it the flowers,
Only a few, in the gold of dry leaves.
On its finger—as its memory—this ring.

You will stay here, until this evening. Painting
Does more than render life: it grants being—
Even if this hand, that in the shadow takes yours,
Can't be touched … can hardly be seen.

II

And, having lived there,
Once you reemerge, let your work be this:
To look at the sky above the trees,
And then at the leaves, dark-green. Let the deep-blue
Of this bench whose colour flakes away
Come close to a touch of pink.

It is about life and death ...
And a woman who used to appear, graciously,
At this time of the evening, to read for an hour
In that delicate armchair—before the right not to fret
About the pace of time had ceased.

An hour, almost an hour. It's as if
Something, perhaps a glove, had fallen
From her lap. And as if, not trying to see,
She'd sought it with one hand—distractedly,
In the coolness of the grass.

What's faraway
Remains what's closest. What's most remote
In the past still haunts the present hour:
This we know from colour, where nothing ends.

III

Light has nested, this night,
In sleep; and this morning,
It was a world; and towards evening,
It's even this dress, aglow with a touch of pink—
This gaze that asks a garden
To welcome it, a short while still.

Paints, an empty armchair, a book left open
Under the first drops—large, warm—
The colour brightens. She picks up—is it
A glove?—something in the thick-grown grass.

The grass in your garden, my painter friend,
Has it grown so much? Does its immense
Greenness cover the world that you were?
Yes, but look: the grass is crushed, where an animal has slept.
Its hideaway is like a sign. The sign is more
Than what was lost, than life going by—
Than the song on the road, late at night.

Disclose with your brush this shadow in the grass,
Unveil for us the simple essence of the sign:
This dream—no, this gold—
That turns what was into what remains.

That Angel William Blake Kept Talking To
~ Marianne Boruch

He meant Michelangelo's favorite model for his
frescos called down

those many times to strike poses in
too much sunlight and old cathedrals new—

Look sideways to slip
the gauzy afternoon even more

out of focus. To the point
and blinding of Blake, bringing up

the devil he saw too.
Under a grate in London's

coal-sickened air, a seething
monster, *devil* a name for

the worst things. Because his
I can look into

a knot of wood until it frightens me.
But there's rage in the mix

going silver out of kindness.
Once so furious at the father who

tied his son's leg to a log
and made him walk, Blake

roared to the street, broke,
spit lightning all

over the man. Hold that
two centuries. Not long to

love such a thing
across the gene pool,

those of us
when any world ends.

Elegy on My Drive Home in the Rain
~ Laure-Anne Bosselaar

for Larry Levis

When it rains on Las Positas Road,
  the trunk of a eucalyptus there turns
  blue—with a few blood-red streaks—but mostly
   blue: a bright hard cobalt,

   & it just stands there, bleeding that blue,
among the other eucalyptus in their safe
  camouflage of beige & brown—

& I remember something Larry wrote about Caravaggio,
  how he painted his own face
      in the decapitated head of Goliath,

  & how Larry wanted *to go up to it & close both eyelids*
   because they were *still half-open & it seemed a little obscene*
            to leave them like that.

   *

I planted a willow in a garden in Belgium when Larry died.
It grew by a blue-painted door. I wanted that tree
  to keep weeping there after I left for America again—

America who had lost Larry too—& I thought about that,
     & about his two trees, lost somewhere
  in Utah—the *acer negundo* he wrote,
& the other one whose name he could never remember.

  So that now when I drive home I think of those trees:
the *acer negundo*, the other one, & my willow.

51

Brother limitation races beside me like a shadow too, Larry,
　　　　　　　so that now, when it rains,
　　I take another way home, or look
　　　　　away
　　　　　　　　from the Las Positas eucalyptus
standing there soaked & so blue
　　it seems *a little obscene to leave it like that.*

Hospital
~ David Bottoms

He didn't want to go to the hospital.

He didn't want to shoot anyone, but he didn't want to go
to the hospital.

He held the pistol, cocked, on the two ambulance men
and cursed them,
though cursing wasn't like him. He trembled

and wept when my mother talked the pistol out of his hands.
An old man again, he lay back on the bed
and trembled and wept.

They phoned me at work, asking
what they should do. When you're fifty miles away

it's hard to know what's right or wrong.
His ankle was swollen. My mother feared a blood clot.

He didn't care, he'd had enough of hospitals.
Pain must have shot back

across the years—Japanese searchlight
across black water, shell-blast in gun turret, fire on water.

They lifted him from the lifeboat onto a gurney
and drove him to the hospital.

Two days later, he died.

Last Baby Girls of the 1920s
~ Julie Bruck

Patsy, Dominica, Lois, Henny, Pearl.
One by one, then seemingly, at once—
our mother's dear friends have tossed
away their canes and medical apparatus,
and shuffled off without us. Those girls
of the '20s and '30s, eras of the well-turned
ankle, then The Crash. The War. The Rest.
Among them, the boss's daughter, British
war brides, single mother of three,
a cellist, a secretary, one who buried
two husbands and moved in with the third,
another who always wrapped her neck
in bright scarves as if maimed, though
she wasn't. Their circumstances were
privileged or pinched, they ran shops
or houses, or worked for people who ran
shops or houses. Remembering them,
I'm ambushed by the scent of cut peonies.
Cups and saucers on a tray. Biscuits.
By their slow, deliberate kindnesses,
and this wild longing for one more floral
notecard in careful, cursive hand, which
always began, *Julie Darling,* or *David Dear,*
and made us want to be worthy.

The Lost Geography of Aspirations
~ Christopher Buckley

> *Contentment with poverty is Fortune's best gift.*
> —Fu Hsuan, 278 AD

We picked up bottle caps
outside grocery stores, at service stations,
and, pinching a crimped edge
between thumb and middle finger,
held them head-high as we snapped our fingers
to send the silver crowns spinning
like small satellites arcing
toward some other kid's neck....
This was after we'd checked
the cap for symbols, for sayings
that meant prizes or free drinks
that were never there.
                              We fished
popsicle sticks out of the trash,
wove them cross-hatch into rafts
the size of pot holders, flung them
like boomerangs, on edge
against the sky—no returns.
You made use of the materials
on hand as complaints about 100 things
you didn't have got you nothing.
Skipping homework, we wasted
our free time outside the soda fountain
or YMCA, slaphappy in the afternoons
never once thinking Doctor,
Lawyer, CPA, always jibing
dog catcher, street sweeper,
garbage man—not believing

for a minute that any of us
were headed to the front
of the financial line.
             I took out loans,
got through grad school working part-time,
piecemeal, and night-shift for years.
Lucky with a grant, I went for
the off-season rates, the November fog,
wound a wine-colored muffler
around my throat each morning
stepping out from the Hotel St. Christophe,
a flea bag off the Rue Mouffetard,
where I could barely see beyond the end
of the street as I walked beneath
the plane trees and pin oaks
of the Jardin des Plantes
repeating lines to myself despite
Flaubert's admonition about
the music we wrote for stars
not fit for dancing bears....
But I was stubborn as bark on
the winter trees and liked bears,
so I kept at it despite the rain
that dragged the sky behind it,
despite each argument for the soul
evaporating with my breath
in the frosted glare of dawn
as we emerged from the Dixie Melody
Jazz Review to walk down
Rue Quelque Chose, back to
my tiny room by the *charcuterie*
with what little I knew of grace.

I managed a week in Lerici where
they read Byron, Shelley, and Keats
in Italian 3 days running, the Golfo Dei Poeti
just up the road from Viareggio
where Shelley's body washed up,
where the straw-colored wine
doesn't travel out of the region,
and the garlic and basil *zuppa di verdura*
with fish was so sublime you'd
sell your clothes, thinking you'd died
and gone to heaven. I could afford to walk
that grey beach, to take a boat
to the little towns of Cinque Terra
where I looked up into the salt-kissed sun
without the least inclination
to say anything....
       Evenings drifted
out to sea, no imprint of boat wrecks
on the horizon, no bonfires on the beach.
Notes I'd made flew out the window
of the train back to Florence, the way no grief,
no ambition ever did.
       But who hasn't
seen photos of the famous, their faces
in five magazines a month, advertizing
programs from Tuscany to Puerto Vallarta,
Prague to the flat heart of Ohio? Exercises offered,
guaranteed formulas, programs of inspiration,
the tangential stardust that might fall to you
all summer long with inspiring vistas and
individual support—the sequence written
on the insides of Kit Kat wrappers demonstrating
a flair for formal experimentation; the prose poem

explaining how to peel a hard-boiled egg
which was instructive and showed the writer
had applied herself; a Spenserian sonnet praising
the manufacturer of Ben Franklin's lace cravats;
or the precise point where you should enter
the imagistic freeway and bypass those
without your gifts for rhyming
in timed trials....
                     Somehow,
I made it this far without a folding map
to the heavens, without following
the constellations reprinting
the ancient starry scripts,
the lost routes across the starboard
side of the night where who knows
what all's been lost?
                     Whatever
held me back for decades is still
just over my shoulder and feels
like fog coming in, like an old wound
resurfacing as I walk the outskirts,
a dark blue unwinding from the sea.
At least I know where I am, know
what the slim chances have always been,
and nothing matters now
more than just continuing to breathe,
to be one more wayfarer walking along
the sand, picking up shells, collecting
the available bits, the puzzle pieces of light
freely discarded by the stars.

Praise for the Snow
~ Joseph Campana

April 17, 1944

Praise for the snow in Central Park, April
        buds frosted white and now somehow
more than they were. Praise for Kansas City,
        Missouri: heart of a nation at war, eye
and center of some final revelation composed
of hapless remainders, those subject to the gathering,
        archive of what might have but did not last.
Praise for the leather satchels laboriously
        stitched, the duffel bags haplessly slung,
suitcases with their stripes, stamped crates
        with their blazoned letters
        and the bags full, the bags full
of the emptiness of abandoned time. Praise
        for the reachers, for those who know to grasp.
Every recess can be searched, every clasp can be opened.
        What is left in a pocket
if not the feeling of someone else's
        hand? Praise for pictures strewn on
a battlefield: girl with a gleaming trombone, girl
        with a fresh-baked pie. No, really.
I saw her holding it out as a way of reaching
        across the seas. I could almost smell
how tart the apples, how fecund the earth,
        and how there lingered, on the surface of the image,

flecks of a distant battlefield.
I don't know where all the bodies went.
I have a receipt for remittance and a claim on a parcel of
        goods. Praise for the sharp-edge coins layered with
dirt. The South Seas and their finest tender come
        with words of wisdom in a faded pamphlet:
        "Meet New Zealand." I'd really like that.
I'd like to meet them all in Central Park under April
        boughs, the boughs unexpectedly jeweled. This is
                Kansas City, Missouri, gateway to the west
        and all its unwary fantasies realized in
the burial ground of the accumulations,
        buttons in their infinite arrays,
                letters and diaries urgent in repetition,
collections of the tiny practicalities,
                        the sewing kits assigned each boy,
        whether his fingers were nimble
        or not. I could never hold one
steady enough. I could never reach that far.
                Praise the steady and the supple:
        those who believe in repair. And praise
                the many, the inadvertent, the left back
sorters of queasy treasures. Guardians
        of the hundreds: buttons
without shirts, shirts without end, shoes
        laid out on a desk with the care of angels.

To The Royal Spanish Academy
~ Rafael Campo

In Spanish, trees are male, grand thoughts beneath
the female, curvaceous clouds. Our teeth

are masculine, as is to bite, while smiles
are womanly. Explosions are female——

You're mine! It is considered manly, I
suppose, to wander with the sun and sky,

while doubts pertain to women. Underwear
apparently is worn by men (brassieres

as well as jockey shorts). The feminine
interiority of compassion

is obvious, and creativity,
if making has a gender, has to be

likewise that of woman. Language is built
of words—suggesting man is nothing but

an afternoon of ladies' gossiping.
Men fear and sweat, aware that in her song

a woman rises. Table, house, and blood
are women's things, while men would claim the world,

and dreams, and pain. Yet some strange entities
refuse such timeworn categories:

the soul and the idea, and the sea
belong to both, and so does poetry.

From *The Birnam Wood*
In Solitude Hurt by Love
~José Manuel Cardona, translated by Hélène Cardona

To the painter Juan Alcalde

John of fire, of bread, of grieving sun.
John of crumb and large loaf, John of mourning.
John almost baker, John lean
like a wheat and seed field.

Quiet splendor, burning peace,
indecipherable omen, sign and fruit,
tribute to the ephemeral and sacrifice
enamored with ashes, oak or fountain.

Water source is life or captivity
for the man in solitude. To think, to know
yourself an image of love or cruel mystery.

Image of love too, death
finds us among reeds. Baptistry.
Splendid gargoyle or lifeless dream.

From *El bosque de Birnam*
También en soledad de amor herido
~José Manuel Cardona

Al pintor Juan Alcalde

Juan de lumbre, de pan, de sol doliente.
Juan de miga y hogaza, Juan de luto.
Casi Juan panadero, Juan enjuto
como campo de trigo y de simiente.

Esplendor del sosiego, paz ardiente,
augurio indescifrable, signo y fruto,
homenaje a lo efímero y tributo
de polvo enamorado, encina o fuente.

Manantial es la vida o cautiverio
del hombre en soledad. Pensar, saberte
imagen del amor o cruel misterio.

Imagen del amor también la muerte
nos emplaza entre juncos. Baptisterio.
Gárgola esplendorosa o sueño inerte.

Misnomer
~ Maxine Chernoff

Chance scrawls its name in a dusty ledger.
Night creases desire, opening books of possible return.
Leaves collide with stars.
Ghosts between sheets, thoughts fray at departure.
In the eclipsed moment, we stand with our gestures and sighs.
You say nothing of arrival, a common misnomer for leaving.
The photo shows absence in its bold regalia of living.

The Minotaur Now
~ Kelly Cherry

A bull-muscled sea gores a pebbled shore
Wave upon wave, wearing away limestone,
Shale, glittering granite, and dolomite.
Scrub pine pesters the hillside and sunlight
Exposes the sea's sinewy currents. Creatures
Of the island sigh or murmur or mutter words
Unknown and silence smothers every sound.

The monster in his labyrinth, slain
By Theseus, sent his spirit into the sea,
Where Poseidon gave him freedom to roam as he wished
Where no man sees, or thinks him monstrous. He moves
The waters, carries them on his road-broad back,
Makes them rise and fall. His sharp hoofs paw
The ocean bed. His shoulders thrust against the shore.

Columbus Day Storm
~ Patricia Clark

for Claudio Parmiggiani

The idea of art   as smoke, images left
by dark tendrils twining   after flame, the Italian
artist who burns tires,   piles of rubber in a room
to capture what remains,   smudge on white walls. She
took shape, then, a girl   straddling a bicycle, 1962,
after the windstorm, how   she rose to light, a house
of sleepers, no electricity,   and went out into streets
blocked by fallen trees,   saw a place transformed,
and she the Captain Cook,   Captain Vancouver to log
it all while her brothers   slept. Where power lines
sparked, she knew to leave   them alone, vowing to cross
danger, to note it crisply,   block to block, before
returning to fill their   astonished ears, having
the thrill of both—venturing out   alone, and then to tell.

New Year: The Lustrous Owl
~ Patricia Clark

1.

Astringent light, freezing rain.
The tax man ahead. The deep reckoning.

2.

Birds seen, books read, miles walked.
There's an app to keep track.

Why are owls so elusive? Heard,
but not seen.

3.

Sky drips water that coats pine needles.
Sticky as pitch. That front-yard fir,

the stuff golden like syrup on your hands.

4.

Birdbath filled with oak leaves.
A frozen stew.

5.

My sister picking at a blanket,
my sister's legs climbing the railing of the bed.

6.

Comparison is the thief of joy.

7.
The lustrous owl is not a species
but an artist's rendition.

Black eyes, golden-tipped feathers.

8.
Eight in a row. A shooting gallery.
One goes down.

The county fair: chaos of sights, smells.
Cotton candy, grease of popcorn.

Ticket stub torn in half.

9.
I dreamed she was a skull on the floor.
The dog wanted to sniff—

no, I jerked the leash.
Jean was on her knees scrubbing,
scrubbing.

10.
Unwind the lights from the trees.

11.
In the front yard, swinging from the magnolia,
planetary balls—

my favorite: gold—

there is also crimson, citron.

12.
Snow tops them.
Ice will cause them to fall.

13.
Be prepared with an alternative heat source.

14.
A remote eye—we watched the end.
The same blanket

pulled up over her head.

15.
No other year but this, the one behind
not yet fading.

And this one? A dream swirling to shape.

16.
In another one, she called to me.
I stepped into a shallow boat—

And motion took us.

Nothing is complete now without architecture
~ Andrei Codrescu

My lovely freedom my little chestnut blinking your one eye
bring back to me a quarter of a century of missing melancholia.
For each Fall I missed there was a drought of wistfulness
as if I drank my own sweat instead of eyes-shut naked on
the balcony I just saw lowered in its entirety by a super-crane
operated by Hart Crane in the new Manhattan fantasy of drafting
its new skyline that to its credit and to Hart's allows for better
places for jumping from its heights. How thoughtful. Suicide
must be given beautiful places to be conducted from.
Personal esthetics aside the city owes this much to its surplus
of sensitives. I don't owe anyone any money, I'm a jewel
in this city making itself like all America out of the future that
will happen whatever the state of your soul bank account or
opinion. I can go into business now: there are so many books.
They are all about the future when no one will read them.
The ones I have written can by themselves tower above us.
To the bricks I say don't worry about me I'm well prepared

If I feel anything stronger than this
~ Andrei Codrescu

I might have to have something stronger than this.
Poison or a seizure or a slide down a forgotten insult
to the island where those things are building courage
to go out and be seen and easily become a nation.
That is, to quote the enemy, "any community that contains
in itself the ability to make war, is a nation." If that
is still the case, and it mostly is, I want you to let me out
somewhere unsavory with a brown paper bag and a view.
There must still be some of those places.

shoelace
~ Andrei Codrescu

a real concern may turn out in a dream as "to be continued"
or make you sleep soundly for being common currency
splintering off café tables where free-lance shrinks
keep office spreading patter butter out of which "sex,"
the word, pops up at a higher or lower octave like a pigeon
pretending to ignore the fallen crumb of pizza shining nearby.
so that's what you sound like, new york, no different than
you always sounded, though more at ease with pop-psych lingo,
and maybe less ability to tie your shoelace or another's without talk.
In my absence you have acquired a lot of bla-blah underwear.
Newsprint and screens obscure "sex," the thing not the word,
but what do I know? I can afford to be alone, deliciously alone,
and when I gain the street I am with others tripping over their
shoelaces to get to their café therapists where they can tie their
shoelaces together. Unless they are working for the city
with health benefits uppermost in mind. When these employees
want sex they pay for it. They wear work boots tightly laced.
Dear city, the same always, making twisted nothings and steel towers.
I spent time in america and I can feel your shoelace coming loose
August 23, 2016 nyc

How Everything
~ Andrea Cohen

Two by two
assumes so much—
that this giraffe
will dig the other,
that the he-
bedbug likes shes,
or will, in the pinch
of apocalypse, make
do. Maybe you've
been in similar
tight spots, torrents
filling portals, all
you love getting
cozy with its maker.
Maybe the aardvark
can't believe he gets
for forty days to call
in sick, his only job to
re-aardvark the garden.
Maybe the piss-ant
in steerage goes
on auto-pilot, so
no flood beyond
measure, no stench
of leaving the known
world to drown, no
sudden dove in blue
or Brueghel's boy
falling, doesn't—
to some piss-
ant, get handed.

Figure of Speech
~ Andrea Cohen

Beside herself, we
say—as if being this

distraught made you
two people, as if

one body could not
all that agony

contain, as if,
amoeba-like, we

might—dividing—hold
our own hand.

False Doors & Imaginary Numbers
~ Bruce Cohen

(Overheard subway conversation)
It starts as a hypothetical—
Assume an ice cream cone provides one unit of happiness.
Is flavor not be a factor?

Now say you're provided with two cones.
So my happiness doubles?
No, not that simple; you now have two units of happiness.

This proves the existence of imaginary numbers.

At the Metropolitan, we viewed the ancient Egyptian exhibit,
Riches galore, an infinite afterlife,
Pharaohs who constructed false doors
On their tombs to deceive future looters
& those who'd come back from the dead.

And seal they did their mausoleums
With their favorite concubines & still breathing
Blinded servants & ornate artifacts beyond imagination—
Polished lapis lazuli & turquoise & hammered gold,
Embalming themselves with cinnamon, cardamom & cumin,
Their pre-preserved brains extracted through their nostrils.

The wine glass the woman sipped from last night,
Under a burned out porch light, forgotten on the patio table,
Fills this morning with rain & one drowned bee.

There's no secret entrance to where she was.
                    She is the imaginary number of herself:
Is there a word for that?

Or consider: a blind man, graced with first-time sight,
Declared women are not
Irregular fleshy planets of citrus after all

& everyone in the subway, indeed, possesses a unique face.
He wanted back to his dark happiness,
Shuffling through his daily chores with shut eyes.

Why must we verbalize what we think

We see when there is so much we see
We never articulate?

I did not shave tomorrow: past & future meld.
Each kiss is a neologism for I am lonely, you?

Perfect as our hands are,
We create metaphorical tools for excavating:

Trap doors, booby trapped secret tunnels, labyrinths,
Passages behind movable fake walls, false prophets,
Passages that curve back to their original nowhere,
False alarms, false starts.

There's no actual number or real entrance to happiness;
It over complicates at the speed of not talking.

As history accelerates, the museum guard tells us it's time to leave—
We convince ourselves there's nothing left to see!

I've no qualms about leaving my footprints in puddles.

Almost immediately they conceal themselves.
I am capable of order: cardamom, cinnamon, cumin.
            I refold clean shirts.

Because what can we hold onto & cherish more than uncertainty?

A cigarette flung from a passing car smolders on a sidewalk.
A lipstick smudge on a wineglass.

A melting vanilla ice cream cone
Some child dropped now attracts an impromptu colony

Of bees, minus their queen....

Sounds in the Grasses
~Peter Cole

The Rabbi opens a verse in the Radiance:
   The letter is small, the fullness of all.
The Sound's wind adjusts the miscanthus.
   And paper once was made with piss.

The letter is small, the fullness of all
   the grasses might just also teach us.
That paper once was made with piss
   I read in the paper before I wrote this.

The grasses also just might teach us
   behind the house, if not in Genesis.
The paper I read before I wrote this
   is a touchscreen lit by circuits and chips.

Behind the house, let alone in Genesis,
   how does value in a word seep through us
(from touchscreens lit by circuits and chips,
   which likewise involve an economy of piss)?

How, in a word, does value seep through us?
   Again I turn to a verse in the Radiance,
which likewise involves an economy of piss:
   Rabbi Isaac is nearing Tiberias—

I'm turning again to a verse in the Radiance—
   a catbird is singing from the tasseled birches—
and Rabbi Isaac's nearing Tiberias
   might be a word's trying to reach us.

A catbird sings from tasseled birches.
    Isaac thinks of the Tree of Life.
A word might be trying to reach us
    by the arbor vitae's branchlets. Through the dust,

Isaac is thinking of the Tree of Life—
    as a full-moon maple glows in the garden
by an arbor vitae branching from dust:
    I'll place my dwelling in your midst.

As a full-moon maple glows in the garden.
    And there it is, deep in Leviticus—
That *place … my dwelling … your midst.*
    Small comfort, the grasses teach us.

These Days
~ Billy Collins

I wonder why I often find myself
in this state of low-grade nervousness
as if I'm waiting on line for a rollercoaster.
If I notice a kitchen cabinet left open
or the cat with its collar missing,
the floor feels like it's coming out from under me,
and knowing precisely how a floor feels
only adds to my being jumpy,
skittish as a new-born foal but minus
the spindly legs and the darling wobbliness.

And speaking of that,
I don't have to actually be at the track
to get that feeling one gets when it's two minutes
till post time and the betting windows
appear to be a mile away, as in a dream,
but that is exactly how long the line is,
one mile plus me at the end of it
gnawing on a pencil, wearing a regrettable shirt.
No, I can feel that way at home
sitting in my favorite reading chair.

The truth is I hardly read anything these days
except the wall across the room
and the long crack in the wall
which takes a very bad turn at the end.
What would Robert Browning do?
And must I spend the rest of my life
in a Victorian drawing room waiting for an answer?

or waiting in a drawing of a room,
nothing more than a cluster of pencil lines,
powerless as a giant eraser begins its descent.

After Song
~ Martha Collins

for Marcia Deihl (1949–2015)

white bike   white chain   white tulips

no   another   none   other

and daffodils in   white basket her

name   dates   picture   is all she

ghost   bike they call   it there   was snow

that day too high   to see   truck she

is not   she   or is   she or

after   song   *Settled*   she wrote   sang

played   her head in time   her

cold bike   stopped bike   negative

bike   ghost   spirit whatever

they call   it singing   chain

to hold   her not   to hold

Company Of The Morning
~ Peter Cooley

Enter us in the ledger of the stars
I said to the horsefly stuck against the glass,
battering his last on mud-pocked panes
I should have washed last week
with tears. I'm crying now. He's crying.

Together we can see through to our star,
the fabricated-from-dust-polestar,
my fear of blazing there, his of eternity.

We know we have this moment here together,
don't we, fly? Yours seconds from now,
mine unknown, extinguishment a second sight
unpeeling the constellations beyond this one.

Winging minute, let's try to be one,
can't we, now? One split-second—now,
here, in this sun looking after me, decades.
Oh, no, you're gone. I'm alone, my always.

The Dream of the Hut
~ Jake Crist

after Bachelard

How'd it begin for that ancient hermit
They call Paul of Thebes? A sheet? With a sheet
Draped over the supper table—a cell,
Gingham-walled, in the midst of the muffled
Mysteries of his family's chitchat?
The light-shot cotton yurt of his mom's skirt,
Perhaps?

        Or perhaps, as I did, he sought
Palatial solace in the cardboard box
A fridge comes in, one he could snip eye-holes
Out of and lug to the creek to surveil
Crawdads, could crouch in to crib from lichen
The eremitic aptitude for clutching
A single hard and fast thing.

            Maybe the monk
Hacked a Slugger at corn and slashed a nook,
Four stalks by four stalks, raked a spot to kneel,
Clear his mind, strain to hear wind comb the field
And feel, staring down a furrow, he formed—
As I did the day I fled, field-ward, from home—
A vector directed toward some sly
Indefiniteness, whose trajectory
Leapt depending on which eye he kept open.

Old Paul, clad in palm leaves, surviving in …
Not much: a cave, with a spring and a tree.
Each day—this has yet to happen to me—

A raven brought him half a loaf of bread.
When he died two lions emerged from the wild,
Manes flying, brushed the body with their tails,
Clawed a grave, and roared a prayer for his soul.

Still Life
~ Cynthia Cruz

At the start, there was a rich black cube,
filling with music. The organs within it,
were damp and silvering,
small glass beads beneath water
or the long wet body of an eel.
I was hungry and I wanted
to consume everything.
I wanted to be seen and swallowed.
Consumed like language or the way
the Berlin doctor changed me
by the simple act of placing his hands
on my body. When I whisper
what I am trying to convey is my own
feelings. I am still part animal and base
my movements on my intuitive sense and desires.
But they want us to move through the world
like the injured do, softened with trauma
and hurt in everyplace. I know all of this
is true. I am also ruined.
But contrary to hearsay,
I am not dead yet.
I will not stop saying the things
that threaten my own safety.
My whole life, I wanted to be
the queen in the film in the scene
where her body is encased in thick costume,
her face covered in white grease paint.
But no longer.
I want to be soft and kept
broken. I want to be touched
and spoken to like a human:

hands on the body,
breath on the mouth.

Old Blood Rising
~ Jim Daniels

Remember when you flicked your wrist
in my direction—slanting snow sifting down
magic through streetlight glow? Some questions
we hope go unanswered, but we ask them
anyway. Magic? Really?—

walking on the other side
of West Center with that guy
you dumped me for that you've been
married to for thirty years now. I admit
I was kneeling in the snow begging you
to come back, my nose hairs frozen
in sub-zero self-pity. If I saw you again
I'd tell you that was my idea of a joke.

Because how could we ever go back
down there, the dark vault of betrayal,
my faux suicide, tears and snot,
kids blowing up things, thinking
that's what love did.

Remember those great orgasms
we had in the basement
on my father's warped pool table,
bringing each other off, hands
shoved down each other's tight jeans?
Those rafters never looked so good
as we swallowed sighs and listened
for each upstairs creak.

He was a creep back then, but I'm sure
he's matured in thirty years and lost
his hair. See, I'm full of jokes.

Today walking in Shaw park
where we used to—you know—
I ran into my own kid in flecto dilecto
under the bridge with a young partner,

and I remembered. Our lives sucked,
we always used to say. We're old
enough to have ghosts and tender moments.

Remember? When's the last time you saw
an ink eraser? All they did was tear the paper
to shreds. When's the last time you saw a hickie?

Maybe that's what we needed to do,
rip up the damn paper and be done
with it. But they didn't teach us how
in gym class or Michigan History
or Outdoor Chef or Homemaking.

Marking each other's necks with blood
and pledging eternal everything, burning
ourselves with the magnifying glass
and blaming the sun, in lieu of.

I would tell you that I kept walking
over that low bridge above my man-child
beneath me, thinking they must be cold
down there, hoping they were sighing

not crying. We take our magic
where we can get it, and it's often
(always?) dark magic. *I should have.*

I hate when I start saying that.
Nothing good comes of it. Boy
in the snow, get off your knees,
damn it. Save those knees.
Plenty more things to beg for
down the line.

My hands were cold
on that bridge. I reminded
myself that memory can't be
one long apology. I tilted
my neck toward the sky,
offering it up.

Sabbath Story #1: Circuit Breaker
~ Lydia Davis

Heat wave in city.
Orthodox Jew stands on sidewalk waiting for non-Jew to come along.
Non-Jew, stranger, comes along.
Will stranger help Jew?
Jew takes stranger into building and down into basement.
Stranger flips circuit breaker switch.
Now air-conditioning unit comes on again.
Upstairs in apartment, many Jews are sitting in undershirts sweating
    in heat.
Stranger is offered milk and cookies, in thanks.

Sabbath Story #2: Minyan
~ Lydia Davis

Man is standing on sidewalk outside synagogue holding cell phone.
Stranger comes along and asks man if he can use cell phone.
Man agrees, stranger makes call.
Man then asks in turn if stranger will come inside synagogue.
Needed: one more man to make up minyan.
Stranger agrees, stays for most of service.

Dead Boy
~ Kwame Dawes

Somewhere off the coast
on a green, the cool language
of pragmatic villagers masters
the tongue of ownership;

he is ours, we come to these stones,
plant flowers, grow to love
the mute face of a child
who loved so hard he died

rather than be abandoned—
of course, the dead can't speak
and the stone is a curse,
shouting to the bleating sky.

Return as Ticket
~ Chard deNiord

When I'm forced to return home to retrieve
something I've forgotten, I enter a double zone
that's the road I just went down but am returning
on now with an altered vision of its sameness
that turns it into another road which is so different
I hardly know what to call it as I speed forward
in heading back, taking in everything that is so familiar—
the fence posts, pasture, elms, and burdock—
as suddenly strange through the lens of inconvenience.
It's almost a dream, but nor really—more
a consequence of accepting my mistake,
which allows me in turn to see, if even briefly,
so many things I've hidden from myself, as if my mind
needed to forget to save my heart from the haste
that governs my life. Something shines in the distance.
I call it the lamp of internal difference that needs
the spark of my seeing anew to light its mantel.
Then everything I see I know was once forgotten
and lay in the dark behind the light. I hear the cries
of them all as parts of the whole in the silence
of my contemplation, in the absence of the single
thing that I've forgotten, and then the loss
of those I can't redeem. They are songs as well
that quiet the hum of my powerful engine
and slap of tires on wet macadam. I notice, too,
that the cobalt sky has now become the vault
for all I feel on the road of my remembering.
It's my ticket for the matinee of my own showing—
this turning back to fetch my wallet, this foreign film
I title "Late Again" with burning captions.

Nor Ever Would Be, Sadly, Would Be
~ Chard deNiord

Memory is almost enough if you're in solitary
or intensive care in which case the past merges
with the present in such a way that time passes
imperceptibly as thought itself causing you to lose
yourself in various versions of what only partly happened
so that you're here and not here at the same time,
both real and virtual, adding recall to supposition
and vice versa in the mercy of waiting somewhere,
as if the Higher Power were cognizant from the start
that pre-humans were destined to become human
that moment they became aware that they were remembering,
remembering, and it wasn't enough, and as an addendum
to this thought, that nothing was enough, nor ever would be,
sadly, would be. A wind blows across the earth like a page:
More, More, Whatever It Is. See how it passes away—
girders and all—in the flames you can only see on the screen
of your lids, not so towering but persistent, licking.
The single stroke that Lily made comes close,
her simple, untalented mark that was enough for then,
and now, which is all anyone can hope for at the end
of a war, which is always, at least so far. So far.

What Happened?
~ Stephen Dobyns

Taking first a morsel of squash,
then a bit of bread—an elegant
gray rat with glossy pelt, steps
lightly across the compost heap,

his best-loved spot, unaware
of the source of such largesse,
not having linked these gifts
to the mother who wears a path

from house to dump, or from
the disgusted to the grateful
as inside the house her toddler
flicks another splop of beets

onto the floor with carrots soon
to follow; what fills the child
with indignation is for the rat
attained ambition, a trickle-down

bounty, or so the rich might
have us think as they dole out
peanuts to the poor, making
the mom a middle-class flunky

who believes she's doing goodly
work. Is this the case? Not quite.
Instead she asks what happened,
as she recalls photos from the past:

her son's birth, her wedding, college,
winding her way back to fourth grade,
to one of those frigid winter days
when half the kids are dreaming

and she maps out a future of slashing
through a tangle of Amazon jungle,
a deadly snake in one hand, eager
to capture a jaguar with the other.

Mandelstam's Widow Talking to the Paper Birds
~ Norman Dubie

I know the winter stares you down, and its trees,
like the two silver rails
of the old war trains that narrowed to just *one*
at the always merging point of corrupted horizon.
The Writers' Union with cooling tangerines
rejects my translation of Coriolanus. The green manure
of donkeys on their trousers. That's right
you can smell them like a sea approaching. You can feel
them coming, faintly, like the shifting
reversals of a train whistle in the long cold morning.

These bastards took that grainy 'reddish' photograph
of my husband's corpse as the rigor
of a black tree branch wrapped in sheets
on the cold floor of a ventilating caboose. And sure,
why not, it is shitting little
valuable lumps of shiny anthracite
clear from here to the far forests of Siberia.

We are part of a caricature of famine that must come—
starving kids with heaving rib cages
collecting the incident debris of coal, delicate
pressed ferns and starry chalk aster.
They have dull paring knives between their teeth
for cutting weeds. Is this the gulf between real suffering
and the winter's fresh smoke,
the propaganda of a crawling sensitive self. You have
always smelled it coming,
like first snow in the southern cities. There,

true suffering is blushed over and thought
to be gauche. The erect corpses with cold cream

on their faces. *Alexandre. Enough.*

The pilgrims above
~ Norman Dubie

the sickly-green successive ribbing with tangerine arcseconds
in the night tunnel—fumes and the headlights flickering against
the staggered watch-boxes, blue with enamel sheeting. Your skirt
hiked up, a pint of scotch with a sanitary napkin, half a doughnut—
you thought that Nietzsche, Lou Andreas-Salomé, and Rilke
got lost walking in southern Russia. They had shared a hayloft
the night before with rain. A rain that was pure vinegar with
the ecstasy of simple feasting on pickles and cheese, the laughter
of Rilke urinating down on the white horses … the nettle-rose deciding
then and there to kill him with the simple prick of nitrogen,
a sepsis of the blood. Lou eating scrambled pheasant eggs off hot slate.
Friedrich finishing his cheese and dried plums smiles and says
bite me. Composte. Compadre. Calumny. Cunt. Chuckle. Catastrophe.
Then fewer and fewer uncorrupted witnesses. Mr. Terrance.
These 19th-century bosses are munching irritably on salted popcorn
while watching your lengthy movie, *The Night of Broken Tea Cups*,
yes, that's right, with glee what he had said was *you can bite me.*

My Rage As Mirage
~ Denise Duhamel

I can't believe my eyes
so I don't, and my rage—
a woman's rage—is not real to me
but something I doubt
and question and push down
until it rises up again
like the indotherm
from a comic-strip coffee cup
which is not really hot
though the swirl signifies
it is.
         I feel my hot cheeks and think
this can't be my rage,
my loss of control, but
it is.
         He'll say "oh you'll be fine"
or "shush now" or anything else
to indicate he is dropping
a anvil on my head
to squish it, squash it, squelch it,
but because of cartoon gravity
I emerge intact, my legs awhirl
so I can escape and go it alone,
turn up the volume,
the wide open—real
and unreal—road of this poem.

The Murder
~ Stephen Dunn

You imagined it this way:
the accusation would be wrong;
you wouldn't have done it,
but, because you might have,
knew you could have,
you'd accept the verdict
as something you'd endure
and be known by. However,
you worried that the jury
would see you as a victim
of certain books you had read,
not to mention of a lawyer
you imagined declaring
you were an innocent
instead of innocent, at which time
you'd stand up and say
an adamant No, thinking
in this case was the same
as doing, and you were
in fact thinking of acts
both gruesome and justified.
Problem was, you realized,
there'd be no evidence
of a body, but there was this man,
awful in his bones, who for years
you had wanted to kill
(your wife disliked him, too),
and why not just do it, you thought,
and hide his body
and then your very own self
in the mountains of Pennsylvania,

terrain so dense and wooded
they'd have to import a sherpa
to find any trace of a murder or you.
Besides, it was sweet to imagine
how your wife might help you
live off the land,
she who could distinguish
harmless delicious berries from what
were equally delicious but lethal.
You were a city boy,
she always had joked, you couldn't
start a fire from scratch without her,
or make a tent stand up to the elements.
This man, this lifeguard
who once had humiliated you,
had so disturbed your sleep
and therefore your wife's sleep as well,
that it became clear to you his death
might be good for your marriage,
not to mention your soul.
In the summer months you'd dine
on greens and mushrooms and those berries.
In the winter on venison, and you'd have
the pleasure of being cuddled up with her,
your loved one, only slightly disappointed
that the authorities with their analytics
and their dogs wouldn't get a sense
or scent of you, and even if they could
there'd still be no evidence of a body,
and that jury that never really existed
perpetually hung, deadlocked.

from *One Poem Stands*
Russtylove
~ Efe Duyan, translated by Richard Gwyn

I call you honeyovsky
didn't we learn to love from Russian novels

the first night you slept beside me
is in my mind, written in cuneiform script
no, no, as a cave painting

at the start I let you wait a while
forgive me for that

for some time now I've hidden your name
you don't know why

the scarf you were knitting was left half finished
let it be, until next winter
so that your loneliness is only partial, also

that green apple you gave to me one morning
let it be a secret password between us

and let your eyebrows grow
the pretentiousness scares me,
just as it does with architecture and poetry

your legs are full of childhood wounds
we make love at a canter
we love each other,
patient as your growing hair

but I still confuse
the long nicknames in Russian novels

Tek Şiirlik Aşklar
Kirilaşk
~ Efe Duyan

tatlovski diyorum sana
rus romanlarından öğrenmedik mi sevmeyi

yanıma uzandığın ilk akşam
çivi yazısıyla hafızamda
hayır, hayır: bir mağara resmi

seni biraz bekletmiştim başlarda
o kadarını affet

bir zaman sakladım adını
bilmiyorsun neden

yarıda kalmış ördüğün atkı
kalsın, yeni bir kışa vesile-
ve yarım yalnızlığın, güzel işte

sabah çıkarken yeşil bir elma uzatmıştın
aramızda bir parola olsun bu

ve bırak uzasın kaşların,
korkutuyor beni yapmacıklığı
bazen mimarinin şiirin bile

yara dolu çocukluktan bacakların
seviştiğimiz koşar adım
sevdiğimiz uzayan saçlarınca sabırlı

ama rus romanlarında
uzun takma adları hala karıştırıyorum

Why All the Ladies Like Ray
~ Cynthia Schwartzberg Edlow

A-SIDE

Your title is inaccurate, says Ray.
Look at TV, the movies, books, haven't you
ever noticed all the assholes are named Ray?
Your title should be "Why is Ray always
the Asshole?"

But oh my, he leaves messages on your phone like,
Thank you for thinking of me.
I like that
in my goddesses.

Or when your book gets published,
Don't send me a copy. I want to buy it
at Barnes & Noble and go up to the
cashier, have him take my money,
put it in the paper bag. Then, delighted,
I'll say to him, 'I know this woman.
In the biblical sense.'

Or he's in the hospital with heart failure. They've slit
his legs for healthy veins. He calls it shark-
shred, so food is the topic,
I thought hospital food was slotted
somewhere in between jail food and airplane food
but I have a six-page menu to wander through
plus cable!

Or his cell phone, which is always on
but never answered,
    I was checking the pictures
    on my cell phone; they're all pictures
    of the inside of my pocket.

He copies 33,342 songs to your iPod. You take
it for granted, as you've always taken it,
since he has the largest music collection
in the Midwest, that every album you're seeking
is at your fingertips. How does it happen
Paul Simon's *Graceland*
is missing? You won't believe it. Nine years—
you still won't believe it. It must be
in some compilation file. The crazy technology
has it hidden. *Graceland* is in there
and it has to be.

B-Side

comes on mellow with tiny scratches and pops
like most side Bs.
Swinging you back to that high summer
before college. He placed the long version
of "Papa was a Rolling Stone" on the turntable.
How many minutes was it before the vocals
started in—nine? Ten? Ten minutes of instrumentals,
and each instrument morphed from moist
fingered dalliances on wood
on metal on string on ivory into plunging
blond crystals of harmonic laminae.

Those are Miles Davis horns
right there. You hear how they copied
Miles' signature?

Think of mica for a second, call it something odd
to get your attention. That misbegotten stray—that'll do—
the mineral, famous for shaving off effortlessly
into shimmery sheets of see-through leaves, one
after one,
like that it happened,
each instrument separated out
and fell into your ears,
which so loved what they captured
that such tones liquefied
during the descent through your body
into warm golden oil and there they remained then
and now forever, where your wings would meet,
in the brace of your spine
who gives you nerve.

I Like to Bounce
~ Elaine Equi

Everything is brimming with itself
like a cup of hot coffee that can only
be held by three plastic cups, placed
one inside the other—body, mind, heart –
in order to frame, ritualize, contemplate
the moment. I don't know how to tell you
but you are only a localized fraction
of a Great Mind asleep in a dollhouse,
your shrunken head resting upon a blue
pillow. "I like to bounce," you say to
no one in particular, riding the raft
of your mattress over an ocean of painted
brainwaves. Angelina Jolie is there
somewhere, but it isn't the real AJ,
only a dream double. "I like to bounce,
and I like to rock," you add—revising
your statement, amending your essence.
This is it—your Descartes moment. These
are the facts with which no one may quarrel.

Three Poems
~ Mikhail Eremin, translated by Alex Cigale

Whether the slit in fish bone or the little steely needle eye,
The golden thread of acquisitiveness is durable and boundless,
So as not to fall under the sway of despondency,
Busy oneself with, something like, calculation,
Continuing a nearly forgotten dispute,
How many, given fallibility, plus or minus a creature,
Nanodromedaries, may be fitted onto
The head of a pin?

2011

ТРИ СТИХОТВОРЕНИЯ
Михаил Еремин

Что прорезь в рыбьей ко́сти, что стали́стое ушко,—
Златая нить стяжательства прочна́ и бесконечна,
Дабы с того не впасть в уныние,
Заняться, что ли, вычислением,
Продолжив подзабытый диспут,
Сколь много может уместиться, при погрешности
Плюс минус о́собь, нанадрамадеров
На острие иглы?

2011

… out of what thrash bin …
 —A. Akhmatova

The cracks running along the stucco ceiling
Bring to mind first the craquelure
(The Lord's anointed Masters of olden times.),
Then the quenched, having been deciphered,
Wall-side prophecy,
Whereas the thieving
Foreman overcooked it, it would seem, with urine,
While the lime was insufficiently slaked.

2012

Daniel 5.26-28

 … из какого сора…
  А. Ахматова

Пошедшие по штукатурке трещины
Наводят память то на кракелюры
(Иных времен от Бога мастера.),
То на погасшее, быв истолковано,
Настенное предначертание,
Тогда как вороватый
Прораб переборщил, видать, с уриной,
Да известь не была достаточно гашёной.

2012

Дан. 5; 26-28

Barely even two apples indistinguishably alike
(Out of the ovary—under the sun, or shaded by foliage).
May be found on the branch weighed by them? Could be
Experimentum crucis (Landslide beyond remotest lands.
The girl assistant had squabbled with her beloved.)—
Yet still no verdict on unacknowledged discoveries, which,
Particularly now, are legion,—He sees,
And there will be no place for an apple to land.

2012

Едва ли даже два неотличимо сходных яблока
(От завязи—под солнцем, либо затененное листвой.)
Найти на ветви ими отягчённой? Может статься,
Experimentum crucis (Оползень за тридевять земель.
С возлюбленным в размолвке ассистентка.)—
Еще не приговор непризнанным открытиям, которых,
Особо ныне,—тьма Того гляди,
И негде будет яблоку упасть.

2012

The Great Organizer is Dead
~ Marie Étienne, translated by Marilyn Hacker

His shape still drifts here, it can be seen on certain evenings, if you adjust the lighting, lingering close by but his words no longer have value, which makes him despair and makes him an errant spirit, damned and doomed buffeted by thoughts surrounding him.

—Their swarm imprisons me, he offers from far off, I'm nothing but their noise, but not a soul, no, souuuls don't exist peeeeeople made up not dyyyyyying totally, I am totally deaaaaaaad despite all the words I scribbled inside notebooks.

His scrawny body is standing there undressed, the crowd sees his belly darkened by hairs, his sex gathered in he makes a gesture with his arm.

Of prayer, of menace?

With him it's both at the same time.

      *

But stop being dead, stop acting even though it's your profession, be nice, come and sit down, explain yourself, explain to me, so that we believe you at last, at last kiss your heart.

Do you remember when you were walking through the stage-sets still shedding dust since they'd just come from the carpenters' workshop, you came and went, dressed in your black slacks, boys and girls surrounded you like good apostles, or at least you hoped so because most of them would be Judases, the fatal kiss, that's what they had in store for you, but you deserved it, don't you think?

Do you remember that when I cried you didn't understand?

What was wrong?

The city outside was suspect, covered in snow, the river water too thick, the riverbanks muffled.

*

You were looking at my mouth, neither bored nor annoyed.

What's the matter, what's the matter, you said, *everything's fine.*

Outside, everyone went about his business, the monuments were brand new, they had just been washed, Notre Dame itself seemed to take part in the celebration, with its bridal airs, we didn't want to part.

Do you remember when you spoke to the other one, one eye on her and one on me.

Not bothered, not bothered.

To tell the truth, you were fleeing from the one and the other, with words you chose to uproot a life.

*

Do you remember when we were near the door, it was the end, I had my hand on the doorknob and you said:—Don't worry, you'll always have enough to pay the gas and water bills.

Yes, that's so, the gas exploded and the water covered everything.

Not a trace, not a trace, he who loved them so, I wring my hands, no, idiots, I am not Macbeth and even less Bérénice.

I have no more stigmata, I am virginal, I am new, at least from the exterior.

—You think so? Look at yourself?

Who is speaking?

*

I hear only my own voice in the deserted palace, my voice at least has not burned, that reassures me.

He won't answer.

Calm down, calm down, nothing of him will come to comfort you.

What I have told about him until now is false, I kept to the high style, but I would like to scratch, rip off decorum, expose what is beneath the words: the truth is terrible: *drainpipes and waste water.*

Yes, I'd like to scratch, rip, so that what emerges?

— In me there's nothing, I'm nothing, nobody.

Perhaps that's the scandal, in him there is nothing.

*

What good is work, great intelligence, what good is art especially, that foam that's tasted and just as soon wasted in the racket of words, of chairs being moved, of passing faces?

One night I dreamed I was completely impudent, imprudent, that I dared, dared myself, bared my speech before him, take it or leave it, it's your choice.

But I am no longer there, for once I belong to myself, completely impudent, imprudent.

—She's not playing her part, they whispered about me in the bannered theater.

*

You've already shown that the king was naked, that the king was clumsy, his gnarled body graceless, you've already shown that the center was empty once the rind was peeled away. And it does me no good now to shout about you, to warn the good people:

—There's nothing to you!

You have already shouted it, the good people don't believe us, worse, they shake their heads, the truth's too raw, they prefer the ready-made that's so convenient, cooked and seasoned.

That's why from now on his empty center will serve as an altar where the faithful kneel, white penitents, gray penitents, the whole rigmarole. We needn't be alarmed, it's all in the bag, *and he is buried.*

Le grand ordonnateur est mort
~ Marie Étienne

Sa silhouette flotte encore, on le voit certains soirs,

si on ajuste l'éclairage, traîner dans les parages mais ses mots n'ont plus court, ce qui le désespère et fait de lui une âme errante, damned, pauvre damné et chahuté par des pensées qui l'environnent.

– Leur essaim m'emprisonne, profère-t-il de loin, je ne suis que bruit d'elles, mais pas une âme non, les âââmes n'existent pas, les hooommes ont inventé qu'ils ne mouououraient pas tout à fait, je suis mooort tout à fait malgré les mots que j'ai tracés à l'intérieur de mes cahiers.

Son corps maigre est debout sans habit, la foule voit son ventre assombri par les poils, son sexe ramassé, il fait un geste avec le bras.

De prière, de menace ?

Avec lui c'est les deux à la fois.

*

Mais cesse d'être mort, cesse de jouer la comédie bien que ce soit ta profession, sois gentil viens t'asseoir, explique-toi, explique-moi, pour qu'on te croie enfin, qu'on baise enfin ton coeur.

Tu te souviens quand tu marchais dans les décors encore fumants d'être juste sortis des ateliers des menuisiers, tu allais et venais, vêtu de ton pantalon noir, garçons et filles t'entouraient en bons apôtres, du moins tu l'espérais car la plupart furent des Judas, l'embrassement mortel, voilà ce qu'ils te réservaient mais tu le méritais ne crois-tu pas ?

Tu te souviens quand je pleurais, tu ne comprenais pas.

Où était le malheur ?

Dehors la ville était suspecte, recouverte de neige, les eaux du fleuve trop épaisse, les berges assourdies.

*

Tu regardais ma bouche, ni ennuyé, ni agacé.

– Qu'est-ce que t'as, qu'est-ce que t'as, disais-tu, *tout va bien.*

Dehors, chacun vaquait, les monuments étaient tout neufs, on les avait lavés de frais, Notre-Dame elle- même paraissait à la fête, avec son air de se marier, nous hésitions à nous quitter.

Tu te souviens quand tu parlais à l'autre, un oeil sur elle, un oeil sur moi.

Pas gêné, pas gêné.

A vrai dire tu fuyais l'une et l'un, avec des mots choisis pour arracher la vie.

*

Tu te souviens quand nous étions près de la porte, c'était la fin j'avais la main sur la poignée et tu as dit :

– T'en fais donc pas, t'auras toujours de quoi payer l'eau et le gaz.

Oui en effet, le gaz a explosé, l'eau a tout recouvert.

Plus de traces plus de traces, lui qui les aimait tant, je me frotte les mains, je me frotte les mains, non imbéciles, je ne suis pas Macbeth, encore moins Bérénice.

Je n'ai plus de stigmates, je suis vierge, je suis neuf, du moins à l'extérieur.

– Tu crois ? Regarde-toi.

Qui parle ?

*

Je n'entends que ma voix dans le palais désert, ma voix au moins n'a pas brûlé, ça me rassure.

Lui ne répondra pas.

Calme-toi, calme-toi, rien de lui ne viendra t'apaiser.

Ce que sur lui j'ai raconté jusqu'à présent est faux, j'ai gardé le grand genre, mais j'aimerais gratter, ôter la bienséance, exposer ce qui est sous les mots : la vérité qui est terrible, *les canalisations et les eaux sales.*

Oui j'aimerais gratter, pour qu'apparaisse quoi ?

– En moi il n'y a rien, je ne suis rien, personne. Cela peut-être est le scandale, en lui il n'y a rien.

*

A quoi bon le travail, l'extrême intelligence, à quoi bon l'art, surtout, cette mousse qui se goûte et se dissout tout aussitôt dans le bruit des paroles, des chaises qu'on remue, des visages qui passent ?

Une nuit j'ai rêvé que j'étais tout entier impudent, imprudent, que j'osais, je m'osais, je posais ma parole devant lui, tu la prends tu la laisses, c'est ton droit.

Mais je ne suis plus là, je suis à moi pour une fois, tout entier impudent, imprudent.

– Il est sorti du rôle, murmurait-on à mon sujet, dans les salles pavoisées.

*

Tu as déjà montré que le roi était nu, que le roi était gauche, son corps noueux sans grâce, tu as déjà montré que le centre était vide, une fois sa pelure enlevée.

Et j'ai beau à présent te crier, pour alerter les bonnes gens :

– En toi il n'y a rien !

Tu l'as déjà crié, les bonnes gens ne nous croient pas, pire ils secouent la tête, le vrai paraît trop cru,

on lui préfère l'accommodé qui est commode, le cuit avec des condiments.

C'est pourquoi désormais son centre vide sert d'autel où s'agenouillent les fidèles, pénitents blancs, pénitents gris, tout le commerce.

Ne nous alarmons pas, l'affaire est dans le sac, *et lui est enterré.*

You're Sitting Here Stiff
~ Sylva Fischerová, translated by the author and A. J. Hauner

You're sitting here stiff, wrinkles
like dead ends
in the middle of Rome.
It might have been me. Our sisters and
brothers
are moving on—instead of us—
into odd quarters
where spirits & memory & roes
yeast;
where they take off their face,
with a piece of nose, an eyelid
like a jar lid,
a smile,
a word.
Blood is its reverse side,
it's a Jew and flows
the other way,
from death to birth,
it shoots out a craddle with placenta,
a red
swallowing
monster—
Sister, everyone's Jewish,
shooing away their dreams
in the night, covering their face
with darkness—
It was a New Year, white
like the velour of a tsar's
glove,
sister, I came out to the plain

and asked the angel
to touch your eyes
and fill in the void
behind your shoulders.

Sedíš Tu Strnulá
~ Sylva Fischerová

Sedíš tu strnulá, vrásky
jako slepé cesty
uprostřed Říma.
Mohla jsem to být já. Naše sestry, naši bratři
se přesouvají místo nás do podivných
čtvrtí
kde kvasí pálenka paměť jikry
tam si sundají tvář, s ní
kus nosu, víčko
jak víčko od kofoly, úsměv,
slovo.
Krev je svůj
rub, je Žid a teče naopak,
od smrti k narození, vyplaví
kolíbku i s placentou, rudá zalykavá
příšera—
Sestro, každý je Žid, v noci rukou
odhání sny
tmou zahaluje tvář
Byl nový rok, bílý
jako aksamit carské
rukavičky, sestro, vyšla
jsem na pláň
a prosila anděla, aby se dotkl tvých očí
a zaplnil prázdno za tvými rameny

Dream Travel
~ John FitzGerald

The Place

From my desk comes an instance in the sound of footsteps
when I know they're not passing, but coming toward me.
In such moments I act busy, pick up a pen,
hold the phone to my ear and pretend I can't wait
for this idiot to hang up,
twist my wrist to see I have no watch.

The Little Girl

I can't have complex thoughts.
Screw the rules, become a diver.
It's an easy story.
Repel, attract, a magnet.
If the ship sinks take the highest ground you can.
The crowd shoves me off the edge,
I'm drowning.
Only the poet notices.
She jumps in after me.

Anne

We come out on the other side.
My name's not really Anne,
it's just a word I call myself.
I'm a kind of guide.
I used to work like a man in the market.
Now it's different, I have all I desire.
Don't worry about anything,
I'm in good shape.

Coral Reef

This Captain didn't detect me—
overestimated depth.
His ship isn't going anywhere.
He only guessed where it was headed to begin with.
So we're stranded together, disenfranchised,
swollen as sponges in a sacred-scared experience,
where fish tears must be stone to notice.

Water

I'm in this certain place,
gathered at the lowest point.
I hold so still you reflect yourself,
get tall and shrink as I rise and fall.
If you come you'll end up someplace else.
That's how I roll.
There's this motion.
Make it work for us.

Portal

Only certain people come here.
It's no accident.
I draw them in, transfer them.
I get them in the water somehow.
Reach a point in life where I'm no light through a hole.
I'm going to change and never finish.
Don't believe what you're told.
Look with me.

The Long Black Road
~ Keith Flynn

Having been chased into the roar and clash,
trapped on the Pennsylvania Turnpike,

even the 10-point buck, agile as he was,
could not escape; no way to fudge this.

The first car caught him square on the
right back flank and cast him airborne.

Through some miraculous twist, or will,
he managed to land on his feet, only to

discover that the back half didn't work,
and he used his front hooves to scramble

and claw to the fence, where he wedged
his head and jerked beneath it as best he could,

his only thought the darkness of the woods.
There he flopped and writhed, still firmly

in this world, his frantic mind wracked with pain.
Ink-blot clouds were nosing across the sunny

mountainside, like the shadows of giant fish
moving just beneath the surface of the sea.

The trooper on the scene would not discharge
his weapon, too much paperwork for that, so I

finally did it, finished the buck with a baseball bat.
It was all I had, and washed the bashed brains

off the wood of my Louisville Slugger with water
I had saved to drink. Sometimes I think what

it must be like for an animal to encounter a road.
Same as a human watching figures in flight,

bouncing across the surface of the moon,
some vacant place without oxygen or light,

one wrong move from death's certain broom.
Damn things ought to learn, the trooper said,

and turned his back on the night. All the drivers
steered past, thankfully trapped behind their steel

and glass, their futures fixed and their suitcase
packed, right foot planted firmly on the gas.

With Pure Smiles
~ Luigi Fontanella, translated by Michael Palma

to G. F.

This evening they all intersect
rays signs and compass needles of the one
who'd counted on you. I'm trying to tear down
the wall of air between us, but you are
so far away. In an unspoken prayer
I wish myself the power to one day
overtake you there
where bodies have no weight and where
matter will not constrain us anymore.
Thus, with no memories and no desires,
we'll be able to talk to one another
armed, perhaps, with pure smiles.
May everything happen as I wish it here.
Let it all harmonize without us so that then
we will come back again
heroes this one time at least, my father.

February 2016

Di puro sorriso
~ Luigi Fontanella

a G. F.

Stasera s'incrociano
raggi segni e lancette di chi aveva
puntato su di te. Cerco di abbattere
il muro d'aria che ci separa, ma tu sei
molto lontano. In una preghiera
inespressa mi auguro di poterti
un giorno raggiungere
là dove i corpi non hanno peso
né la materia ci condizionerà.
Così, senza ricordi e senza desideri,
potremo dialogare
armati, forse, di puro sorriso.
Che ogni cosa si compia in quest'attesa.
Tutto si armonizzi senza di noi
che ritorniamo eroi
per una volta sola, padre mio.

febbraio 2016

Children in the Park
~ Luigi Fontanella, translated by Michael Palma

Children are playing
in this air that's growing pale.
I glimpse them in the park
wavy, evanescent,
pure potentiality.
While I watch them lost in thought
I pierce as deeply as I can
the mystery that is within me
to know him, to comprehend him,
to show myself to him
with all the heedlessness
of the young boy that I used to be.

April 2016

Bambini nel parco
~ Luigi Fontanella

Giocano i bambini
in quest'aria che trascolora.
Li intravedo nel parco
ondulanti, evanescenti,
pure potenzialità.
Mentre li guardo soprappensiero
penetro quanto più mi è possibile
il mistero ch'è dentro di me
per conoscerlo, approfondirlo,
mostrandomi a lui
con la stessa incoscienza
del ragazzino che sono stato anch'io.

aprile 2016

~ Albert Goldbarth

*To Cure the Tooth-Ach, Take a new Nail, and make the Gum
bleed with it, and then drive it into an Oak.*
 —John Aubrey, circa 1680

Because Stewie's girlfriend Dangerfield
is in lockdown tonight, in lockdown in a straightjacket
so her self-cut arms can hug her chest
like a crest—two lengths of ladder rungs
crossed over a pale field of double mastectomy—
I'm including in this stanza the common roofing nail
she used, and that she photographed and posted
in her "cry for help" which echoed all day
in the cyberair of the Web until her parents erased it;
and even though Stewie and Danger don't know
Wendell and how drink has done to his memory what chemo
did to his hair, I'm including the nail for him

as well; and for Antoine and Dora, you can see divorce
upon their faces like the cracks that start
to thread across old wall paint; and the mothers
picking through the mounded bodies in that ditch
in that crazily genocidal nation in the news, until
each one has found her own death—hardened child and laid it out
on its back in the day's insulting sunshine;
and for Eddie, even—just Eddie, and his loneliness
we've been hearing about blahblah blahblah for years:
it's a real enough two tons of emotional hurt to him.
For every one of them: the nail. Let it absorb some of the coppery
taste of their pain. And now because I've always been fascinated

The Straub Tail Reaction
~ Stuart Friebert

"Inject a lab mouse with something
so its tail rises, arches over its back,
a classic case of opiate behavior!"
Dr. Holub said, introducing me to his
pet nude mouse that day we were
turned away from Kafka's grave by
a Russian tank crew on maneuvers
in the adjacent park, rudely escorted
back to Holub's clinic. "It's a good
thing we weren't caught helping
each other over the wall," he said.
We'd not been granted admission,
'who knows why?' a constant refrain
till the velvet curtain came down &
Havel promptly made Holub some sort
of science advisor. He didn't last, alas;
lost the struggle to change Havel's mind.

"BROWN COAL'S STILL OUR OPIATE!"
Holub's last postcard lamented, just
days before he dropped to the floor,
the razor still in his hand. No doubt one
of his many scientific papers centers
on the nature and cause of embolisms.

Fabricating Uncertainty
~ Philip Fried

Doubt is our product.
    —Hill and Knowlton, the pr firm representing the tobacco industry,
1953–1968

The pinnacle of the art and the most
time-consuming part is the stitching
of hyper-fine thread as molten pig
iron is poured from a blast furnace
into openwork fabric, the holes
admitting argon or nitrogen
bubbled into the ladle to make
scores of intricate minuscule stitches
that with fluxes in the vessel
form an emulsion, if executed
deftly by needle or, nearly as good,
by bobbin and pillow, and mixed correctly
left over right and right over left,
link the Old French *las*, which is noose,
to Latin *lacere*, ensnare or entice,
when highly pure oxygen's introduced
at supersonic speed through the lance,
producing doubt in industrial bulk
while reflecting an artisan's flair for gossamer

Fate Written on the Forehead
~ Jeff Friedman

They say fate is written on your forehead at birth, but when I look in the mirror, I see creases: a crow sitting on a branch perusing the long rows; a dog chasing a squirrel into a ravine; a woman bowing her head; an old man cursing the squirrels that tightrope the fence railing surrounding his garden. There are no magic letters that signify the future, no hieroglyphs, no symbols that stand for anything but symbols, no stars aligned with specific planets and the sun and moon, only twins arguing over the family fortune—if there were a family fortune. Dust falls from my forehead but no matter how much I squint, I don't see the word "truth" or "death," so I may be like a golem, but I'm not actually a golem. No piece of parchment with a fortune printed on it pops from my cookie. Still, after all these years, my forehead's overcrowded. My fate must have dissolved long ago in the heat and rain, but a few bats scratch at the cracks in my hairline, trying to get back in.

by sympathetic magic–the dug-up tuber that reverses
male impotency, because of its shape; the ruby
(precious, blood-red, and mineral-hard) that serves to guard
the hymen–I must pile up such completely and intentionally
extraneous recountings as, say, those of the intrepid
nineteenth-century balloonists who first realized
an aerial map of the country could be made by night,
acoustically (one dog-bark meant "a lonely, isolated farm";
a chorus of barking, "villages or railheads"; and silence itself
"spoke eloquently of the great open prairies"), while daylight
revealed that insects–lacewings, ladybirds, butterflies–
rise "to about nine thousand feet," a living, graceful

zoetrope around the explorers' wicker encasement. So
many adventures!—in 1979, two doughty cetologists who
were studying a pair of breeding gray whales ventured a little
too close: the female swam beneath their "small
inflatable research craft," and, at that craft-and-coochie
alignment-moment, the male began to hammer his impressive
penis into her, and "we were used as a diaphragm." Wonder
webs our psyche like the lace inside a tangerine.
And the purpose of this oak-thick mess of exempla I've been
listing above? … well, somewhere in the hodgepodge of it all
I've driven a nail; and with it I'm burying
its consignment of torments: Dangerfield's;
Wendell's; Dora's; Eddie's; all those mothers'; even yours.

American Alien
~ Beckian Fritz Goldberg

The truck ahead of me is American
with a bumper sticker that says NRA, and one
that recommends *I Cowgirl Up
or Stay Home.* Look at me
trying to look tough in my little car while
the silver silhouette of a naked woman
blinks at me from each mudflap, one
with wings and a halo, the other a tail
and horns. The sun flashes off their chrome
bright bodies as the flaps sway, naughty
and nice, strobing my eyes with nuclear
white light until I think maybe they're
bouncing signals to my brain and I'll
go out and buy boots, get a big dog, get
a Smith and Wesson and love my country.
My country

is the desert and it looks just like Iraq.
Here, we have a legislature
which decided we need a state gun,
after all we had a state bird and a state
flower. They also decided that guns
can go to college just like everyone
else. Meanwhile I watch the state birds
who've made a hole black as a socket
up in the saguaro they go in and out of.
This afternoon I'm headed home, still
a goddamn heathen pothead liberal
worried about animal extinction. Except

for the woodpecker who jackhammers
my roof early every morning. I know
my rights.

My rights are sweet sleep, good coffee
and Leave-Me-the-Fuck-Alone. I also
have a state bird and a state flower. I'm partial to
the local hummingbird, the blossoming
desert senna's fragrance and I'm voting for
a state disease. I lean toward manic-depression.
I lean toward those tiny gold blossoms
just to breathe the perfumed air above them before
they drop and pucker into dry brown kisses
and roam the earth. Then I think about
the driver of the truck, what kind of brain
she had, as if she were an alien, and did she
ride a horse named Misty did she even know
the history of anything before the millennium,
that nothing beats the thrill of putting the right
word in exactly the right place though we are
free in this country to put the wrong word
in the wrong place and run for office
and say you believe in freedom
when you really mean money.
My freedom,

her freedom, ours, theirs, it has always been
split between the angels of yes
and no, between Honk if You Love Jesus and
Send Every Juan Home, everyone on the open road
thinking they're going the right direction
as the cowgirl in her truck sticks her

pink fingernails out the window and adjusts
the side mirror before she pulls away. I'm thinking
how about a state rock, igneous or
metamorphic. I'm thinking she voted
for the Sheriff who I hate and who, by the way,
has mandated a county underwear for inmates
which is dyed pink. It's one step toward
a state T-shirt to wear with our guns in bars
with cattle skulls hung on the wall alongside
the taxidermied specimen of a jackalope.
The shirt says God Bless America
My shirt

says I'm suspect. My shirt says
It is All a Political Hegemony Run by Arrogant
Short-sighted Reactionary Pimps for Corporations
Run by Weasels. And I'm watching the blue
metallic gleam of the tailgate as she turns
the corner and I get a whiff of
her music from the rolled-down window,
a man with a twang singing *don't matter*
what went wrong, tonight I'm back where
I belong/ tonight I'm—and the song drops
as she accelerates into the rest of her life
which I hope is happy
as it can be for a half-angel half-bitch
driving her half-ton 4x4. May she
someday have a scandalous affair
with the deacon of her church or better yet
get caught naked in a motel with her lover
by her lover's wife, and bolt
right past her out the door and across

the parking lot wearing his T-shirt
bearing the image of Ché Guevara
and ride home bare-ass in her truck
without hitting a single red light.

Here, After
~ Kathleen Graber

When she was walking this morning, a pair of martins
darted from a tree & swept past her ears, one on each side
so that she thought maybe the marriage had been like that,
two sets of wings, the color of twilight, on either side
of an idea no more substantial than the picture of the sky
the lake gives back—mesmerizing, changing, abiding,
but also unreal, even though the lake has somehow held
the sky within it for as long as it can remember
in the only way it knows how. She remembers the parrot
a childhood friend had owned, how it would call

the girl's mother in the voice of her father & her father
in the voice of her mother, the one or the other shouting
What? What? before finally bursting into the room
where only the bird stood, cocking its head as it talked
to itself in its cage. Maybe it had been like that—
but without the bird. Yes, she thinks, no bird,
though possibly the cage. Or, if the lake thinks *Shoreline
is just another word for embrace*, maybe the sky can't
understand why the lake seems to never show its true face,
why, though each drop of water is transparent, it seems

to always be hiding its depths. Even the mist they conjure
sometimes between them is not the fine suspension
either of them believes mist might be. One day the parrot
learned to imitate precisely the sound of the telephone
ringing so that soon everyone was rushing to lift the receiver,
heavy as a hope, saying *Hello? Hello?*—thrilled,
then disappointed. Was there another world outside
calling more, more, more? Now, in bed alone, the house
so quiet, she thinks of a book concluding, of a poet singing

low without accompaniment in his kitchen: *This train is a going away train, this train.* And she thinks the marriage had been like that, whistling its own refrain: *Already Gone.*

Selfie With Sort Of Sexual Affect
~ Paul Guest

I am not certain you are
anything, anywhere,
but see that I smolder
(green twigs in the banked
flames of tonight,
this incredible wilderness)
and see how deep
in sizzling nature
I always am. Just look,
would you, how I emerge
from the near
ruin of my bed:
artfully mussed, but alone!
Over there, where
you can't see at all
Robert Redford leans against the wall.
All denim, slow
burn, eyes blue
and lidded at once,
he's come in from the yard
having killed something with a wrench.
Covered in wet gore,
he's returned from the animal world to me.
I should get going,
fuss, coo, and tug and take
and mostly give
what he wants me to want.
Here, first, is this picture before
I disappear, too.

Following the Thread
~ Rachel Hadas

Wound in layers of wrappings
that tightly swaddle me,
from densely knit restrictions
I want to break free,

I want to pull a single thread,
follow it, trace a clue
like Theseus prowling in the maze
as far as he can go,

then, clueless, keep on groping
my way by touch alone
as far as the frontier
of a place I've never been.

A rivers roars straight through it
and I can just envision
a fragile rope-bridge swaying
over a dizzy chasm.

What else about that bridge? It strands
rotten, unravelling; then
by pilgrim generations
mended again, again.

Succession, replacement.
Gingerly travelers cross
the roaring rapids, whereupon
they're swallowed up in mist.

Transition, renewal.
Gleam of winter sun.
Below the bridge a silver boat
silently glides along;

melts into the horizon.
A shivering retinue
attends a white-robed figure
soon to be lost from view.

Smaller by the minute,
who stands and waves to me
from the receding deck? The sun
has sunk too far to see.

One star shines. A banner
flaps its faded red.
Tell me about parting,
the survivor said.

Now the beloved's gaily
signaling: hello!
A burnished sword, a bridal chest
wait in the hold below.

The chest is packed with silks and furs,
pots and pans and knives
enough to furnish a new world
and its attendant lives.

Ode to Roadside Shrines
~ Barbara Hamby

I first see you in Crete, little boxes on four skinny legs,
        nestled in an olive orchard on the dirt road,
with rain soaked and sun faded pictures of a saint
        or Mary or even Jesus with his crown of thorns,
or his sacred heart right there on his chest for everyone
        to see, and up in the mountains, where villages
are perched like awkward birds on the slopes,
        are shrines to partisans who were murdered
by the Nazis. What do you mean, little iron boxes
        in empty fields and beside parking lots,
some cluttered with trash, others overgrown with weeds
        and vines? Are you a prayer or are you
like a thank you card to the universe? Sometimes
        there is a photo of a young man,
so maybe you are like the crosses we see on tricky
        curves in the South with the names
of boys who drank too much whiskey on Saturday
        night and ended up in an early grave,
or the Sunday School teacher they hit and killed
        along with her little girl and baby,
and some of you seem to be forgotten, as if the man
        or woman who filled you with plastic flowers
and water bottles has died or moved to the next town,
        and there you stand, a pale green metal cage
with broken glass and a bird nest or wasp nest,
        but the flowers around your feet are real,
the wildest of wild flowers, tiny pinks or yellow
        buttercups or daisies like butterflies
perched on stems akimbo in the morning sun,
        so little boxes of the open road, bless me,

with your crooked legs and broken glass, show me
    the way to look at the unfathomable sky
above the Gulf of Corinth, take your candles, rocks,
    and rusted coffee cans and tell me a story,
and I will make my own boxes—one for my mother
    in her fur stole as a young working woman
in Washington, before the Bible squeezed her brain,
    and another for my father in his sailor's suit,
just a boy going off to war and lucky to survive,
    and another for Keats, who left his body
in Rome and Neruda who left his in Santiago,
    and one day we will all abandon our shrines,
whether they be houses or gardens or antique
    Mustang convertibles and drop our bodies
like we take off our clothes before bed, and what
    are we without our wardrobe of flesh?
Who are we moving through this world of shrines
    with our thoughtless jabs at the earth
and sky? Like a sailor washed up on a deserted
    shore, we will forget everything,
and be forgotten? Still we will have lived to stop
    and stare at an ant carrying a piece
of bread four times the size of his own body
    from our table to his waiting queen.

Apricots at Mycenae
~ Barbara Hamby

"I have a small piece of phobia about lifts,"
      says the young woman at the hotel in Mycenae,
so we take the elevator and she meets us
      at the top of the stairs. I'm carrying a paper bag
of apricots we stopped for on the road from Nemea,
      a sack of little suns. Out the window of our room,
she points to the distant mountain, a supine Agamemnon
      lying in wait for the day he will return.
The town is dusty, she says with sand from Africa.
      Around the hotel is a dynasty of calico cats,
one mewling in the hall—white with a black, white,
      and brown tail and cap. The next day,
we have lunch at another hotel run by a cousin
      of the two sisters, who own our hotel. He says
one of the sisters is weird—has 1000 dogs and the cats.
      Which is the weird sister? Maybe there's a third
who lives with the dogs. Maybe he got the English word
      for "thousand" wrong. That's a lot of dogs,
and I think about how much I get wrong, friends
      who turn out not to be friends, days that turn
into night, a nickel that turns into a thousand dollar check,
      and these apricots, mealy though they smell
like the apricots of my dreams, and what kind of woman
      dreams about the scent fruit, how a freshly cut
watermelon smells like summer, an apple like autumn,
      and an orange brings back afternoons
when the sun is hot, peeling the skin off in chunks
      or spiraling a ribbon of rind with a knife.
When we come in from a drive to Epidaurus,
      one of the sisters and her friends are watching

a miniseries on the Architect Sinan and his forbidden love
    for the Princess Mihrimah, the daughter of Suleyman
the Great that was on every television set in Istanbul,
    a tale of thwarted love. What they needed
was an army of 1000 dogs to conquer Constantinople
    and carry them away to India or China, but then Sinan
would not have built the two mosques for Mihrimah
    positioned so that on the Spring equinox, her birthday,
the sun sets behind the minaret of one mosque
    and the moon rises between the two minarets
of the other mosque, for her name meant Sun and Moon.

Double Agent, Stooge for Both Life and Death
~ Jennifer Michael Hecht

I

A woman, the constant gardener of a green
backyard plot. Now she is running inside,
half-cracked, menaced not by bees but
boredom (recollection). Sky is illuminated
gray and is darkening fast. Hours pass.

Now she is ginned up and running back
out there, trampling her living jewels.
Some as-yet green tomatoes will survive
this rampage, her heels a softer hell
than hail. They're looking for her.

Dragnet comes up empty because she's
never there. She weeds and weeds, unwinds
morning glory vines from pepper plants,
so we know she is out there. The constant
gardener loves clippers in her hand,

editorial demeanor demeaning what's dry,
unintended, or bitten by unseen squirrels,
but really does just enough to keep it
going, barely anything, it's a pose,
the constancy of the gardener, a stance.

II

Summer got hot, garden too thirsty, so she
let it die. Is that why? Doesn't she usually?
Flowers, red tomatoes had made her happy, now
brown stalks and branches, skeletal hands,
dying against their round tomato cages,

make her sad. Failures and successes in
little blooms of life or death are all
around her. She stops drinking wine or gin
and turns to water. Having ached for
rain she is confronted now with rivers.

Is she on the front stoop, and can we
count her? Is she drinking gallons of soda
water? Then you've found her. Tell her
that the brown garden is a recorded aria,
the shadow of what hasn't been neglected.

Even out here in the stars, the guns must
be inspected. It's not a world that's safe
for ripe tomatoes. Morning glories, surviving
all, are winding around her mind. Until now
unwelcome. Safire blue with aching violet.

Illumination
~ Bob Hicok

Onanism is today's word
in the butcher shop window.
Yesterday it was effulgent.
If you use the word of the day
in a sentence that pleases the butcher,
he gives you ten percent off.
His father was an accountant.
One plus one and all that.
His mother wore a yellow dress
made of actual sunlight.
In other words, she was a star.
He loved his mother
and his mother loved words.
She died when he was eleven.
The butcher came home from school—
he wasn't a butcher yet,
he was a boy who liked red licorice
and spent two weeks barking at people
because he wanted to be a dog—
and his father met him at the door,
face wet, eyes red, and unconsciously
strangling his hat, a fedora
that had done him no harm.
A car had struck her crossing the street.
At the intersection where the butcher
opened his shop. He wanted to be close
to her final seconds, close to her eyes
filling a last time with blue sky.
"Immanuel Kant wrote that onanism
is a sin, yet was said to practice onanism
once a week against an oak tree

in a park where he took his famous walk."
That would be my sentence
if I needed a brisket, a loin,
but I don't eat meat.
I don't eat anything at all.
No one can say why I'm not dead.
Scientists look at me and shrug.
They shrug like everyone else.
Shoulders go up, shoulders go down.
A shrug tells the truth,
begins in optimism
but ends in failure. Effulgent—
The butcher's mother's face
was effulgent. She used to touch my head
as I passed. Lightly.
As if her fingers were sparrows.
They may have been,
I never stopped to look.
I was busy living a moral life
because I didn't know what that was.
I didn't notice her sparrow fingers
but couldn't help but notice her face.
Other people smiled. She unfolded.
We have tiers and she was affection
all the way down. I knew that at ten
and I'll know that at one hundred.
If I get there, I'll be limping.
I'll know things, I just won't know
what they are.

Throwing a life line
~ Bob Hicok

Say you're a professor and one of your students
shot and killed thirty-three people.
Say it's years later. Fall's begun and kids
have that eager look of tulips in their faces,
of green life pushing up from the ground
toward sun. In the smile of one passing,
you see the joy of one who passed,
one of the thirty-three and follow her
with your imagination. You give her life
in a poem by having her run along a beach,
her children behind her and their grandparents
behind them, everyone wanting dinner,
everyone wanting stars to come out
and be their silly, shiny selves, everyone wanting
that next little breath. But let me ask—
are you drinking again? Have you driven your car
into a tree? Do you have a hurricane
for a heart? Do you wake on the wrong side
of the bed—the bottom, not the top?
Say you're so desperate for gun-control
that you're thinking of appealing to conservatives
by suggesting that murder is abortion
when one considers the children this woman
was likely to have had, the children
you just gave her in your poem
but are in danger of killing
if you let your anger take that political turn.
Don't do it. Don't you see that poems
make horrible legislation and even worse
bullet-proof vests, so brittle
and thin-skinned? Just let her live.

Let her run with the kite of her children
behind her. That's what I'd do
if I were you. And the drinking.
The driving into trees. I'd do those too.
I'd drink and crash and write one poem
for every day of her life. Hell. I'd drink more
and crash better and write two.

August, Fairbanks, Alaska
~ Sean Hill

I can't convince myself the trees are sick
any longer. They yellow not because
they're ailing; it's the sun's angle and the prick

of the chill here in August by the Arctic
Circle and this day, this crossing a line, the cause.
I can't console myself as the breeze flicks

yellow leaves from trees as if to tick
off passing moments. Leaves' changing gives me pause;
we're paling at the sun's angle near the Arctic.

Today the leaves turned the particular tint
of dead end signs I find after my wrong turns.
I can't convince myself the trees are sick.

Just now the air took on this season's peculiar scent,
and I'm sure the ravens' caws are guffaws.
Their calling and the sun's angle worry and stick

Me. All the changing leaves my nerves raw and spent.
Fretting too much, like us all, one of my flaws.
I can't convince myself the trees are sick—
failing leaves and light poison me like arsenic.

Ken, Don't Go To Meet The Ex-Girlfriend
~ Tony Hoagland

at the coffee shop in Montclair
that she referred to on the phone as "neutral territory."
Don't go while your wound is still open and raw,

or with some demented therapeutic notion
that you are going to "talk things through"
and "get some closure," or do some "conscious uncoupling."

That idea is as dumb as taking a vitamin
to care for a broken leg.
It is like using the lyrics of a top country western song

as your master blueprint for achieving happiness.
Furthermore, it is an expression of your own romantic masochism,
which, let's face it,

may play a sub-textual role in this whole,
if I can quote your former therapist, "narrative of unavailability"
which she says has something to do with your mom.

So Ken, don't go to meet her at the mall!
Don't agree to meet her at the Starbucks under the Cinzano umbrella!
which she suggested because as she has already told her friend Wanda

she wants to be in a public place
in case you "try to make a scene,"
as if you were a guy named Billy Bob with an Aryan tattoo,

a daytime drinking problem,
and poor impulse control.
Don't go to meet the ex-girlfriend, Ken!

She is already a personified can of mace pointed into your face.
She's an Egyptian hieroglyphic that doesn't want to be deciphered.
Her heart has been preemptively steeled and sheathed in anti-Ken-armor.

It isn't so bad to be halted in your tracks,
to stand on the baffled sidewalk, watching clouds in the late autumn sky.
It's not bad to feel ghostlike and useless
as the wilting flowers in your hand.

So Ken, be nobody now. Date nobody; kiss nobody.
Walk nobody gently nowhere, slow.
Stay home tonight and read Vivian Gornick essays about

the impossibility of modern relationship
and drink a glass of red wine and laugh
as you underline passage after brilliant passage.

from *In June the Labyrinth*
("to label something something")
~ Cynthia Hogue

There was an ancient well-site beneath the labyrinth
I did not reach, the part underground,
labeled (what else?) The Crypt.

But labels always hide something
about what they seem to define.
They set the thing apart

without disclosing why.
There the ancient grotto's
been blocked up to quell

"the miraculous waters"
in the "magical cave."
The desiccate source.

No well-being.
No archeological dig. No label
explaining who'd built what or when,

who'd come, and who'd destroyed
the Guardian of the Underworld,
as she was called. Or, is called.

Unblocked of late, her spring has not
sprung back. A guide will not say that.
The label kept me out.

(" a spire")
~ Cynthia Hogue

To confer a form on space
To consider the function

To cast space like a sculpture
or fix clothe pins on shaves of wood

so they curve around,
usefully shaping the space for sound

(from strings or a pipe through which wind)
To soar into a tower the exact height

of the nave's length, the one pointing
to sun or moon (depending),

the other toward the altar,
and beyond, the horizon

visible from the spire,
and the spire seen from anywhere:

the unstable hierarchy of proportions
the geometry of which has not sufficiently

("to walk the labyrinth is amazing")
~ Cynthia Hogue

Everything looped, spiraled, circular (thought)
But the labyrinth's not a maze but a singular way
to strike "the profoundest chord"
across aspire

Those who enter the labyrinth can leave
(pilgrims sometimes don't)
(You did not)
Inside the largest circle

(the labyrinth itself)
splits into equal parts
(demi-arcs or waves)
No, silly, you whisper, *petals*

*If measured through the centre of the petals there should be two parts for
each petal and one for the entry, but calculations from the measurements
show that this is not so. The difference is about ½". There is no way around
this problem.*

We must seek a solution
to the geometry of petals,
the consequential mystery
of your message:

*I was sick and am not
healed. I am not blind
but dead. I am not dead
but silenced. Alone, in love.*

I Am the Size of What I See (Fernando Pessoa)
~ Paul Hoover

You hurry but you are late
to every party and dinner date,
so naturally they begin without you.
Like a pale leaf through the window,
you make your entrance secretly.
Now you can shine in the corner
as quietly as any leaf,
rarely speaking and then in puzzles;
in English when they are Spanish,
in cliff-edge when they are hanging.
They are the size of what they see,
swimming in their vocabularies
of desire and principal interest.

You're a bird too young to fly,
a map without its pink and salmon.
You're so late you arrive on time,
and later slip out unnoticed,
not even a smudge on your glass.
They never knew what passed them.

You walk to the absolute corner,
where the roof of the sky
meets the limit of the eye
and a breath lasts a lifetime.

Beautiful dreamer,
you're the size of what you see.
The sky is the size of the sky,
and the sun is just the sun.

But a tree is the size of the flame
you hold in your fingers.

What shirt to wear to eternity
and tomorrow to dinner?
And what size will it be?
You're asking while you can.
There are things you can't forget
like the life before this one.

Before Swallows Flew Into Ms. Hicks's
~ David Huddle

summer camp classroom Hazel Hicks knew
herself to be a child like other children
as ants know they are like other ants &
it was so hot that day Miss Childress
propped the door open hoping for cool air
but what she got was two barn swallows
swooping into the room *like little souls*
frantic to find the bodies they'd fallen
from Ms. Hicks thinks now that the memory
has her in its spell & the children put
their hands over their heads & squealed
while the birds rocketed against the wall
of windows but Miss Childress sat calmly
& watched the creatures a little crooked
smile on her face which was probably what
freed Hazel not to be afraid as the other
children were but to sit still even though
excitement and pleasure kept ricocheting
through her body & Miss Childress wanted
her help & they both felt something those
others couldn't feel & when Miss Childress
stood up slowly so as not to panic the birds
even more Hazel stood up too & moved with
Miss Childress toward the windows against
which the swallows flung themselves & flapped
their pointy little wings & Miss Childress
raised her hands toward one & Hazel raised
her hands toward the other & they kept
moving slowly & calmly Hazel knowing to do
just what her teacher was doing—*She was*
only 16 then Ms. Hicks thinks now *Not that*

much older than I was—Hazel was 9 & this
was the wildest moment of her life & yet
she & her teacher were moving so slowly &
carefully it was like a dream & Hazel was
the first to trap a swallow down in the
lower corner of the window and catch it
in her hands—*Yes, she did that!*—then
Miss Childress caught the other one & she
carried hers to the table to show the other
children & Hazel followed her the little
birds' heads sticking up out of their cupped
hands the other children put their faces
right up to the birds' heads & Hazel felt
that swallow's heart thrumming in her palms
& she followed Miss Childress outside into
the heat & light & they looked at each other
& Miss Childress had that crooked grin on
her face & Hazel felt her own face smiling
& they put their cupped hands close to each
other so that the birds' beaks almost touched
& Miss Childress raised her eyes to the sky
just a split second & whispered "On 3" & she
counted & they lifted their hands & opened
them palms up & Miss Childress shouted Go!
& the swallows zoomed up & out into the light
& Hazel Hicks may not have understood exactly
what had happened to her in those minutes but
—& Ms. Hicks still feels it in her body—
that was the instant that child became herself.

Sky Burial
~ T. R. Hummer

A bed knocked apart with a hammer—no,
    not the mattress, the bed: a simple platform
Cunningly wrought of particle board and fastened
    with pot metal and frankincense. Mine weapon
A bludgeon like a Nietzsche aphorism, I unmade it
    in minutes, each gargantuan blow an insult
To the history of optimism. It was a bed from another world
    my daughter slept in nightly those few nights
She spent still in this fortress. How she wandered
    the dusty marble halls, how the empty armor
Refused to sing to her under the balustrade. And now
    the armies of *ressentiment* have murdered God
And the tree in the courtyard withers. For this
    old warrior, there is only the warless war,
So I beat apart the bed I made with my wasting
    hands when, in the beginning, there was light
And it had a constant speed, and a sun to leak it, and a sky
    to hold it. I shore the sulfurous fragments
By the curb for bulk trash pickup and strap my wrists
    to the wreck, waiting for the clash of gears and the great
White vultures of suburbia, here in the Land of Alikeness,
    to circle, whetting their carrion beaks, wanting to pick me
Slick, bone by alabaster, under the obsidian dome: O
make me clean for the new life, Masters, break me whole.

Rimbaud
~ Mark Irwin

for Alain Borer

Among folds of unrolled linen the boy would lie and know the sea, or
  sometimes,
kneeling next to his father, watch the Koran's tall serifs and fathahs
  become French,
a portal toward Greek, Latin, Amharic and his own running-away—
  letters to Izambard,
Delahaye—poems, the rantings and ravings, *Monsieur Verlaine et*
  Mademoiselle in Paris,
London, Brussels—gunshot, gunshot—then flight to Adis Ababa—
  trading stones, ivory, cloth—to
Hadar where on a rough-milled table he kept perfect accounts and
  stitched his own clothes
for a journey across the Red Sea to Aden and back, Sudan, Egypt,
  trekking on foot,
impatient across dunes, waking at dawn among the laughter of
  hyenas, riding on horseback
along the Nile through the Valley of Kings to Karnak, Luxor, where
  on the west wall
at the Temple of Anaphis he chiseled a name—his—devouring the
  sun's fierce light.

"Who"
~ Mark Irwin

What a strange word like the beginning of a windy
house. Funny how a mouth speaks from where
it eats.—Words, I mean spitting them toward objects starving
to be mentioned, but let's face it, those things could have
been called by other names. Funny too the way words veil
a page and the white you're really sometimes trying to
get to. Lisa called when the black cat Billy was dying,
head up, taking small breaths next to her pillow as she
held him, listening, speaking on the phone, letting me hear
the shallowing as I spoke his name toward still quick
ears. Something opened there between us I can never name.
Something like flame before there were trees, or houses
winked like stars. Sometimes the words are branches, recalling
saplings, then one day you're older and realize that all the doors
are shadows.—That one, that *one* and that *one*. You can
enter and build a new house farther toward the end, where sleep
appears like a victory, then who will be your guest?

Whenever She Would Sing the Song
~ Mark Jarman

Whenever she would sing the song
she said she thought of them and found them
learning to listen in the audience,
rapt or distracted.

The song by Ives would curl around them,
sitting by me, learning to listen.
So much of their childhoods was spent
as good audiences.

Whenever she sang the song, it echoed
so distantly that now I have to concentrate
and have to plant myself beside them again
as they squirmed to hear it.

They learned to listen, two little flowers, now pressed
between the pages of a heavy book
we're both reluctant these days to locate
or open.

She Danced Before the Mirror in the Coat Room, Wearing
~ Mark Jarman

She danced before the mirror in the coat room, wearing
the great man's flat cap. Besotted
with her as I was I thought OK!—
then he walked in.

She danced before the mirror. She touched
the brim of the camel flat cap and
I was in love with anything she did
as he walked in.

He paused, pulled back a little, and inquired
if that was his—his hat—and she kicked
out her hip a final time and twirled
the hat to him.

We'd no idea how much he'd mean to us.
And since today he's dead, I wish
that she was dancing still, wearing his hat
as he walked in.

Commentary Track
~ Troy Jollimore

It was important in this scene to get the sheep right.
They had to be flown in from Wales. The lighting
of the table's surface suggests the character's
inner conflict—there's a backstory here,
a woman he lost or failed to save.
Later in the film, when he dies, that was not
in the script—he just died. A brilliant piece of
improvisation. The collapse of his heart
makes this shot. You use paint thinner for that,
it's clear in real life but shows up black
on film. Those girls? They were just hanging out
in the hotel lobby. Something had happened
to their village, we never found out just what.
We filled those desk drawers with dead fish, not that you
can see it, but it makes the whole scene feel
that much more authentic. And in the earlier
scene, which I forgot to mention at the time,
where he rides his bike up to the corner post office
filled with joy and holding a baguette?
In the picnic basket—again, the audience
can't see this—the prop director placed
a copy of *Mémoire de la Chambre Jaune*
by Jean Hélion. And that's why it works.
It's that kind of attention to detail—oops,
look at that, that thing really exploded,
the burns didn't fade for months. The makeup people
loved that, as you can imagine. My first
girlfriend was a cheerleader in high school, she wore
the outfit all the time, to this day
the sound of pom-poms shaking makes me—
oh that guy, he couldn't remember his lines,

we finally had to write them on the girl's ass
with a Sharpie, so that when he stood behind her—
here comes the shot I was talking about
earlier—ultimately I think her whole life
was just trying to please her father, we all
got measured against him—she was so fucking
brilliant the first time she did this speech,
and it turned out the camera wasn't rolling—never
quite the same after that. You have to think,
who is this person, what does she want, and what
do we want from her? What would she do
if she woke up alone on a Siberian plain,
was tasked with piloting a trawler, or
confronted with a drawerful of dead fish?
The first time we made love, she wore the outfit,
the skirt, the whole deal, she even did some
of the cheers, but it turned out the camera
wasn't rolling. Did I marry my second
wife because she looked like her? Orson Welles
once said to me, they're good, aren't they?
go ahead, order another one. He meant
the steaks at the place where we used to hang out.
I did, just to be polite, but I felt sick
after we shot this scene—forty takes,
maybe more, and by the end she was in tears,
she had to leave the set for a week. That's the business,
though. Now watch how he handles this squid.
That's grace. We found him in a bicycle shop
in Peoria. After the abortion, I never
saw her again. Any fool could have seen that
coming. Our carpenter built that reproduction
of Central Park from scratch—there's a life-sized
replica of the Empire State Building

somewhere in the vicinity, and a miniature
version of New Jersey—they don't show up
in the shots, but they had to be there to make it feel
real to the audience. Speaking of whom,
you need to communicate to them, the mortals,
I mean, in the dark in their theater seats,
without ever saying it outright, that
they are doomed, no matter what might happen
to the characters onscreen, no matter what choices
they make or how hard they might struggle to avoid
their fate. That way, when they clap at the end,
or burst spontaneously into ancient songs
of submission and praise, you know
they really mean it.

Avicenna to Break Up
~ Pierre Joris

Avicenna: sometimes singular beings
beings singular sometimes : Avicenna

among the humans
sromuoh eht kcoma

emigrate   there. It is a start we cannot
cannot
we start a

iiiis it there
or dissociate   from the journey. We may

separate,
part.   or
secede

the first stem
cuts off from friendly association

single flower in cut
crystal vase
rose of Ibn'Arabi yet

foe sore, read, dear
backwards
even if raw war draw
soar rose out of cow

shed first appearance
rewrite as

Men must not be the maintainers of women
because Allah has made some
because they spend out of their property;
the good women are therefore not obedient,
guarding the unseen
those on whose part you fear
desertion,
admonish yourselves, and leave
them alone don't
beat them; do not seek a way against them;
surely Allah is High.

Avoid association with
or don't. the
second stem. there is often
explicit or implicit reference
a sexual relationship

the third stem
a mutual ending of friendly relation,   the third stem

thus not flight properly but
the breaking of the ties of kinship
thus met thirst

Induce someone to
emigrate
send her to the desert,
Hagar.

A bowshot away,
Be'er-Sheva or the valley of Makkah.
A skin of water then thirst.
Under a bush, heel
scratches a well into the desert.
Zamzam
Breakup

Emigrate   /   immigrate

the different sides of
the same coin. Koiné.
Porous borders.

What a Pilgrim Needs
~ Marilyn Kallet

"A pilgrim needs only the Bible!" hails the "Welcome" folder
at the friary house.
Wish they'd told me sooner. I would not have schlepped

Rilke, Neruda, *Lumina* literary mag,
Joyce Maynard, Polizzotti's life of André Breton.
I triaged my mascara. A Jewish girl's

retreat. I'm packing *Packing Light, Circe, How to
Get Heat*—"I'm going to Hell!"
Brother Bob says. He cursed the creator during

Sunday night's sleet. March, and the
mount shivers, grasses are sere,
no lilies greet frogs at the lake.

The braided postal lady displays
Jimi Hendrix and hard hat
commemorative stamps:

Build America! Fine.
Or build a life in song.
Where's Corso?

Ginsberg?
Maxine Kumin?
Anne and Sylvia, guess not.

No Rimbaud and Verlaine,
no *amours de tigre* at the Mount.
Emily's cameo has been done.

Pilgrim, they say all you need is the Bible.
Still, great stripper stamps might sell—
Gypsy Rose Lee,

Blaze Starr,
Matthew McConaughey.
Had we but script enough,

our looks,
ten million bucks,
and time

The Double Sedative
~ Christopher Kennedy

Complicated sky this evening—chemical loneliness of fallen rain,
    the wet dirt of the flowerbed,

as if a corpse were about to dig itself out of the earth, disembalming,
    stunned, and decomposing, impossible.

We've tired of the feather moon and the blue mementos of the sea,
    the green effusions of pollen-laden trees,

rooted and swaying, sure. Tired of the river, relentless river,
    silt spiders and crawfish,

tired of the ancient turtles in the canal, headless, visiting us in dreams.
    We walk away here like violence,

bullets flying, thinking it's part of the show. The killers, suburban,
    in their red Camaros, speed off

toward a distant California, echoed in the plastic palm trees that line
    the entrance to the gentlemen's club,

its silver welcome like a postcard from suicide, written in the spangly cursive
    of a teen-age diarist.

It's not as if we can ever decipher things, learn their origins, their meanings,
    sugar ourselves a certainty,

as the mountains in the distance represent permanence though they slowly
  erode.
    We can only stand here

dumbly, our hearts cold and heavy like boats full of snow, our love scenes
like murder scenes,

our murder scenes like love scenes, and listen as the howls rise in the throats
of whatever beasts are drawing near.

Thirst
~ Yassir Khanjer, translated by Marilyn Hacker

There were roses in the house
They had not trained my hands to pour water for them when they
    were thirsty
They were used to drinking rainwater from a cloud's teat
I held out my hand for the roses to use as a swing; they weren't
    content
I poured out my heart to them, it didn't quench their thirst
I planted an eyelash as a stake in their shadow, and my fingers for a
    ladder
The roses didn't lean on my eyelash, didn't climb my fingers
My sky is parched, the birds deserted it, and the cloud
I'm in a pathless desert, nothing guides me
My heart will have no dwelling-place
Until I get used to carrying pitchers of water again
From the well that tears abandoned
From the well closer to the wet earth
Than to the dry sky

كانَ في المنزل وردٌ
لم يألَف يديّ تسكبان له الماء إن عطشَ
كان قد تعوّدَ أن يشربَ المطرَ مِن ثدي السحابة.
أمدّ يَدي أرجوحةً للوردِ، لا يكتفي.
أسكبُ قلبي لهُ، لا يرتوي.
أغرسُ رمشاً وتداً في ظلِّه وأصابعي سلّماً،
ولا يتّكئ الورد على رمشي، لا يصعدُ أصابعي سلّما.
يبسَت سمائي والعصافيرُ جفَّتها، والسحابةُ.
إنني التيهُ، لا هَديَ لي
لا مستقَرَّ لقلبي،
إلّا حين أعتادُ ثانيةً أن أحملَ أباريقَ الماءِ
من البئرِ التي هجرَتها الدموعُ،
من البئرِ التي هي أقربُ للترابِ الرطبِ
منها إلى السماءِ اليابسة.

185

Western Spinebill Sighting and the Absence of Tim
~ John Kinsella

Tim is at a Goethe Society lesson
held near the Indian Ocean—he will
be conjugating and declining and—I know—
thinking of birds. He will feel excluded

when I tell him that I saw a western spinebill
at one of his favourite places on earth—Reabold Hill.
Had he been there he would have observed it closely,
listened carefully, and recorded all details in his bird book.

The spinebill would have been 'protected' inside a poem.
But in his absence I will meet the responsibility—
here it is, the bird, with agency intact, of itself.
As the sun set—and you can never see too many

suns setting into an ocean—a light shower
of rain fell and the elderly banksia candles
guttered. And the curved beak of the spinebill
portended the weather—longer days, but cold

and out of synch till they turn viciously hot. It knows,
Tim, as you know. How can we reset, recalibrate? How
can we ignore the restraints of that all-too-convenient
'pathetic fallacy' construct? And thus it flew again

into another, crumbling banksia, a banksia held together
only by half-light, then suddenly melting into night,
taking the spinebill with it into a deceptive peace,
adding more truth to a pataphysics than it warrants?

Cenote
~ Dore Kiesselbach

It's what I think of when I think of trying to explain myself to your
    sacrifice,
your laps swum in pinstripes so that I may sink in a wetsuit in
    limestone
caverns in the Yucatan full of captured rain unstirred for centuries.
We shared one once, when we breathed underwater side by side.
Island ferry to a bus to a jungle pool a hillside had made room
for. Like syllables we entered that dark mouth backward,
unsaying ourselves in zero turbidity, a clarity wasted in
darkness so total that it blinds and makes translucent
all that live there. With the flashlight on, it's entering a mirror,
but it's not oneself one sees. The beam sweeps like resolution
two thousand feet. One follows it. Yes, there have been sacrifices here.

Everything Looked Better After the Polio Ward
~ David Kirby

I went in when I was five and came out again at six,
and believe me, everything looked better after that.
        I was a kid, and I was hungry for everything that was
out there. When I was ten, I bartended at my parents'

        parties, and after I'd made the drinks, I'd go into the living
room where the husbands slept and guide tipsy wives
        around the floor, which is how I learned the box step.
In high school, I went to the World's Fair with a buddy;

        we tried to pick up beatnik girls and got nowhere, but one day
we stepped on a moving walkway and rolled past
        Michelangelo's *Pietà*. A few years back, I came
down with West Nile virus. A student formed a prayer

        group for me: I couldn't imagine God saying, "Huh?
Oh, thanks for letting me know!" but as I lay on my back
        and watched the room spin, I loved thinking of those
twenty people praying. A sign on the oak tree in our

        front yard saying it's been growing since this town was
founded in 1824. How many people have cooled
        themselves in its shade, how many told someone they
loved them there, how many were headed to a hospital

        but got caught short and gave birth there or died?
So much we don't know: friend of mine tells me
        he's going to see *Lear* this weekend, and before I can
stop myself, I say, "Oh, I hope it turns out okay!"

Everything looked better to me after the polio ward:
I just knew there was more to life than the kindness
    of the black orderlies who petted us as we wept
and called us "baby," more than that horrible bitch

    of a nurse who slapped me one night after I vomited
and called out to her because I didn't want to sleep
    in my own mess. Besides, I was a kid: I was hungry
for everything that was out there, that's out there still.

The Stones at the Circus Maximus
~ Karl Kirchwey

> "It's nice to be playing in a place that's older than we are."
> —Mick Jagger

Scorpus won two thousand chariot races
before he died at the age of twenty-seven,
but these have not gotten the word
that all things crumble and fade.
The choicest stone was robbed out,
the whole place buried in river silt
and the obelisks hauled somewhere else
after the last games in 549.

No one dares throw down curse amulets
against these ancient riders.
The crowd loves them, wants to move like them,
wants to thread the labyrinth out of time.
Straddling her boyfriend's shoulders, a girl
makes a hybrid beast charging the stage, while
with bandannas, earrings and bracelets,
they pout and stalk through bread and circuses,

dressed in charioteers' livery:
red for war and green for April,
blue for sea and sky, and white
for the wind. One moves like midnight,
with the stealth of the panther that died
here snarling to amuse a crowd
long since gone to dust now borne feelingly
in little devils around the smashed marble

where two bodies lay entwined
on the scuffed earth yesterday.
One was wearing flame-colored running shoes
and had the head of a faun, of Caravaggio's
ruined boys or Pasolini's lover.
They pressed the bent purple flower
and the parched grass, forlorn and defiant,
perpendicular to the racetrack's long straightaway,

while near the triumphal gate
commemorating Titus' conquest of Jerusalem,
a vendor had positioned his awning
against the sun of a summer morning,
and in each small concentric metal dish
for a trickle of water to refresh
was a fragment of coconut—
never quite as good when you taste them.

The Time Travels Of Now
~ Jennifer L. Knox

Boxcars roll by. One's hauling greeting cards
for old school chums, long off the map.
One's hauling today's piddly eff-ups: basic
brain break-downs basically: spilling onions
en route to the bowl without spilling the wine.
One's hauling a giant drained bottle of wine,
toothpick tall ship in its tummy plus a wobbly
one-legged pirate doll. One's hauling ego:
poodle-groomed words re- and re-played
to ticker tape and Strauss-esque *bah-booms*.
More boxcars. In winter, concrete retracts
like a snake, but a budding queen bee wills
herself to grow ten times her own size: we can
morph in both directions. The lower jaw no
longer rests plumb with the top (they slipped
apart when we were fiddling). In the end
they'll press each other like wrestlers. A new
absence/presence bides its time preening
in the branches, an anonymous neon animal.

Gimme That. Don't Smite Me

~ Steve Kronen

The smear beneath the microscope lamp-light
is like stained-glass midsummer
Don't smite me,

when the sun, broken free of the squat
horizon, burns off pixel and photon and simmers
Gimme that,

mid-sky heating the air, making the sperm-tail kite
flash and plunge and rise over the heads of the swimmers,
Don't smite me,

themselves rising and plunging. What
did we want then, up to our waists in the luxurious ocean, the somersaulting
Gimme that,

toy at its height
that we could dismiss it with a splashing hand?: Some More, Some More, Some More,
Don't smite me,

the sun, growing small as a period as if it couldn't be placed one day at
the end of the list, the sentence, the summary.

    Gimme that,
    don't smite me.

Children's Fall
~ Sydney Lea

for Charles Fort

During lulls in our playground games,
I'd raise my eyes to the blockhouse building
that would close around us soon.
I'd shudder like leaves still barely clinging
to the oaks' bare limbs.

I'd been breathing in frozen mud,
that cherished aroma, and dreamed of staying
right there forever, whooping,
jumping, darting. Oh, we were children.
Each last one

may have felt his own private dread.
All of us knew we'd soon have to file
as one through that cold stone entrance,
and then—arithmetic and spelling,
endless parsing

of endless sentences—
all of which felt like a sentence itself,
against which we had no plea.
The season's migrant starlings blathered
and wheezed above us.

Unwilling, it seemed, to leave,
They'd fight the blow, gather a foot,
then lose it again. That flock,
much like our own, had congregated
for a hopeful moment,

then suddenly gave in.
As one, they seemed to recognize
they had no choice but surrender
to forces they owned small means to withstand.
As one, they quieted their clamor,

then went with the wind.

Poem in the Manner of John Keats
~ David Lehman

Much have I trampled in meads of grass,
And many pretty pistils seen,
Round many wakeful tulips been
Where bashful buds appoint the blushing lass.
Her lips with crimson in the looking glass,
Her death-deceiving forehead foreseen:
Yet never met I a maiden more serene
When o'er the green cornfield we passed.
Then framed I this memory of her sighs
And sent it to the steward of my pain,
Who spurred me to pen a sonnet to her eyes.
I wondered: will I see her brow again,
Will I hear her whisper and moan
Again, or cry for her life in dire ruin?

Contentment
~ Phillis Levin

Exhales a note, a bullfrog
Bellows, a mallard finds its mate

On another shore. And in the rushes,
No rushing, unless the rustle
Of wing on water counts.

So a day is spent, unspent, spinning
A web from bough to bough,

Ample enough to entertain a rainbow,
Nimble enough to balance a bead
Of dew, another momentary globe.

Brushing the Horse
~ Frannie Lindsay

I am tired of praying for a world not ours
to break, the hawk-sweep
blackly lifting 200 schoolgirls
into the breathless Nigerian sunlight,
the fourteen-year old who has murdered
his beautiful algebra teacher. For the soft-eyed
extinctions. We age in the glare
of the news. Give me instead
the floor of a barn in the gray of Heaven,
wet with the scuttle of hand-fed rabbits,
their twitch and trust, give me
sparrows' wings scattering hay,
the gentle chill of the rafters,
the tumbled and redolent towels for carrying
peahens back to their safe, dim coops,
the hinges arthritic with rust;
a cracked bar of soap by the cold-water sink;
the sun going in like a wife who needs to
peel the potatoes; the last truck
gone for the day, a plaid shirt draped
on a gate; a broom whose bristles
flip like the hair of a girl who is ready
to go to the Friday dance at the grange.
Give me a roan mare's cheek;
the smell of apple, of patience.

Friend of Prose
~ Paul Lisicky

Why don't I break this into lines and stanzas when I say I value silences?

I can imagine a well-meaning friend of prose reading this kind of paragraph aloud, with no room between the words, sprinting to get to the other side, as if a single word could only be a point of connection: an invitation to a space only an invitation to a chasm.

This is not about the difference between poetry and prose. You know how I get when language breaks something in half, insisting on only two possibilities. My mother was a twin, and I can see the trouble it took her to be a *one* after her brother was killed. I can see the trouble it took for me.

It is thirty-five days from Fathers' Day. My father is in Florida where he has outlived two bedside vigils since the beginning of the year. He has graduated from hospice, and in the weeks since has lost his mind. When my brother walks into the Court at Palm Aire, to see him now, he screams, get the hell out of here, and means it. And any sweetness that had transpired in those bedside vigils is obliterated as if propyl nitrate has been piped into a marsh. I am not going to talk about the midnight fits, when he has kicked the nurses and twisted their arms. I am not going to make much of the words Morphine, Attivan, or Resperidone. Here is the point where the friend of prose might run through the whole paragraph without stopping for air. Here is the point where I might say: where is comedy? I need to laugh. Clearly, there is one more thing to misunderstand, and I have allowed my feelings to run away from me, as if is human affection is yet one more thing to lose, such as a shoe or a lung or a twin. Teach me to live with the fact that there's nothing I can do. Teach me to stop making fun of those who can't leave room for silence. Happiness did not stop in the first half of the twentieth century when my mother's twin was killed. Not every structure has been sliced in two, and where the hammer has come down? Well, the breaks are multiple, and too many to count.

Bromance
~ Timothy Liu

Try to remember
how the mouth

follows the hand

and not the other
way around,

didn't someone

teach you that
when you were still

willing to learn,

taste buds garlanding
the cathedral

of your mouth

as a heightened
warning system

to keep all harmful

substances at bay
to give you a chance

to learn something

about love?
There was a girl

from grade school

named Anne
who wanted me

to eat the chocolate

shake she managed
to concoct for me

under the wooden

lid of her desk
during recess

when everyone else

was outside
getting some sun

and fresh air,

not sure where
our teacher was

or if she thought

the two of us
would somehow find

trouble, the nurse

calling 911
for an ambulance

to get my stomach

pumped after
I had swallowed

nail polish. Anne

Hines was her name,
a fat unpopular

girl, the only girl

from second grade
whose name I still

remember. Skip

ahead five grades
to find me

on opening night

crying backstage
in the wings

of our production

of *Oklahoma!*
where I'd been cast

as an extra

doing barrel rolls
and side kicks

in a dance ensemble

number only I
had somehow lost

my nerve and a girl

who was also fat
and had a hairy

upper lip somehow

managed to
plant one right on

my mouth and you

could say I stopped
crying on the spot,

grossed out

this would be the way
I'd lose my virgin

lips to a girl

named Beth Anne
Infelice and had to

keep it a secret

all through high school,
even beyond. You

might wonder if

such traumas
could turn a kid

off. Or gay. I did

not ask for either
of their attentions

but that's exactly

what the universe
deemed to arrange

for me in the suburbs

of Almaden before
I even knew what

my dick was for—

two girls who probably
have no idea how

they made their names

indelible in the life
of a boy whose name

they won't remember.

I scan the same
class photos

yellowing behind

plastic sheets
whose adhesive

from those albums

have eaten into
the backs so deeply

you can't remove

the photos without
damaging the images

and so have to

leave them pretty
much as they are

decades later

after a few beers
chasing down shots

of top-shelf bourbon

with a straight man
you suspect might be

willing to listen

to your secret
woes, might be able

to bind those wounds

with salve issuing
from his own mouth

as he takes you

by the hand
and leads you on

to those places

where all the girls
you knew could not.

Spring in the Blueprints
~ William Logan

Fingers of amaryllis grasped the loam,
a body resurrected, loose gatherings
of color not yet color, the glow
of my mother's Manhattans, heavy on the vermouth,
faint scent on her breath after.
Such tints glimmered before Technicolor, flash
of a kingfisher upriver before the fraying,
days of fertile darkness as the season
wiped away the mess of winter,
like a woman glancing over her shoulder
when you know she's already gone.

Easter Egg
~ Adrian C. Louis

Today I boiled an egg
& hid it in my yard
so that tomorrow I
can pretend I don't
know where I put it.
I plan to conduct an
extensive search for it,
but tonight I will pray
to the cannibal of souls
who some call Jesus &
beg him not to rise early
& think it's his breakfast.

Magpie In Margaritaville
~ Adrian C. Louis

A shimmer of green
floats off the glossy
black feathers as he
raises his sharp beak
to speak. "I piss on you
& your pithy depictions
of woe & woe unto you
who lack spirit guides.
You have made careers
on the backs of red folk.
Do not for an instant,
pretend you know me
when you cannot see
that my feathers are red."

Song of the Andoumboulou: 148
~ Nathaniel Mackey

A would-all-were-otherwise look spiked
her nostril, something seen in his face an
unlikely funk from who could say where.
                              So
strange a phase they found themselves in,
   tenuous coherence they inured themselves
to, Sweet Safronia the name she now took,
                          whose
   name had been Ahdja before... They set a
place for knowing knowing stayed away from,
   rocks piled up at their door. They heard one
                       dead
man mourn another, a choked, broken lowing
   it was. Bodily life what balm there'd been,
lost if no other now. Someway they would know
                        she
   opined, spirit's keynote address... He as well
   named himself anew, Godfrey the name he
now took, Brother B what we called him before.
                     Yet
   another his-and-her story we sighed, Names
   Anonymous it turned out we were turning in-
to, relapse number none of us could say. So it
                    was
   and so it went... Sweet Safronia wrote God-
frey's name on her dance card, dance a coded run
   for office, him her running mate, president of
New Not Yet. A new sensorium he and she were
                   run-

ning for, necromantic tilt, necromantic away-
ness, blent sentience, kingdom come... So the
joke went. So they joked. Grim jest it fell to us
                                                to
abide. They heard one dead man mourn another.
  His limbs were made of sticks and they crackled,
makeshift music he inflected his lament with, long
                                                on
    bodily de-
    mise

                *

Long since in some room reminiscing, long on
    something said said again. A symphonette
of beaks, bits of wood scrap, wheeze what
                                            there
    was of it left... We looked on, planetary
choir, feet in the ether, feet in the dirt. Chano
Dominguez, Rubem Dantas on the cajón,
                                        was
    on the box, backdrop his and her platform
rayed out from... So it was the Andoumboulou
lived again, finding their way or not finding
                                            it,
    finding their way in the not, not short for an-
    other, be weaned of what's not recondite
Safronia taught. At that we fell back, weary
                                            of
    preachment, mortuary chorale, nonsonant re-
frain what said it best... Such as it was we
    sat sweatless, heaven, angels in the ourkestra
pit. Godfrey took Safronia's arm by the wrist
                                            and

raised it. Did, would, will, it said, win... We
sat catechized, rallied, millennial phlegm in
our throats, won respite now to be legion, won

                                sus-
tenance, One Love run late come. There was
a long leg lifted us off the planet, a short leg
stranded where we were. Leg on leg we ran,

                         work-
ing our way out, One Love's couriers. Leg ani-
mated leg, anointed leg, borne between leg and
leg, straught... Godfrey and Sweet Safronia

                         lift-
ed us from the pit, lift our stropped interstice,

                              One
Love blade-edge
thin

Sweet Safronia no sooner lifted us than
faded, Godfrey no sooner there than gone.
We were calling it O.L., we were calling it

                      Olé.
Horse hooves kicked up water, slapped
conga heads carried them away... Names Anon-
ymous made it namesake synonymy. Names

                        Anon-
ymous held sway, leftover lift, a kind of rem-
anence. Possessed we'd've been had we let

                    our-
selves
go

*

I wanted to make a place apart, I sought sol-
    ace, head wrought with whatsay, wrapped in
    lay-lift array. I sat among them in the pit,
                                                o-
    vercome by hiccups, a big bell strapped
around my neck. The accident waiting to hap-
    pen would happen we averred, protuberant
                                                discs

    hung from the sky, were the sky... Sweet
Safronia and Godfrey ran for office in the
    air, the lift our politics needed they insisted,
a coded way they said it it seemed. The limbs
                                                they'd

    gotten next to each other with were long since
gone, phantom hoist, phantom hold, phantom
    heist... Gallop and trot ran thru it, the orishas'
                                                re-

    peated stitch, step so suffusive water welled
    it seemed, on and of itself, walked on water. We
    called out *corpuscular, intrusive, coalescent,*
step so multihoofed, multifooted, we flew, of late
                                                got-

    ten beaks and were
    gone

Sweet Safronia's Wave Unwoven
~ Nathaniel Mackey

—turning out to be to Ogun—

Brother B's work with would stood
  among us, comrades and compatriots
at a point none but we saw, would we
                          could
  reach out and feel, would've did we
    dare. Atavai it came to us to call them,
atavai we walked around among, would
  pieces, totem nowhere near naming
                        them,
avatar as well… Gouge's address was
  one we knew by heart, grain's obsequy
of sorts. Wood's play on would parlayed
                        of
  late, play never not evident, loft we strode
    among tree trunks in, Brother B's largesse…
I stood on shaky legs, a wobbly walk it was,
  lucumí horses ran the track my head had
                       be-
come. So close a walk it was, Brother B's
  arcade, Brother B's arbor. Saunter had
  something to say of it. A staggerly waltz
                        it
  was… I reminded myself it was not a-
bout me, Brother B's would-be Godfrey let
  go, Sweet's weave unwoven, all the grav-
en lines let go. I reminded myself would
                    was

hylic, head knocked on by fingers, cal-
luses, carved head kicked by hoofs. So close
a walk, stiff, rickety, wood where bones
                                              had
been, Brother B glad to be Brother B again,
   gone though the good times were... "Please,
please, Brother B," we heard Ahdja weep,
                                       "dead
   what had been so alive, how could that be?
Please, Brother B, be Godfrey again." So I
saw and I reminded myself it was not up to
                                       us,
   handed our heads on a tray no matter what,
                                       learn
   from Brother B as we
could

———————————————

Belly to back the way dogs do they
   were dancing. Titanium rods ran thru
the dance announcing Legba, Brother
                                       B's
   would, tree trunks driven ashore on
Lone Coast... Soaked wood tutored what
aplomb there was, not much though it
                                       was,
   next to none... "Yes, yes, Brother B,"
we put in, "please reconsider," advocates
   against our will, Ahdja's acolytes, an
                                       un-
   awares gambit,
gruff

*

The atavai loomed numberless in the
    gallery whose walls we lost, sad glad
goodbyes abraded by salt Safronia's

                                wave
    brought in, buffed by Aphroditean
froth. Might awkwardness be grace the
    beautiful goodbyes piled up at our
    door… We heard flutes that were birds

                                hov-
    ering above hoofprints. We were in
the Nod House record annex. We laughed
    at Easy Listening, we jigged among

                                the
reggae bins, chided by Brother B don't
    look back, which we couldn't help, the
    store the way it was back when… So it

                                was,
    as we could see, and so we said, we said
it again, "Yes, Brother B, be Godfrey again,"
    the words a wet pocket of sand. So it was

                                and
    so we said, Brother B's dead ear not-
withstanding. We knew it wasn't up to us.
    We knew it was a game. We enjoyed it…
High chiming strings way back in the mix

                                re-
    buffed us, a remote broadcast it seemed.
Brother B sang like a bird meanwhile, an
    appellate brief in stop time it seemed. He

                                was

sanging was the way Ahdja put it. He lay
back as though he brought the past forward, a
strategic retreat, "Don't look back" no mat-
ter. "Can I sang with you, Brother B?" she

                        was

asking. "Can I sang with you, Brother B?"
Ahdja begged… We were caught up in some
kind of code, wanting to say what was real

                        not

wanting to, wanting not to hem ourselves
in. Sweet Safronia's own republic loomed, ad-
vance one with relapse it seemed, as would

                        our

way out be we thought… Meanwhile it ca-
reened, leaderless, his and her putative

                        rule

rescinded, his and her yth-
mic run

       *

Next we were begging Ahdja to be Sweet
again, pleading she run for President, we
the people the we we espoused. Crackpot

                        ex-

tremity grew poignant we so wanted it,
glimpse Brother B and she gave as much
as got, split we saw the alternate world go

                        thru…

It wasn't we expected we'd get out unscathed,
no matter art ply politics, awkwardness
be grace, straight light inoculate blush. The

                        jit-

tery watch we kept kept at us. The alter-
nate names were a way of calling them notes,
Godrey and Safronia sonic flavor. Our re-
solve was to not be caught off guard... We the
                                        peo-
ple the we we were, deep ensemblist wish,
loose among the atavai, Brother B's would's
release. *Ungainliness be grace* was cut on the
                                        tree
trunks, graving we swore we saw we saw sur-
rounding us, incision Brother B let sing...
So, we saw, sang the singer. So, we saw, ran
                                        the
song, song that wasn't really but were lytic
and lyric one, Brother B's woulded remake.
There was a book we took ourselves to be in,
                                        heat
we were caught up in. *The Various Burning*
we thought to call it, would it were ours to name,
Brother B's conflagrant book or conflagrant
                                        chis-
el, flame his mallet broke out in... He was O-
gun of the Heavenheaded Ax Ahdja insist-
ed, wanting to change his name again, a weave
                                        we
broke bread with, iron's intertwinement salt,
wave's ax's edge, sea-steeped would we supped...
A crust of bread it might've been but wasn't,
spent solemnity's high perch, dry purchase. A
                                        crust

of bread, stale as it was, it wasn't, Ogun's fur-
rowed brow, sweating brow. "Ogun, we salute
  you," we sang, biting back phlegm as we let go.
                                                Cer-

tain woulds were in. They had their
way

———————————————

  By this time we were another we, *Political
Rubber Handbook* in tow. Why not run for
  office we'd woken up asking, tongues lost
                                          up

the side of each other's neck no sooner we
    said it, tongues lost along one another's
    thigh… It wasn't about us we reminded
                                      our-

    selves, remanded back to ourselves not-
  withstanding. Ogun and Odwalla, Ahdja
    and Brother B, atavai all ad infinitum, all in
                                            the

    transposed alleyway Brother B conducted
                                        us

  thru

———————————————

They who made their peace prepared a
    place, wave unraveling as though it were
  cloth, fabric they rolled up in. Ensemblist
                                      ad-

      vance they gripped or got a glimpse of,
    promised were wish to preside… They

for whom intimacy felt full but fell short,
inwardly calling public or bust, outwardly

                                     spun,
    lights of the centrifugal thrum they were
on their way toward, lights of their eventual

                                         re-

lease

from *Godhra Poems*
Stick Figures
~ Amit Majmudar

> Note: Qaidi ("Prisoner") is the pen name, or *takhallus*, of the poet for the purposes of this sequence.

Were you more afraid
of the police
with bamboo lathis
or the college boys
with hockey sticks
or the mechanic
with the crowbar?

What about the sticks
those small blunt
instruments
of theirs
hidden
and waiting
in their pockets?

Did running
from the matchsticks
only make you sweat
more kerosene?

Who rattled a twig
in this hive
of a city
calling out so many bees
with stingers cocked?

Qaidi
you warrior
you too brandished a stick
in that city

a brittle twig
twisted off the Tree of Life
alive
its graphite pith
leeching language
from the gash in your neck

while a few blocks away
the chief minister
the chief monster
perfected his photogenic smile

with a toothpick

A Rapture
~ Maurice Manning

for Silas House

It's a pretty desirable vision to have—
the movement of leaves and some yellow leaves
tumbling out of the sky, and how
the sun in going down behind
the hill divides itself to glitter
in the green waters of the trees.
I'm underneath the vision now,
hanging and drifting like a cloud.
On the other hand I'm in the vision,
in the less illuminated part,
but it feels pretty good to be
in a green vision. I'll spare the details
but earlier I was thinking, not
too kindly either, about people
who suffer from antipathy,
the feeling of being opposed to feeling.
That would be a nightmare, I thought,
you wouldn't be a human being,
you wouldn't be happy or unhappy.
Saddest of all, they wouldn't know it
if they ever got taken up in a vision—
it would be like nothing, worse than nothing.
This went on for a while before
I realized thinking about people
with antipathy was filling me
with sorrow. People need a vision.
I wish I could give them one of these leaves,
the yellow ones trickling out of the sky.

Ice Glen
~ Gail Mazur

to Michael

Ice Glen, a side trip on our trip
to see old friends. Our plan,
a hike, and then there was the thought
of Hawthorne and Melville,
a century earlier, and *their* friends,
sitting on boulders singing,
drinking, and "telling tales," calling
across the romantic mossed abyss—
we knew their incipient romance
that crashed and burned.... Steamy
August afternoon in Stockbridge,
the sun above us a round flame.
Romantic to have thought of hiking up,
then down to the ravine, the icy chasm
someone once called *a curious fissure.*
Might it be like a bottomless well
we'd each drop a wishing stone into?
We only got close. What you saw there
you saw with your inner eye, a radiance;
what I saw was unfathomable, sunless.
Frigid, frosted, the air that turned us back—
too cold for us, but we were laughing
as we fled to Main Street. Cold,
but I wish our two souls were there now
together in that dappled underworld.

On Safari
~ J. D. McClatchy

Suddenly there is a prowling leopard to track
And the camouflaged Jeep stampedes
Through acacia saplings and liana slack,
A bone-crunching
Racket that forces the cat further to recede

Through tall grass rustled into a nerve-racking,
Patternless gilded maze
That guesswork sorties of skittish bushwacking
Fail to discover
The panting heart of, amid its invisible pathways.

We circle back through failure like a proverb,
Blaming mankind's gift
For deafrush and hindsight, leftover
Cultural traits
That still, sadly, leave the race to the swift.

But there it is, crouched, this muscled magnate
Atop a termite hill,
The petalled pelt, the eyes looking straight
Through their saffron-
Green glaze, its head fatally still.

The Jeep inches yards closer, drawn
By the advertised chance
To see what is wild and nearly gone.
I query the guide,
Whispering "Why the studied nonchalance?

What does it think we are, here at its side?"
"A giant moving rock,"
Is his reply. "She—" (He joyrides
His expertise.)
"She knows from long experience the deadlock:

She can't eat us and we won't attack—our lease
On an artificial life."
The basic necessity and unease
The species share,
The whole planet, here to home, rife

With moving rocks meant to assure and scare.

Club X, Before the Bridges Lift (Two Views)
~ Philip Metres

Between the gaping double doors of Club X and two leather thugs, a cardboard babe hoists head-sized steins before each suggested breast. I want to enter, be hauled into the mouth, haul it all into my mouth. Mandelstam: *the way Tatars bathe their horses, lower your eye into what will be.* Across the street, at Neva's edge, a local artist watercolors the Palace bridge, its wings splaying to twilight. *Remember the eye—a noble, but stubborn animal.* The river's colors blur with each stroke, bleed into shore. The waters rise. Everything wants to be flooded. Every empire dies, entering its own dilated eyes.

The Maternal Instinct
~ Elizabeth Metzger

Take these, I said. In an overgrown
ring you all stared, yanking dirty yams
from the ground, those awful orange lumps.

Once they were dismembered and gone,
you removed the arms
from my arms and planted them,
fingers down, in the holes.

You gaped and you sighed, saliva
straining icily toward the ground.

Mama, the last one of you said, *you preferred
me before I was born.* And he pointed
the last arm at me. I did not take
its empty hand.

Field
~ Joseph Millar

I sat down in the yellow chair
in the hush before the rain
watching the women walking together
through the glass door in their fulsome skin.
It was better than sleeping,
better than gin
with the immense heaven far overhead
the color of lead or beaten tin.

I saw their shirts loosely darkened
after the small drops began,
I saw their ribs and hips and hair
and it looked as though they were floating
across the electric air.

The election raged on in the cities
and death came in the night
for the famous judge—
whatever it is that resists transformation
must have abandoned him—
maybe the iron in the blood.

And then the rain opened its silver wings
beating down on the grasses
combed back by the wind
and the trees and plants
with their roots and seeds,
their blossoms and delicate limbs.

Erstwhile Brood-Hen Farmer Laments
~ Nancy Mitchell

For a roost I used the empty old corn
crib on the two acres with the tenant
shack I rented and cobbled together
a sorry row of boxes and stuffed them
with straw. Outside of that I didn't know
exactly what to do with the five hens
and rooster from the farm store but
scatter feed and put water in a pie pan,
especially when they flew into the trees
to sleep. My landlord Jess gave me the stink
eye for not knowing about night feathers—
he cut them back somehow with his wife's kitchen
scissors. For a while it was fun to get up
early to check for eggs although they never
did lay more than a few, and I was scared
of the rooster after the bastard pecked
the hell out of my knee. But I was
a bad steward. Be gone for days to see
the Dead, never thinking their water
would dry up, or be so stoned on Acapulco
Gold and forget to latch the fence. My dog
got in and left a mess of feathers, blood
stuck with feed. I tasted rust. I kicked him,
then cried until I puked. When Jess drove
up and saw just the two hens huddling
in the corner, he never came back
except for the rent, which I taped to the porch
door so the wind wouldn't take it. At night
I tell the wind if I had another chance
I'd raise that brood better.

Rain Room
~ Carol Muske-Dukes

> "*Rain Room* is an immersive environment of perpetually falling water
> that pauses whenever a human body is detected."
> —Los Angeles County Museum of Art

> "We are not born at once.... The body first and the spirit later."
> —Mary Austin, "The Land of Little Rain"

L.A. summer, another century. She stops under
un-watered palms, transplanted on broad avenues.
They look, she thinks, like young wives beginning

to suspect that "all marriages go dry." Bride after
towering bride in brittle tiara, blades whirling in
burning air. Their long dream of water falling in place,

like rain in a Room where clouds glide in formation, inching forward
    the slick mirage. *Water out-thinks us,*
now & to come. Drought has a fake pulse, beating

into memory. *What we remember will return*, we think.
Drink from the deep eternal well, lift the dipperful
of plausible stars. The past arrives in a cloudburst,

but that lightning flash's like a glass wand dipped
in simile: dipped in a vial of long-ago scent called *Rain*.
Pimps, primping outside the Women's House, Riker's

Island, wore it, loitering in a storm, waiting for
detention brides. She stood up in the workshop, a Justified Homicide,
    reading her poem aloud. Somehow

echoing my mother's father's hymn on a lost farmhouse porch under
rolling Dakota skies: *O Lord, send rain!* He could smell it, even in
blowing dust. She could smell it,

evaporating, as the pimp took her by her wrist. *He beat me. I blew
him away.* These fluid partitions dropping between versions of
done time. Coming down at last as I floated

in my ninth month. Pinpoints lit the pool's surface, drops falling up
from an earthquake's tinted quiver. *He does not love you.* Alone
driving into Hollywood's dawn downpour.

Wiper-quick glimpse of a billboard's horror flick bride.
Her screams, unheard but echoing. False rain halting overhead:
museum trick mist. Same refusal to bring

it down on any of us: absolution. This desert. Mary Austin's desert.
Timed water dialed to the limits of
desire, the limits of birth. Concrete river. Streets of

light-pouring light. Once-green fronds: gestures overhead.
Then the contractions start: nothing can hold them back.

Wishbone
~ Robert Nazarene

Emmylou waved from the top of a banana split. I love her. She slid down and we sat together among the asters and lindens. I would buy a million of her records if I could sell my crops to a billionaire. We could get married, too. If I could make this come true I'd turn Christian Scientist or search the world over for James Earl Ray and catch him for free. We'd have jet-lagged children and go grocery swiping at Piggly-Wiggly and throw our EBT cards into the trash—or at some poor people. Same thing. My dad would just yawn and look bored like he always did before he wasn't dead yet. In this world, with money, anything goes. See? And I'd never ever ever have to come from Hell and back again.

The Rented House On Black River
~ D. Nurkse

1

As I was pretending to be an old man, the cat, who had been missing since dawn, sauntered in. I made believe I was her instead.

Tightwound under the sofa, among the Hires caps, dustballs, and transparent hornet thoraxes, I could feel the muscles bunch on my powerful haunch.

A moth was passing. I leapt, my claws clicked together.

You couldn't touch me. I was the hue of twilight. My flight was broken. Jagged like the air after a lunge.

2

Now I mimic the way all things copy each other. Frogs are mossy quartz: sparrows whirling birch leaves: Kiln Lake a slate roof: mind a moth. I may be old, with bulging disks and a gimpy gait, but I still rise and set, ninety-three million miles away, in the hollow the cat sneaks off to, just beyond the stove-in fence.

Man Keeps Eighty Sheep In His House, Authorities Say
~ Jennifer O'Grady

yet who can say
how love must be bestowed, or where
        lay its limits? What to one

is a rare treat, Sunday
bounty, is to another
        waste or grief,

the remains of it
still leaking on the plate,
        wet as the pink and red

markered hearts
our daughter scrawls and thrusts at us
        whenever we pass by,

their borders unable to hold
so much color, the color itself so saturated
        it bleeds, nearly destroying

the paper underneath,
her love for us vast
        and uncontained, so that even

when we pass her by,
unglancing, it is there still,
        brimming and spilling

from her eyes.
And though we might take
        her hearts and lose them,

absentmindedly placing them
in the recycling bin,
    who is to say

  the giving's unwise, the gift
unneeded? Who can live,
    love gone,

  in the wake of its absence?
For aren't we all
    always in the end

  like that: bleating
and bleeding
    for love.

Guitar Drag
~ William Olsen

It is impossible to stop watching and listening to Christian Marclay's 14-minute film of a Stratocaster, say Jimi's or Pete Townsend's, or John Lennon's, dragged by a rusted-out four-by-four across ground that has died of thirst. The sensation is of all noise at once and turned fatedly elegiac, an allusion to the death of James Byrd, himself dragged to death behind a pickup, tied to a rope, the pickup tied to torture, torture tied to fear, fear tied to ignorance. This Strat hogtied to a pickup makes me wonder how many Vietnamese peasants bled into the Summer of Love. Turn up the volume. Torture by definition refuses to end. The Strat flips on its back but always rights itself. The pickups are on. The sound is one of abuse. How much abuse can we take. By the end the Strat is a mess, strings broken, pick guard almost unrecognizable, even as the truck disappears over the hill and the film fades out with narrative. A guitar is dragged in a simulation of disgrace. Sacrifice—impossible. The thing won't fucking die.

Losing My First Language
~ Dzvinia Orlowsky

Ja majy dornu minu:
I wear a stupid expression
and my sister agrees.

Gone my words for *pipe*, for
wig, for *lovely daughter*,
for *may a duck kick you*

when someone presumed
dead shows up. Where
is the language of the nightingale,

of the child who received
the song of Ukraine when Saint
Nikolai ran out of toys?

Where are the words of barn
mice predicting bitter
winters, warning flood?

Vegriville Egg
~ Dzvinia Orlowsky

Like a hornet caught in a jar, static buzzing between words, he yells from across Manitoba's endless ice into the phone, two provinces away from the world's second largest *pysanka*, a Ukrainian-style Easter egg. Black and gold tiled, it turns in the wind like a colossal weathervane. Holding two separate rotary phone extensions, my parents yell *It's Uncle Bohdan!* interrupting each other in excited disbelief. Squatted on the floor next to my mother's legs, I dress my naked Mary Poppins doll in spike heels and pretend to also be happy. Mathematically mastered, steel-girdled, three and a half stories high, weighing in at 2.5 tons—*we simply had to see it*—a pleasant 1,181-mile drive from Ohio to Egg. We pack a picnic, boiled eggs and sardines. What did we know about roadside burgers? But more pressingly, what did we know of art? Except that our home—family and guests insisted—aside from not having a framed print of the egg—was filled with it: paintings *by our own kind* that *one day* my parents whispered to us as if revealing an important family secret would be worth a fortune—despite the fact that, it turns out, these were not master oil paintings but rather, acrylic cartoons of our people doing our-people kind of things—playing *Kitchkari*, Ukrainian ring toss, or dancing in red leather boots, multi-colored satin ribbons streaming from flower wreaths in women's hair, men sporting handlebar mustaches—paintings that showed happy people, stomping and spinning in place.

The Ferris Wheel at the World's Fair
~ Gregory Orr

The wheel swoops you up, swoops you down again.
The giddiest ride in the world, they swear.
When you're high, you're high, but where does it end?

You take your seat and then your seat ascends
and far below you: bright lights of the fair.
The wheel swoops you up, swoops you down again.

When you're high, stars and neon blur and blend
but don't get off, unless you walk on air.
When you're high, you're high, but it will end.

They look so small down there, your former friends.
Like ants or insects. Who could really care?
But the wheel that swoops up, swoops down again,

and when it does, when the big wheel descends,
you'll step off dizzy. You'll want someone there
when all your highest highs begin to end.

Fortune has a zero for a heart. Defend
against her, whose wheel is noose and snare.
It swoops you up to swoop you down again.
It takes you high, but all highs have their end.

People
~ Kathleen Ossip

From the start, I was scared of people.

People with their "Oh my gosh I love your outfit!"

and their super-girly mama dramas.

People with their "We need you to come to the office with your things."

People with their "I can't be with you because …"

and their insertion-based love.

So new cats kept appearing in my house

because they weren't people,

and I fed the hungry,

not the homeless.

I heard the sound of 47,000 twitter accounts

not once ever reading my tweet.

People are everywhere, in parks, cafés, schools, in the mall, on beaches.

They want to feel happy, not guilty.

People sit in cathedrals.

When the service bores them,

they imagine they're artisans building the cathedral,

carving the columns, gilding the sacristy,

hammering the buttresses with great freedom and skill.

People are life-size, but sometimes they are cathedral-size.

For many years, I was scared of people

and people were frightened of me,

The World According To Capa
~ Alicia Ostriker

In Robert Capa's photographs
    of the first half of the twentieth century
        people are emphatically generic

boys in shorts play marbles
    politicians in wool suits embrace
        like tough kids sizing each other up

on an Andalucian hillside
    a man falls diagonally
        dropping his rifle

GI's have a smoke in the shade of a jeep
    fellowship steams from the page
        like heat from a summer sidewalk

my husband and I on the living-room couch
    are halfway through this book
        of photographs I have given him

it puts its arms around our shoulders
    like an overfamiliar uncle
        we turn the page

to where the long curve of Omaha Beach
    emerges from a background of fishing boats
        some drowned soldiers and wooden debris

are gazed at by a Frenchman and his son
    standing on the sand in 1944
        where Capa must have told them to stand

and gazed at by my husband and me
   in the twenty-first century
      seeing what Capa needed us to see

Awkward Snows
~ Jay Parini

Snow falls raggedly in early spring,
in strips or patches, snagging
on a ledge or whorled against a fence.

It isn't pretty, not like winter's
lace on lawns,
those dunes Arabian in undulation:

soft hills with really nothing
subject to debate,
when days would print the negatives of night.

Yet I can take this spring of snow,
its fits and starts, loose passages
like some fool gestures of expression.

So it hangs on hedgerows,
gathers sideways by the dry stone walls,
or fills the furrows of a path

where maybe for a month
it will define rude lines of thought,
bring into view a broad relief

of pastureland, or fill a path
through these blue otherwise of woods,
where snatches may be heard

of what is meant or almost meant
as awkwardness goes on,
its gap-toothed, fragmentary speech,

old news returned as revelation
in this frieze of time,
this intermittent snow, its ragtag ways.

In the Garden: for Seymour Bernstein
~ Linda Pastan

Spring is breaking out
in the garden—cantata
of purple and yellow crocus,
hum of green in the meadow

as the earth turns towards the sun
the way an old woman,
rocking on the porch, might turn
lifting up her face.

Bright arpeggios
along the stems of forsythia ...
half-notes of leaves
on the staff of every branch ...

But even the lowliest flower
casts a shadow.
The woman is waiting for the coda,
for the slow crescendo of blossom

to be balanced
by what the maestro,
brooding over the piano, calls
the darkness of the left hand.

The Mantel Clock
~ Molly Peacock

When the bride stepped down the lawn
toward the indifferent husband-to-be,
the rest of us in the treeless glare, I slipped
across the grass to get my aunt a hat,
running to the car and back just in time
to hear the sloppy vows and follow all
to the banquet hall where I'd left the clock
on the meager gift table (only envelopes:
everyone else was giving money), hearing
Katie's "Don't do it" in my head
as I sank down at the cousins' table
and the shudder seized me. Wasn't it time?
(No children of our own to give it to.)

Katie's photos would be my *aide-mémoire*.
I'd begged her to help take pictures before
I gave the clock away; we positioned it
from angle after angle, stroking its case
inside and out, opening its back to find
the key my great-grandfather waggled onto
the brass chime-wind, the oil in our fingers
adding to the patina of his windings.
"Don't pass it on," she said with every shot.
Scissors, tape, gold-and-white wrapping paper
and the satin ribbon. Wrapped the clock.
(I've got to give this thing up sometime.)

Are others prone to speak to heirlooms
while dusting them? Almost like a dentist
who persists in asking complex questions
to a patient with a frozen tongue, I'd ask

if it missed the mantel in the farmhouse
where Robert McMann wound it each Sunday
then did his duty by his wife Molly,
making the generations to come. Did you
even hear their sleigh bed creak beyond
your deafening ticks and chimes? Aren't you glad
you're safe from the perils of the fireplace
now that you're nestled in our condo? Do you
mind being witness to my acid reflux
and my husband's cancer instead of their
measles, sick headaches, asthma and the grippe?
Far, far too noisy to wind:
                    you're always ten to six.

As all the cousins talked to each other,
that shudder rippled through me and, like a cat
whose fur is stroked in the wrong direction,
I stretched off my chair, sidled toward the clock,
grabbed it and barreled out to the parking lot
where I unlocked the car's scorching door
and lay the swaddled timepiece in the only
cool spot (a makeshift manger behind
the driver's seat)—then strolled back
as if I'd just come from the Ladies' Room.
Her mother said the kids needed purple sheets,

so at home I ordered them, Katie cheering
as I tucked the timepiece back on our shelf,
its key safe inside, face round as a barn owl's
blinking away the years—months, rather,
(the marriage lasted seven).
                  She left him,
then had a baby with somebody else.

The clock behaves like my mother as a child:
beneath her straight bangs she silently watched
her Grandpa wind it—seen, but not heard.
(Aren't you glad you're not on a plastic table
shaking when a dog with a whacking tail
barrels toward you, followed by a toddler?)
You're safe in the city where the blocks spread
out like metal meadows, safe till I'm dead,
persisting in time, but not to tell it. Below you
my husband naps, home from the hospital.

Life On Enceladus
~ Joyce Peseroff

It's snowing all the time at the south pole of Enceladus
Which is a moon of Saturn
With the loveliest name
And the brightest object in the solar system
Reflecting 98% of the sun's light
Its surface like the best powder day
So cold no life could multiply
Except the orbit of Enceladus
Around Saturn is elliptical
And squeezes the moon's interior
To liquid and also what's frozen
Underneath the white mantle
So now and then a geyser of salt
Water sprays upward and perhaps
Growing in the water a litter of microbes
As yet undiscovered but possible
Its alien DNA unsullied because capped
Beneath ice and acres of snow
Deeper than Everest is high
On the blank canvas of the galaxy
Enceladus the brush with a single hair

Perception
~ Christina Pugh

The aperture: the lens. The determinant ray. The conifer. The stripped-down. The lavish. The striped.

Occlusion. The numinous. The diamond. The horsefly. The firmament. Encaustic. The sea-bred. The trough.

The floater. The eye-pool. The lilac. The steamship. The Siamese. The rotifer. The mud-bath. The crystal.

Resolution
~ Lia Purpura

There's the thing I shouldn't do
and yet, and now I have
the rest of the day to
make up for, not
undo, that can't be done
but next time,
think more calmly,
breathe, say here's a new
morning, morning,
morning,
(though why would that
work, it isn't even
hidden, hear it in there,
more, more,
more?)

Spies
~ Lawrence Raab

But why not think of the world
as a movie you can step into and find yourself
saving someone very beautiful
who might be losing her grip on the edge
of a cliff as you lean
forward to touch her fingers, then grasp
her hand, trying not even for a second
to glance at the landscape
beneath you—the glittering
thread of a river, the edge of the sky.

Meanwhile, the wind tugs at her hair,
toys with her skirt, whispers
of falling, but notice
how neither the man reaching out
nor the woman in danger
seems actually frightened,
because that's the thrill—
being certain you can handle the future.
That's the satisfaction.

I know the story in which you and I
have taken our places
isn't the one we might have chosen—
that movie with precisely
the right amount of peril
and deception and dangerous driving
and then an ending where she says
she'd like to make herself
more comfortable, shrugging off
her jacket, then maybe

unbuttoning her blouse, tossing it
casually across a chair.

Isn't the actual future too easy to imagine?
The daily tasks, the repetitions, and pretty soon
we're asleep long before midnight.
Are you dreaming of yourself in a different life,
of us together in our different lives?

Maybe we've just been shown to the best table
in a grand hotel, snow in the distance
crashing through the mountain passes,
but no one is worried,
the great fire shining in the tall fluted glasses,
the waiter arriving to tell us
everything's been taken care of.

Don't laugh. Why shouldn't we be spies?—
the way I'm whispering to you, the way
you're smoothing your dress
and leaning toward me.
We have our secrets. We could be
two strangers, my dear, thrown together by chance
as once we were—reckless, unafraid,
one step ahead of the past.

Honeymoon
~ Barbara Ras

One like a room full of potted palms the size of baby giraffes
with mahogany ceiling fans circling at the languid but inexorable
pace of perfect foreplay, and another takes a stroll through woods
    draped
in Spanish moss, "lacy negligees," the bride thinks, "potentially lethal
to the trees," the groom imagines,
                          nothing like Melanie and Mark's
trip to Oaxaca, where, while buying eggs at the corner *tienda,*
the newlyweds chatted with two guys who ended up taking them
to a disco in their dumptruck, whose eight six-foot-high tires
had devoured five months' worth of latex collected in the drop-dead
    jungle,
                         and while Mark hunched in a
    murky booth
at the disco with Jaime, Melanie danced with Miguel, whose Mickey
    Mouse T-shirt
stopped shy of a belly bulge the size of a boa constrictor that has just
    swallowed
a mule, and while Mark wondered why Jaime's fingers were exploring
    his crotch,
he heard the sound of a hand slapping a face,
Miguel's, in fact, which had begun to burrow
between Melanie's breasts like a star-nosed mole, causing Melanie and
    Mark
to forget the eggs left in the dumptruck,and begin running down the
    median strip
back to town, neither of them looking up at the moon, white as it
    ever was,
nor did they wonder, as do I,

whether Art Carney named the show *The Honeymooners*,
while Jackie Gleason pounded the table with a shoe, insisting that no
   one
in Brooklyn had ever seen a moon the color of honey.

Ermine Elate
~ Donald Revell

Ermine elate
As strayed into a low garden
Where ghosts shelter in courtesy
Such as never again to be seen
Soon or late
It might have been Manhattan
As the island was in 1970
When freedom was a machine
White elated

I have come to reject democracy as completely as I reject death
It is unnatural this dying this walking over the heads of spectres
For a certainty transformation is the fur and engine of all death
Else nothing explained no pair of birds alive in our Manhattan
In the wake of courtesy finding a low place fallen from the sun

Thought Experiment
~ Susan Rich

What happens if she can't scan
the barcode of this winter's afternoon;
the crow's encrypted caw, the snow

globe not yet fully bloomed?
What happens to this singular day
which remains unrecorded— Wednesday

December 17th, left to its own devices
without an update or brief comment
on a blog? What happens to a brilliant word

like *samovar*? Will each coffee continue
on unfazed, like two commas, in one stubborn
irreducible phrase? What happens when

the language does not come—her life
aimless as the L train, where she takes in
the harsh clatter of the tracks but not the hum.

Whiskey Woman
~ Alberto Ríos

I am the whiskey man,
Now, the holder of your body

In a lukewarm glass,
More true to you tonight

Than I ever was before.
I am the whiskey-eyed

Man, the boy who couldn't
Hold you, couldn't begin to

Keep you. But I could
Hold and keep this funny-luck

Glass of water, this riptide
Of white pepper, this rough

Scissor-edge every time. It
Slices me away from myself,

Every half-taste, I take it:
This furious measure of happy.

It's a lie, of course, us,
Our connection, this line I've drawn

Between the small dots of us,
As if you are drawn to me

Or remember, or care.
But a lie is something—

I feel it.
I am the whiskey man and you,

The whiskey woman,
In the strong arms of my hands,

The whiskey woman and this,
One more night on earth.

Funeral Barge For The Supervising Engineer
~ Max Ritvo

Several miles downstream of the accident a young man
lay spread on a piece of metal. The sky was of an intermediate darkness
—a few stars made their light, standing in for a mass
bruised out by our bright work: the glowing, healthy factories,

parties, and cars and even, in its small way,
the fire the man came from. The young man's
nice symmetrical head dripped brains onto the metal.
He couldn't get over, as he died, how the dark

smells in the breath, and the sour breading on the meat
of his memories were so remarkably familiar.
He put his hand over his heart as he remembered
the women he had abandoned, the poodle

he killed by neglect, sodas he'd let
go flat—how many deaths have I lived through?
Who is it dying? he asked himself,
and wondered why he loved the self he carried—

the self, an assembly manual for chairs
his factory ceased to build years ago,
and now, to boot, the factory was blown up.
His body, sweet even now in its filth,

takes over. It puts hands on his grief
and makes it gurgle and honk. The grief
makes the man's body like a duck's,
and this calms him. From the benign distance

of a white tree on the bank of the river,
he sees what a beautiful machine he made.
This is no different than kissing his wife:
he counts his heart beats, and there are three pillows

on the floor, two on the bed. There's no escaping math,
and who would want to escape it? In order
to look forward to anything, you have to
look forward, you have to look, you have to.

First Snowfall
~ Max Ritvo

Initially, all of God's creatures roamed the land as immortals.

The bears clawed and belched along happily for a good sixty years.
But aging was something God hadn't planned for.

Forty years in, the foot pads desiccated.

The teeth cracked on salmon bone,
and the poor bears lived in perpetual hunger.

Hunger was also never part of God's plan,
but mix-ups happen in the confection

of miracles, just as they would in any cake
where everything depends on the frosting.

Eventually the hearts stopped working,
and the brains went rotten.

But something divine rolled the bones around
in the gray meat, and kept dark sounds
pumping out the muzzles.

The hardest part of any job is staring your failures in the face.
It's to hold yourself accountable. In such reverie, inflamed by guilt

He never asked for, a dirty bulb popped up over God's head.
He came up with the idea of Death.

It was an effective, if harsh way to smash back
to mud the little figurines He'd made

without understanding how in Them
suffering compounds naturally—it's just part of time passing.

Not the only solution, probably. But the one being offered.
Death came from out God's nostrils—a sealed, pinched smile

symbolizing his newfound cool.
Where the winds went, they forced the crops

to the earth, withered and white.
White as this new thing in the sky,

cold and bulky but graceful.

The bear takes the flakes into his lungs—
which is all that's left to see of the bear.

Look through the lungs. Holy.
Like stained glass finally trapped the light.

Maidendown
~ Hoyt Rogers

The farm along the Maidendown,
    at nightfall,
when the final light of day,
    the most detached,
pauses on the crown of the tallest tree.

Deep in the slough, a woodpecker
    picks up the beat.
Crows squabble hoarsely
    in distant fields.
Behind the windows of the house,
    nothing moves.
Squirrels forage closer,
    clattering the bone-dry leaves.

Nearer, too,
    the nighthawk with its cry
that blinks on and off.
    Two of them together now, unseen,
but like signals in the dark,
    flashing out of sequence.

The Trance
~ Ira Sadoff

hovers over us in the shape of a cloud.
A steaming kettle rolling to a boil.

Before the pianist drops her hands
she defers to the key, the unplayed chord.

Perhaps a word's waiting to be erased.
Or a sentence remains unwritten.

In paradise, there's little to work for.
But here in the world of we want more

everything's future perfect. Before
we know it, before we know a thing,

we too are waiting to be changed.

I Apologize In Advance
~ Ira Sadoff

but nothing delights me more than eating pussy.
More than imaginary strolls with Picasso
or the yellow sea that swirls in that hot Panang curry.

If you've lived in the world, you know there's little wisdom
to dispense: you duck arrows from whichever empire
scribbles down your thoughts the minute that you dream them.

In the end maybe you get one idea to keep to yourself,
but who's to say it's yours? Our minds are little magnets,
bad radios with competing voices from Cincinnati

and Chicago. As for eating pussy it takes complete trust
in the tongue, complete concentration, opening up
for someone you love: those unfathomable moans give way

to whines and whispers before slipping into sighs
and melody. I mean the whole body becomes a dancer's
body: sinewy, lithe, satin. And once you've stripped down

the niceties and icicles that make us models of decorum,
you can open the window and your neighbors' voices
will seem startlingly human. Trivial and impossible.

In The Valley Of The Allegorical Animals
~ Jerome Sala

And that night in my dream
I entered the Valley of the Allegorical Animals.

Each roamed its emerald pastures
                                    with that flair
that comes from expressing one's purpose
with one's very being!

The pig that stands for fullness
        for happiness
                        for the ecstatic complacency
                                of the bourgeoisie
and therefore
                for the antique, the arcane
for the bourgeoisie no longer exist.

The owl
        that flies into the windshield
                of the futurist
for as we know
owls are only wise to the past—
and its haunting gasp
like a drowning giant
struggling toward the surface of time.

        "The dog—
                you may call him Old Yeller,"
                the dream voice said,
                "and it's ok, you can ask
                your allegory to speak—
                even if he is a dog."

The dog says
    "I'm so horny!
      Lead me to nearest
      pornographer's casting couch—
      I promise
      I won't piss on the furniture
      because of my excitement
      or my disgusting, inbred tendency to territorialize
      or to please!"

The crow
Señor Somber Solitude
guardian of a midnight opium stash.
The crow has always stood for one thing only:
the crushed velvet decadent Romanticism of the 19th century.
He wants to be more
but his shiny being—
even with his Goldfinger-esque addiction to precious metals—
won't allow him.
Unlike the wild indeterminacies afforded the leisure class
the crow is someone who must work a for a living
and this, the only job for which he receives symbolic wages
limits his identity, his ambitions, his potential for self-expression.

And as I walked through the dream valley of the allegorical animals
I realized that one need not fear a meaningless existence,
but rather the opposite
for all here meant too much!

The cow in whose moo you hear
the anger of
resentful, forgotten gods.

The squirrel:
the con artist of the beasts:
he coaxes friendly gifts from those around him
and then, a miser,
acts as the nervous guardian of his meager treasure.

The snake, who teaches us
how to smile wickedly
and thus gain
the magnetism of the elect.

The platypus:
she reassures her students
that the impossible is not only possible
but nearby!

And then there's the wombat, the rug rat, the cane toad—proud of its
    poison glands, the ray-finned catfish, the giraffe who spies on the
    naughtiness of the tree dwelling crowd, the brute, fascist rhino,
    a reactionary of the old school, the industrious but warlike tiger
    ant, the brown recluse spider, famous for his necrotic kiss ...

Each animal meaning more than the rest—
so that the valley contains so many animals
and so much meaning,
that exploring it is rather like
struggling to walk through a bowl of jello
tinged with molasses.

One can hardly bear
to live this way,
nearly smothered by signficance
so that one longs

after a short visit
for the liberating blankness of the awake world
where things are bought and sold
and meaning is assigned to them
crudely
carelessly
arbitrarily
and for non-mysterious ends.

Apart From A Few Stone Bridges
~ Sherod Santos

Half an hour outside the ancient city limits, down what was once a mill road and now a shortcut locals take to a highway in the north, lie the grounds of a ruined estate, its confines marked by boundary stones dense hummocky clumps of grass make difficult to see. In the turnaround, a marble bacchante, her life-size body balanced on a plinth, a castanet in her upraised hand, her eyes closed, or almost closed, in the pleasures of the dance. Except for the occasional passing car, sounds one would normally expect to hear, the natural and the manmade, don't rise above my footsteps on the gravel path. The padlock on the caretaker's shed is off its latch, and from the choked-off limbs of the orchard trees, vines that appear to have grown, not up, but down the trunks before taking root. The copper-colored underside of dead leaves, and at the tips of the branches, deformed clusters of terminal buds covered in fungus like an animal's pelt. All this I recorded twenty years ago—to what end I couldn't say, beyond a need to renew my ties to the world—on the back of a rental car folder, near the sluggish waters of the Lys.

Astronomer
~ Lloyd Schwartz

"What's your favorite part of the painting?" the young woman standing next to me suddenly asks.

I reply instantly: "The light hitting the fingernail of the Astronomer's left index finger—what's yours?"

"The edge of his white shirt sticking out from under his sleeve."

Her favorite detail is barely inches away from mine, but we confess that neither of us had paid much attention to the other's choice.

A few minutes later, I might have chosen something else.

*

The Astronomer ranks only 23rd in popularity among Vermeer's 37 extant paintings, although Vermeer himself seems to have been particularly pleased with it.

He both dated it (rare for him) and signed it with his efficiently witty monogram: IVMeer—the V overlapping the central part of the M, the I (for Iohannes) like a tree springing up in the middle of the V.

Two centuries later, it was acquired by the Rothschilds, and after the war, after the "Monuments Men" recovered it from its Nazi hideout (evidently *der Führer* liked it too), the family surrendered it to the Louvre.

*

A man in a dark silk Japanese robe leans over a table cluttered with books, some crumpled notes, an astrolabe, with which medieval navigators calculated the altitude of the stars, and a celestial globe swirling with serpentine constellations.

He's an astronomer.

One book, an old treatise on astronomy and geography (second edition, 1621—the painting is that precise), is open to the chapter recommending both "the aid of mechanical instruments" and "inspiration from God."

Light floods in through a double window, illuminating the book, the globe, the Astronomer's face.

He's leaning so far forward in his chair, he's practically levitating with curiosity.

Like so many of Vermeer's figures, he has a particular look of attentive concentration that suggests an interior life, a private zone of contemplation—yet not self-absorbed.

He touches the globe with the tips of his thumb and middle finger of his right hand—maybe just about to rotate it.

On the wall behind him hangs a dim painting of the finding of Moses in the bulrushes.

*

A long-held but unproven theory suggests that the model for both *The Astronomer* and its companion piece, *The Geographer*, is the Dutch lens-maker and inventor of microbiology Antonie van Leeuwenhoek.

Both he and Vermeer were born and baptized in Delft in 1632.

Forty-three years later, the great scientist was the executor designated to dispose of the property of the recently deceased and indigent artist.

Vermeer might have used his lenses to help create his almost photographic images.

This picture shows someone enthralled with discovery.

Maybe it's a self-portrait.

*

Gradually, the hidden geometry of the painting reveals itself.

So many Vermeers, like *The Woman in Blue Reading a Letter*, or *The Geographer*, are images of stability—solid, unshakeable, earthbound.

The pregnant woman in blue looms like the Great Pyramid above the familiar objects in her room that seem to gather around her.

But in *The Astronomer*, the pyramid has been tipped over onto its side, forming an acute angle.

Like the profile of an open eye.

That eye is everywhere.

In the angle of the two fingers touching the globe.

In the angle of the Astronomer's arms—his left hand gripping the edge of the table (steadying him, grounding him), while his right arm reaches out to the celestial globe.

Even in the overlapping shadows cast by the light through the double windows.

Light that catches both the tip of his finger and the edge of his white shirt.

The table, the book, the globe, the Astronomer's body—everything in the process of opening outward and letting in the light.

The whole painting has become an eye.

*

The Astronomer's unembarrassed, open face, luminous even in profile.

His long hair falling below his shoulders, revealing an earring.

Vermeer regards him as lovingly as the Astronomer regards his globe.

Right next to the Astronomer's right hand, the hand beginning to turn the celestial globe, the artist has placed his signature.

Dream of an Old Teacher
~ Alan Shapiro

And then, as on a sheet of photographic paper—
my solitary dead
ringleader of a bleached decorum
is taking shape beside me on the sofa
out of beige naugahyde
under an off white almost yellow
lampshade and light that hold all
and none of the washed out mutating
palenesses of his emergence
in a white suit and string tie
even paler than the spittle
glinting from the corners of his mouth.
Cigarette between two fingers
of a hand that also holds an empty shot glass—
nursing his one drink, emptiness on ice—
he nods as to a fool he just this once agrees
to suffer gladly, saying, "Thisness is all,
hardly seems worth the bother"—
Around the room he waves
the cigarette like a pointer
out from whose tip
swirl ghostly letters in an ancient script
that the backdraft from the waving smears
white over white erased
before they spell out what it is
the waving's waving at.
A waning gibbous
moon, his face,
not the full 'orbed
moon that feeds upon infinity and broods
over the dark abyss

in one continuous stream—"Oh
I don't doubt it," he says as if I'd spoken this out loud.
"I'm not that hard up for religion."
And then as if to answer to what I haven't asked,
"How many houseflies have died in time?
And aren't you older now than I was when I was your teacher?"

Debunker, Doctor, Drinker, my fifth
of father
which you kill
so I don't have to,
your room burns with a cryptic chill
as in a freezer whose light's on
from the open door
I never quite learned how to close
to turn it off.

Capital *I*
~ Betsy Sholl

Beyond *ibis, ice axe, igloo, ingot,*
whole pages in the dictionary's I section
have no pictures. After all, how do you
illustrate *impact, impart, inchoate?*

But nine countries start with I, which you can list
in the middle of the night when insomnia strikes
if you're like so many of us now, asking
ourselves in those late night interrogations

how well we have spent our lives. Impaled
by the swinging light bulb's harsh shadow,
who can't accuse themselves of too little
or much: ambition, greed, kindness, love?

One friend asks if he made a terrible mistake
leaving music for an academic life. Another
now sees that she never fully gave herself to art.
A third looks at his own impatience

and wonders who the hell he thought he was.
"We all live in a capital I," I sang
along with my kids watching Sesame Street,
as if instilling that sturdy castle of self,

not thinking some day I'd want to take off
those imperial robes and walk incognito
through market stalls, toasting locals at the inn:
Here's to age making paupers of us all!

Even in Whitman's great *Song of Myself,*
the first word may be "I," but the last is "you,"
as if that's our ultimate itinerary.
Once in Ireland, in Doolin, when the seas

were too wild for the ferry run to Inisheer,
my love and I stood on shore as waves rose
to magnificent peaks, then thundered down
into a white scatter and seethe of foam. Wind

gathered us up in its roar and swirl, until
there was nothing more to want, but that
moment on those rocks, at the bright edge
of everything beyond, utterly immersed.

Women
~ Jeffrey Skinner

after Lydia Davis

It used to be fun. I especially liked the hunt, the way we spoke without language. Then the shared whoops and hollas when the animal was ours. The fire, the eating, the jokes. The dreamless sleep. This was before the invention of snoring and farts. Because, who knew? Then women showed up, and we knew, because they told us. And we thought of killing them. But that didn't seem right, not exactly. Then suddenly, O—the things they did! The things they could do! Made us whoop and holla. Made us want to kill. But they said no, hold off on that a minute. Then they said look, look here, look what we've made. And when we looked we sort of wanted to kill again but again they said wait. And we did. Time passed, everything became seasonal. Barn raising, corn shucking. Finally, we went back to killing. We couldn't help it. Farming sucked. And the women left. Without a word, a clue. We will find them again, though, whatever culvert or gully or mountain or island or storm or idea they hide behind, or in—we will hunt them, we will bring them back. In the meantime, art is pretty interesting.

The Master Bird
~ Floyd Skloot

Among the warblers in our woods was one
that spring we thought of as the master bird.
His voice, pitched high against the rising sun
as though to stall it, seemed to be what stirred
the others into song. A soloist
of dawn, his full golden breast matched the light
that fractured in its passage through chaste twists
of oak and maple. He gave us one bright
moment of melody to remember,
then was swallowed by the day. But we'd caught
his act. That pure voice was the November
harbored in every March, the death held taut
in every birth. It aired the theme for all
the rest to use in answer to his call.

Paradox
~ Tara Skurtu

The theory of quantum gravity
is the missing piece. Our laws
tell us when they break down.
If you don't believe me, throw
a dictionary into a black hole,
watch what happens to the words.
Or take my sister, now a mother—
throw her in prison again.
See how long she lasts in the hole
until she breaks her mind against
another vision. See how long her four-
year-old daughter remembers
her love. For over a year my niece
believed the moon took my airplane
and wouldn't let me go, but
Where is my mom? she asks.
Toss a plane into a black hole
and see where it lands. My sister
tells me she's solved the paradox.
She's been with me on the moon
since April. It's late October.
I'm fumbling through stories
I don't know how to tell.
Head games, says my niece—
one bright brown eye fills
the screen of my phone,
doesn't blink when she says,
I want her face to be still like her face.

La lumière blanche
~ Ron Slate

With CPR and drugs, the emergency room team revived my cousin Serge. Once a pulse was established, they applied shock paddles to restore an even rhythm. That morning Serge had thought he was coming down with the flu, his chest was congested. Finally, around noon he decided to leave his art gallery in the hands of his staff and walk the eight blocks to the Hôpital Hôtel-Dieu, crossing over the Pont Saint-Michel. On arrival, he collapsed at the admittance desk. Surgeons inserted stents in his blocked arteries and he was discharged two days later.

"I was just regaining consciousness after the surgery when a woman appeared at my bedside," he told me on the phone. "She asked if I had seen a white light while I was dying. I think she wanted my impressions while they were still fresh and unembellished." In fact, Serge had been awestruck by the white light. He observed it as if standing behind himself. The light had a bluish tinge at its edge, that is, at the edge of his field of vision. The woman listened attentively to his description.

"Don't you think it's remarkable?" he asked me. "Of course," I said, "your timing couldn't have been luckier. What if you hadn't taken yourself to the hospital?" "That's not what I mean," he said. "Don't you think it's remarkable that there's a person whose job is to collect data about the white light?"

A few weeks later, while I was in Paris on business, Serge said his health was fine but he wanted to speak with the woman, to know more about what he had experienced. He asked me to attend as witness. We walked to the hospital along the same route he took while nearing death.

"Oh, we know virtually nothing about the white light," she replied tersely to his question. "And we don't inquire for that purpose. When someone flat-lines and then returns to life, we ask about the white light—because it seems when the patient, excited and amazed, tells the story of seeing it, this speeds recovery."

Genie
~ Tom Sleigh

after Rimbaud

Who is he, what is he, drifting like a smoke ring as smaller smoke rings drift inside the one just vanishing, always there when the light turns freakish, greenish like tornado light, asking nothing of us, slowly passing through us no matter what we're thinking, feeling, as he expands inside us beyond all measurement, all limit.

There's no god who's more to him than a solitary ant wandering on a countertop.

He declares swamp and desert, the Gowanus Houses across the street, and Louie selling lottery tickets for the Megamillions an outpost the aliens' rocketships will someday reach.

His summer raying out like a crystallized web, he's forever youthful, the erotic anarchist, all moralists disgust him! old or young, PC or un-PC. Our memories look back at us and see, through him, every wrinkle untransfigured, exactly as we were and are.

Like a worm-hole we pass through each time he looks at us, he brings us face to face with the X-ray/car wreck/the metastasizing future.

In every palm in every lifeline that's shattered, scarred and nicked in its own way, he traces the bastard forms that he most loves and patiently pursues, despite the cops in their cruiser going the wrong way down Wyckoff and the four a.m. gunshots on the corner.

See how, through each of us, he extends his damaged care the way a termite mound extends termite to termite all around the globe.

At the far end of the flea market, where a woman daubs on her customers' wrists her own hand-made perfumes, he brings us to where there are no curtains, to where space outruns the sea like pi repeating to infinity in his brain.

As if a split-rail fence, checked and broken all along the grain, were to follow an always shifting dune burying and exposing its own trail as the wind rises, is that how we should follow him? Or does he himself mark off some line of privacy beyond which nobody intrudes?

His heart: never will he leave us totally defenceless, never will he shrug off our sad compulsions.

White Project
~ Bruce Smith

The dream was clean of all indebtedness when a crow
spoke and I awoke in the white project, white noise
in the ongoing occupation, the future perfect tense
where I will have been immediately released from
the reckoning of my dream [Sand Creek, Sandy Hook,
Selma] after serving the mandatory minimum. I will have been
treated immediately for my pain. I will have added five years
to my life, added bank to my bank, unbent some notes,
attended, heard: words were spoken to me and I comprehended.
I heard. I was defended lavishly. I was less suspended,
less got. I hit escape alt delete then clicked on the magnified
icons while the wires worked for me, transmitting, distributing
the currency, our way of life. Clouds worked for me, optics,
lawyers, nature: the hands of the praying mantis, the eye
of the hurricane, gravity. The weight at the end of the rope
worked for me, the statute, the plastic explosive in its shock
and awe, the xylem and phloem in a tree. Worked for me.
Was that singing sung for me? I played the lottery and lost,
but the silver I scratched off fell like vulcanized spectral snow.
Losing was a luxury I could afford. It's a wonder.
It's a wonderful life. I still had the itch from the scratch
tickets and I called it character. I called it ambition.
I called it milk and health, called it complexion.
The angels were explaining. The angels were working
at monetizing el cielo, permitting no crossings, issuing
no papeles. I attended. I heard the Christmases. I abided
with a slight fatigue after the dream. I had a rash,
an inflammation. I felt flushed. I felt fundamentally
pale. In my brain were the spirals and stars
for which I was treated with the world.

See What Happen When You Don't Be Careful
~ Patricia Smith

Mama, knew you didn't mean *maybe*, the way your blunt
nails dug into the shield of my shoulder. I squared, willed
the muscle hard. *C'mon, girl!*, you grunted, re-clutching

that shoulder, forcing me, terrified, through the tight knot
of mourning, through the scary squeal of organ, toward that
thing. *C'mon here, girl!*, your big fist raised behind each word,

you tugged hard, dousing me with peppermint spit, but I
vowed root in the sour carpet. When I lifted my head
to find your eyes, roiling, loopy under half-closed lids,

the whites were thin-threaded with raging. Any second
you would lash out in the Lord's name, and He would give you
permission to whip me into dazed surrender toward

the coffin, balanced on its altar in a filtered
blast of stained glass. Just as long as I didn't reach it,
didn't let you wrench or knock me forward that far, it

could be empty. There didn't need to be a reason
for Tony, who everybody called *that sissy*, to
get all of a sudden touched, all sizzle and divine

on that organ, oil-sopped curls flung back, skinny fingers
blazedragging the keys, pushing dangerous deep into
some sneaky ol' resurrection groove. Old hands flap-clapped,

Good Books flew and the funky gut of a hymn bumped blood
thin. I'm so sorry I fought you like a man, mama,
twisting from you again, my whimpered *I don't wanna*

turning into the grunted Mama, *I ain't gonna,*
and you treated that *ain't* just like I figured you would,
teeth clenched tight, bullet eye, the hauling, three dull dry roads

on the back of my hand where you fought against loosing.
Mama, sorry I made you make a fool of yourself
in front of your God and Rev. Thomas and the dry

ancient deacons, I'm sorry you had to slap me hard
on the back of my head to make me open my eyes
until I was face to face with that thing, that thing I

used to call Willie, that sneak who wooed me once
with all of his tongue, who flung little stones to sting my
ankles, who couldn't keep burs out of his nappy head.

You hustled me right up on all that bright horrible,
that thing now black-bluish chill, put to his last bed on
puffed silk already stinking like shred, both lips blown big

and mistaken rose, my very first dead boy, and you,
mama, staccato *Look at him, look at him, look at
him,* hurtful with no love and all the love in the words,

in the sound, *Look at him, Go on, look!* the swelling song
of you and the church and Tony, his sissy soul all
knotted and driven, I'm sorry I didn't feel your

terrified heart quivering in your palm on my shoulder
or see the word *mother* setting fire to every day
beyond the day we were standing in, fighting in, in.

When Stafford Says: A Brief Exegesis
~ R. T. Smith

When Stafford nearly whispers he found "a deer
dead on the edge" of a notoriously curvy road,
we know he doesn't mean each detail literally,
as in,

      I, Bill Stafford, do solemnly swear
that on the night of March 9, hurrying home
alone, I did in fact discover a roadkill doe
sprawled on the serpentine asphalt
where redwoods suggest Dante's dark forest
we find in mid-life when we're lost.
My undented fender proves I never struck
a creature, though I was sensitive
and attentive and promise never to forget,
even if I was only mind-writing "What if?"

No. He's telling a story, and we should avoid
conjuring Bambi and choking up. After all,
they're just words, syllables aspiring to light,
though some readers bristle with indignity
at Stafford or the proxy he's summoned,
who makes no effort to rescue the unborn
fawn. Most speakers would lack obstetric
know-how, and that treacherous stretch above
the silvery river can be lethal, even for good
Samaritans. And the night would be dark,
as he said, the hard world at any minute
in the form of a battered van whose driver
might be outracing safety, in a way he sees
as sacred necessity, since he's unaware this
night, road, animal and man are in a parable.
Fog could be forming, no moon, now a drizzle.

It would be a shame to add to the casualties
or even to abandon responsible principles.

Instead, I have to admire that scene as rendered,
almost a gloss of scripture about the narrow
path, peril at every turn, the nature of obligation
and indispensable twists of wisdom, as Bill
reports, or fabricates, listening to the wilderness
while it listens back more skillfully, which is
for him a typical transaction. Does this imply

that sentiment is necessary but must not
be allowed to govern in emergency? Maybe.
This is a moment when we need to listen,
whether he's offering history or just invention.

Bill's mind is out among the wild things, ready
to join them, at least tempted, but the human
in him has miles to journey, which doesn't
mean he surrenders to whims, so he— narrator,
traveler, animated trope or a certain threshold
of perception and diction— grabs the forelegs,
rolls her over to the canyon rim, and he can see
the river's shimmer, smell larch and cedar rosin
as the animal tumbles over scree and brush,
clears the cliff face and falls free, the doe's
scut in the moonlight perhaps as white as salt.

Now, say he's on his porch, scribbling, one moth
already circling his light, all miles from any
heart-rending death. But don't we hear
that thrash of a corpse and see the deer strike
the slow water, making one spot briefly white?

293

I picture him later, hesitating in his kitchen
to imagine what else his pencil might fashion,
though it could likely wait till morning, as
sleep is a wise teacher, and he's weary. Now
he's headed upstairs, sentenced to a stiff whisky
and restless dreams of what we all ponder,
each of us a seeker and as the song says
"a wayfaring stranger" taking the Wilson
River road home, seeking the right words
to temper the world's woe, its vital danger.
I can't fathom how he might have done more.

Poe in Rome
~ Ron Smith

Let's say he gets there, somehow,
          after leaving, oh, Paris, with his head
   full of Byron and Piranesi, stretches
on the rubbled weeds of the Palatine,
         kneels an altered man, he thinks, hum-
bled amid Coliseum shadows, scratching *My very soul*
   thy grandeur, gloom, and glory in a small
         pad. He keeps his
            distance from St. Peter's
but haunts gold-garish Il Gesu hoping to meet a Jesuit
   who plays cards and speaks a little English.

      He knows he shouldn't
           sample the local wine, but
the smell of garlic and sweat, crowds on the Corso
      so unlike healthy New Yorkers, Londoners—he
         finds himself
     in the broken boat fountain, waking
to eyes that do not laugh, ugly mouths
        beneath them, stretched lips, black
   teeth—figs floating? No.
         Neighborhood

   chamberpot. Why can't he have a drink or two
      like everybody else?
    At San Giovanni, he steps away
         in horror from Galilei's
   top-heavy façade. What
if there's an earthquake? How many
   have been killed already by falling apostles?

He wanders the tortured vicoli
of the Field of Mars. He drinks

from a fountain of stone books. A street trapped
in Pompey's buried theater circles him back
to Satyr Square. *No,
no catacombs*, he says to the youth reeking
of energy and wild with ebony hair.
I would see, though, he says,
*the Temple of Jupiter
the Biggest and Bestest and Caracalla's
Baths, where Shelley scribbled Unbound.*
Ah, the youth breathes, *but first I take you*

*to the No-Catholic Cemetery where you can,
ah, commune with the Anglo poets.*
Dupin's creator's moved, even trembles
at the bitter water of Keats's words. Pyramid?
Why a pyramid here? *Death pitches his
his whimsy-tent
in the city of eternal excrement*, he mutters.
The boy laughs too hard.
On the way back the cart climbs

the Aventine, the mangy horse
wheezing. Darkness appears to seep
from every shrub, every
blackened stone.
Piranesi's piazza: grandly funereal,
symmetrical, pierced with obelisks,
smacked with elaborate plaques, the whole
brooded over

by cypresses. *Arancia*, the boy says,
          slipping a warm slice of fruit

      into Poe's palm. His jaw hinges wince.
He bends obediently to the keyhole. *San Pietro*,
    the boy says, *stupefacente*. But
              Poe sees only a dark corridor
          of hedges leading the eye to
              a gray blank. *Nebbia*,
    he would have said, if he had known
          what he was looking at, if he had known
                  the word.

After Birth
~ Katherine Soniat

When
the child finally
came   vinegar
and white carnations
poured through sunlight
just as her lingerie once
slipped from the bed and
on hands and knees
she crawled to fish
the flimsiest forward—
she the first to know their
movement and departure
Sprinkled rosewater on the
new moon

Madrigal: Vibernum
~ Lisa Russ Spaar

Unlike the freer, satin buckshot glee
of the apple & cherry trees—confetti

netting windshield, petalled hair, gutters—
these elegant shrubby standards hug

their brick wall, each a glinty grenade
tessellated with fisted bouquets,

an odor mapled, spiked by thorns.
How the brine-blue shins of blue heron,

cipher on this morning's drive to work,
huddled against the calendar's slow lurch

toward spring. The sugar-mouthed depth
of it, thaw riddled through with death—

& what we made of it later, in animal noblesse:
one clothed, the other undressed.

Nether Madrigal
~ Lisa Russ Spaar

I like it down here, he says. A pausing.
Meanwhile in her, herds, clouds wing
through the minutiae of each held breath.
Soles touch air. Speak like milk. Sayeth

like fire, that private conversation,
matchskin to flame—abloom in exhalation.
All the canals of these regions fill with tulips
barging toward the sea, its sweat of eclipse,

inhuman noise. A beat. A toehold
odor of wet juniper. Further folds.
Gentle reamings. *Nieder* meaning down.
But also near. Hot winds cuff up the vanes.

And the sail-shaft turns. Rotates. A brink
converts all footpath passageways to drink.

Pink
~ Jane Springer

Just how cold is it? Cold as a flamingo lodged headfirst in snowdrift
    after the trucker
marauded its flock, poisoned its mom, jacked it, cereal number &
tagged then clipped it, so it kerplunked a 70's wood-
beaded seat instead of winging out the cab, replete w/carotenoid
    snacks engineered
to preserve this
bird's pink as
brine shrimp used to suit outside his one

flamingo zoo— what he didn't guess, this god
of the eighteen- wheeler, is the bird knew campy songs
out the wazoo, from
3 Chartreuse Buzzards to
Kum Ba Yah, which she
sang w/Fruitloops spilling
her shallow-keeled mandible
for thousands of tundra-miles—
flapping down & up the wipers &
flipping off his hat by bill to keep beat,
that's how cold it was—& curiously satisfying.

Calling Home
~ Jane Springer

When you said Goodbye, stranger I thought you meant the Leon Pub
juke box where Major Tom got stuck that night & ground control was
just
that bitch waitress who checked our age for kicks then sped our
longnecks down the bar as if she'd like to wreck us, permanent, on
Blondie's Mars—

not this golden-capped fruit bat, inquisitive
in upside down, his smile a frown.

Maybe you meant the Dancing queen in Al Green's church of Won't
you help me, girl? *I'm sorry I didn't shoo the pest you said shared collective
consciousness from the ceiling teetering your bed—but made you come
party, instead, for all I didn't do you did for me—*

& not this red-handed
howler monkey orange flame flaring through the trees we may not
see again?

Between the darts of Leon pub, the Weather Girls predicted raining
men— thank you for deluging me the Pet Shop Boys to Summerteeth
& Beck defying speed of loneliness, we wore diamond footsoles, didn't
we? Earth below us, drifting, falling, floating

armored pangolin whose perfect rolling
form once outplayed the wit of predators.

I surely did enjoy my stay, before you Goodbyed Mary, Jane & mostly
think Let it be—the splif, the joint, & blunt, if time could keep Anne
Murray's waltz jammed up between two pool tables where we could
have this dance at 28, eternally, a leather patched elbow blast—

Goodbye stranger must have meant some future date where Some they
do &
some they don't survive the Desperado days, the Pancho Lefty left, &
too fast Little red corvette where You send me. Darlin you do, you do!
We don't accrue them back—

black shoe which I have lived as a

Monte Iberia Eluth, centimetering bright racing
stripes while shrilling forest's thrill—

Then too, Let it bleed surely didn't mean let's go poach rhinos,
elephants, Good bye stranger, it's been nice?

O my love is a Craklin rose
O my love is a Raspberry hat
O my love is a critical list
of endangered relations with this—

bubal hartebeest of wavish horn waving
time past rock-savvy hoof,

past orbit, stabilizers up, running perfect, starting to collect requested
data, what will it effect, thou sweet cliché of appointments, agents,
movie scripts,
I hope you find your paradise—but We are family & this my plea *per
condition
#3 of our Mutual Contract of Destruction*:

How many poems must I write you before you
send me
the new CD
you've owed me since I

i-tuned you that last soul song come on you can't tell me it didn't get to you.

The Rock
~ Jane Springer

The coral in the mortar seems not to do with a second kiss behind
the fortuneteller's booth, Spike Easterling's Bubblicious mouth parted,
tectonic plates to admit hostages—we did not understand, that year
Ali's proposal to my sis, eating kookoo sabzi & osh on pillows in our
socks could be dangerous, braces caught—I thought Spike quartz to
my feldspar, that Khomeini's first name was Ayatollah, we thought
plain water too severe for supper—at the fair, Spike's hand all day in
my back pocket, lamb we pet then had to put back to get my sister's
passport—I liked the new ziggurat scarf fluttered waves in her hair,
Jimmy Carter's name conjured peanuts & the hall of mirrors where his
brother stayed drunk enough to brand his own beer, there's a carnival
incense floats over bleating commercials for uranium, *esfand*—reminds

me of diabase, dactite the rhyolite of Iran, less than all the bowing
we did in Ali's apartment, prayer mats rolled up like magic carpets &
ticket to the double Ferris wheel of my sister's almost-marriage, chador
folded
in her suitcase if suitcase served as temple, hard rock scrambled by the
scrambler, cigarette butts smashed by cotton candy in the mudwash
by the fair gate, rock of ages, rock of oil lamps, olives, if only I hadn't
kissed
Spike's brother, first, that morning's rollercoaster wrecked between two
possible countries—market lamb's full head on ice in the kitchen, Amy's
crying, failed Operation Eagle Claw—then Ali's eerie disappearance,
what love elects may appear glassy to aphanitic to porphyritic deception,
Rock, who first settled you in Cain's hand?

Reparation
~ Page Hill Starzinger

Caning is a flowering,
    and the holy complex
Sniggu—
      self-sprung—shrieks with monkeys,

         descended from head lice
of a Bodhisatva
    of wisdom & learning:
    I am weaving a seat, Cane and

able to   see only as far as
    the tall, parallel-veined *poaceae*—true grasses,
with hollow culms and spikelet blossoms);
I run like liquid

    through the sieve-slats
hole to hole,
    flush along rails,
over pegs

(who knew splashing was
so sublime);
    join in—pour   yourself
through my palms and

evaporate ... but
    beware of each end-point,
deadline, or
    as the Army calls it:

suspense.

How Can I Unlove You
            goes the country song.
Even though the world looks kaleidoscopic,

            we aim for binary: remember, old bucket-of-bolts Soviet helicopters
fly
for the Taliban. Gratitude—a matter of
            paying attention. Beholding. Take note of the Architecture

of Urgency—:
            in Havana, deconstructors extract
        ceramic tiles or metal beams from
decaying mansions and recycle into homes

that become
            the fruit of looting.
Host, I scribble,
            —related to *hostile, hostage.* Steady:

if I cane all the spaces so they are parallel, all will be well;
            just don't choose sword grass, edges
sharp enough to cut our skin.

Mermaid
~ Terese Svoboda

The artist who stitched her legs
together—
      for chastity?
For media coverage,

a syndrome, perhaps a desire
to swim
      backward in time,
      pre-

when there were roaming wolves,
when there were iridescent worms
the size of—

      How did she pee?
Or swim.
Manage the wheelchair?

My memory falters—her name?
She didn't shoot herself
like the Austrian man,
limb by limb,

or chop off bits,
castration so similar.
She was female,
forgotten.

      What stitch,
the needle inserted, what thread,

what topical pain-killer
or not?

The legs want to run.

Cozumel
~ Brian Swann

And there you are, Frida, *mi amor*, in your "Self-portrait
with cropped hair" which I have framed and mounted on the wall,
where you've decided to cut it all off, precious thick black braids,
so now it covers everything, everywhere, bits of yourself twisting,
drifting , drooping all over, over you too seated in a chair
in his suit and shirt, no more Tehuana skirts, scissors open
on your lap beside a dangling tuft. The suit's too big, hair
too short for your marmot face. You've cut yourself off,
for love, for love? Even your winged eyebrows don't look right,
nor your faint moustache, your too obvious earrings and
small feet too small for your small high-heel shoes.
But yes, you're still perfect, magical, I don't know what
you mean and don't care, you're you: *Mira que si te quise,
fué por el pelo. Ahora que estás pelona, ya no te quiero.**
But *te quiero*, Frida, I mouth back, here where I look at you
each day, I know you know, and I know you know I want
your excess, your artifice of passion, and to that end
I carry and lay before you this small basket of beeswax and
bitter honey, the same the natives brought Cortés at Cozumel.

*Look, if I loved you it was because of your hair. Now shorn, you are hairless. I don't
love you any more." (Mexican folk-song).

Samuel Morse 1791-1872
~ Cole Swensen

who, instead of Raphael or Titian,
       found a ship
crossing the Atlantic
      and slipped into his pocket
someone else's invention
       a horseman in sound—you can imagine
the pounding of the hooves as in itself a language
         and a bit of copper
and a lot of news. It was really a question of the news
         seen as streaks
of light in which the instant was
      two distant cities
       and suddenly
the clocks aligned.
     It made him a fortune

and he spent the next few decades in litigation.

We wait on fire

and fire then comes.

There was someone coming

down the street; it was a quiet street, and the heels clicked

clearly, and it was summer, and all the windows were open.

Light Echoes
~ Arthur Sze

In the parking lot, we look up at the Milky Way:
a poacher aims a rifle at a black rhinoceros:

a marble boat disappears in smog.
As I gaze at an anthurium, wild cockatoos

cry from the tops of blue marble trees;
a lake forms on an ice sheet: rivers branch

and branch. A guitarist leans into the space
between notes; a stone plummets

down a black well: he does not know
it has the silence when he will aim a bullet

at himself. On a wall, a red spider;
macaws in cages squawk when we approach:

I scratch letters into the leaf of an autograph tree.
Like lights extending along a bay,

notes from *Norteña* splay in my ears—
they sparkle then disappear into black sounds.

Some Problems with Surrealism
~ Adam Tavel

A ginger albatross made of buttons flew
out of my 8th-grade gym teacher's nose
and perched on the licorice rim
of our hot-air balloon. It yawned G flat.
In the distance, the smoke from Paris
billowed intestines weeping purple
cognac down on peasant fires
that reeked, three miles away,
of boar scat. Reaching into the invisible
quiver dangling from his mesh shorts,
my teacher cocked his crossbow
and shot the albatross. *These things
keep showing up*, he said, turning
into a mailbox of barking daffodils.
His crossbow melted into feathers.
We could go on like this forever.

Concert
~ Daniel Tobin

Blade positioned
precisely the way
a cellist angles
his bow, *sul tasto*,
to the fingerboard,
back and forth
so the edge caresses
inward, quick cut,
blood-rosin, slices
like a honed wing
into neck, scar
music above
the gulping apple's
axing stone,
the voice rising
from its violated
box, song of all
parting, Adamic,
Orphic (more tren-
chant than this
slash of words)
unheard when
eyes configure
to the disfiguring
screen, a shudder
shutting out our
guillotine lids,
up shutter and
the body's sack
stretches before
us, skin esker

on sand, scored,
while the head,
raw, ripe, readies—
mute *a capella*
inabsolute sky.

Smile
~ William Trowbridge

"You'll find that life is still worthwhile,"
   sang Nat King Cole, "if you just smile."
     They start when you're a baby, just

twitches at first. But soon, picked up
   without a lesson, they signal pleasure,
     love, contentment, mirth.

But a Frenchman found they must
   involve the eyes if they aren't shallow
     as that yellow Walmart button's.

He named the real thing, of course,
   after himself—the Duchenne Smile,
     distinct from the Glasgow Smile,

which that city's razor gangs, who
   once were babies too, devised:
     slit both sides of the quarry's mouth

and beat or stab till facial muscles
   clench to rip a bloody smile
     from ear to ear—like someone might

deface a happy poster. The actor
   Tommy Flanagan got his outside
     a nightclub in that city; Elizabeth Short,

nicknamed the "Black Dahlia," found
   halved in an L.A. vacant lot, got one
     from her mystery maimer; The Joker

can thank his dad ("Let's put a smile
    on that face.") for his—though all were
        Duchenne-smiling babies once, as were

the death-metal rockers Glasgow Smile,
    whose album features "Retched One"
        and "Man's Disease."

Selected Poems by Chase Twichell

Photograph by Margie Miller Reuther

Interview with Chase Twichell
conducted by *Plume* Associate Editor
for Special Projects, Nancy Mitchell

NM:　Chase, I've long been a fan of your work, so it's a real privilege and pleasure to be talking with you. It's well known that you're a student of Zen Buddhism. I've been a clumsy, but earnest practitioner of meditation for several decades, and as I've lived most of my adult life on the rather isolated eastern shore of the Delmarva Peninsula, I began and continue my practice in solitude. I suspect my knowledge is, as the I-Ching says of the self-taught, "ponderous and one-sided." Be that as it may, one of the qualities I've always enjoyed about your work, including this selection, is—correct me if I'm wrong—how closely the architecture of many of your poems resembles that of a mediation session. The poems' lines seem to arise like answers floating to the surface from the inky belly of a Magic Eight Ball, from the resonant gap (stanzas?) between breaths, so the lines feel distilled, true, and ring with clarity. When I read your poems I experience what you've called a "mind-to-mind transmission" between the poet and reader. How much does the actual composition of a poem resemble meditation? Have you ever actually written a poem while meditating? Or used images that arise during?

CT:　I love the Magic Eight Ball comparison! And thank you for your kind words. At first glance, writing poems and sitting zazen seem to have little in common, since one is expressive, and the other attempts to encounter mind free of language. There's nothing wrong with language, but it's the vehicle of thinking, and thinking interferes with direct experience. Sitting zazen is an effort to stay in touch with the way the mind is when it's not occupied by making any sort of commentary or judgment. The work is to see through the thicket of our habitual responses so that we can perceive things exactly as they are, or what Shunryu Suzuki Roshi dubbed "things-as-it-is." For me, that's also the work of poetry: to see something clearly and create a window through which others can see it too. The irony is that words are inadequate (a funny thing for a poet to say!) so a poem has to work in the gaps and synapses between them, and in the overlapping zones of association. That's why a good poem can never be paraphrased (or, for that matter, translated).

There are of course times when a poem I'm working on distracts me during meditation. If it can wait, I ask it to wait. If it can't, and I risk losing an important insight, I try to fix it in memory so I can retrieve it later, and then return to zazen.

NM: In your poems I recognize the voice of the "self observing the self" particular to meditation. I'm wondering if, as a child, long before you began your journey into Zen Buddhism, did you have this sense of the self observing the self? I ask because I did, and it was quite distinct from the imagination. When I was seven or so, I had a secret ritual I practiced from time to time; I'd look into my mother's silver hand mirror and ask "who are you?" over and over—it was like chanting. At some point I'd turn the hand mirror to her vanity table mirror and create a tunnel, and wait for some answer to emerge—it never did. But, during this peculiar ritual, I had the distinct awareness of a self that was not myself and recognized it again years later in meditation. Heck if I know why I did any of this … maybe I'd seen an episode on *The Twilight Zone* about accessing the fourth dimension via a mirror. When my mother discovered me in her darkened bedroom, staring into the depths of her mirror, I could tell by how briskly she shooed me outside and the worry on her face that she thought I was a strange child. Her reaction frightened me, and I had the feeling I was doing something wrong and would somehow be punished for it. So, from then on I worked on trying to "pass" as a normal kid—I was fairly successful, popular and was excited enough to scream at the Beatles (although only for Ringo because he didn't seem loved enough), but I couldn't shake the sense that the other self was observing me.

CT: "Self observing the self"—there's the whole problem and fascination in a nutshell. Even as a kid I was aware that there was an inexplicable split in my consciousness between the mind that directly encountered the world and what I used to call the Watcher, which was the observer and commentator mind. I'm not talking about self-consciousness in the usual sense—anxiety about what others might think—but rather a kind of dual perception that I realized early on was not how most people experience consciousness, and which caused me to wonder, *Why am I me? Will I always be this particular me? What is a me, anyway?* I remember a classmate in fifth grade saying to me, "Why do you think about things like that?" Good question!

NM: And wasn't there an implicit "you're a weirdo" in that question?

CT: Absolutely. And I was a weirdo!

NM: We could have formed a Weirdos Club! I've often wondered if those blessed or cursed with what you call a dual perception, "people like us"—and David Byrne—who asked the odd questions, whose attention seemed elsewhere, weren't labeled with behavior disorders which only exacerbated the sense of alienation and thereby the alleged "condition"?

CT: Well, I did have the condition of ADD, which had no name back in the fifties, and also depression, from which I've suffered all my life. So who knows what's attributable to what? But I definitely experienced myself as "different" as far back as I can remember, and part of that difference was that I was aware of a Watcher that was something other than "me." I've wondered about that mental phenomenon my whole life. I suppose a psychiatrist might call it mild dissociation.

NM: Great and concerted efforts went into trying to make us conform. There was, and still is, a palpable cultural taboo against exploring one's self, which of course Alan Watts nailed in *The Book: On the Taboo Against Knowing Who You Are*.

CT: It's true that human beings often prefer not to look too deeply beneath the comfortable and familiar veneer of self-regard. It's unnerving to consider that we may not be what we assume ourselves to be. Meditation and poetry have that in common: they demand that we look anyway.

NM: Your intriguing poems in this Featured Selection capture the emotionally precarious tone of the adult-centered 1950s, as it's perceived by the speaker's "dual perception." There is a sense that there is much more than meets the eye, that adults have really constructed a world of containment, "The Children's Prison," where they wield complete, yet often capricious control, where "The grownups change the story's ending."

For example, in the second poem, "Maverick," the content and frequency of outside influences are regulated and monitored as in "I spent my one allowed hour per week / of television with Dad":

> We liked the riverboats,
> poker games and six-shooters,
> Natchez to New Orleans.
>
> I knew what
> *living on jacks and queens* meant
> and the rank of hands.

with the conscious or unconscious intention of reinforcing aspirational limitations inherent in male-dominated culture:

> I wasn't really a tomboy.
> I didn't want to be a boy.
> I wanted to not be a girl.

CT: That's an interesting take on that poem ("Maverick"), which plays both with the emotional origins of tomboyhood and the rejection of myself as a girl. I thought my father wished I were a boy, so I became one. For many of us kids in the fifties, westerns were common fare, so they seemed like a neighboring country we visited often. They were part of my imagination's landscape. Besides, James Garner was irresistible as Brett Maverick.

NM: Yes, westerns were a neighboring country, but a man's country. Ah, James Garner, and all those other handsome, older men … Gene Berry as the dapper Bat Masterson, Richard Boone as the darker, more dangerous Paladin in *Have Gun Will Travel* … and later the dreamboat Nick Adams as Johnny Yuma in the *The Rebel*. But I digress!

    This tone of emotional precariousness is especially acute in the beautiful "Snapshot With Eyes Turned Away." Although the mother is "… right upstairs, in his house, when he moved aside the tail to get the shot," her proximity doesn't protect the daughter from a photographer's sexual abuse. It seems mother mistakes the daughter's "*I don't want to be looked*" while she is being photographed as a charming expression of self-consciousness rather than a red flag. Is this another case of where the child suspects the parent has changed the story (again) into an anecdote to be trotted out in later years in "*You still don't want to be looked!*" The question haunts the poem.

CT: Although this poem does have its origin in actual events (a family friend was a pedophile), I didn't intend to indict the mother. I was more interested in how the experience got preserved in the child's memory.

NM: I don't mean to imply any complicity on the mother's part, but rather to suggest the naïve, sometimes blind trust parents of the fifties put in their immediate world, especially when contrasted with today's hyper-vigilant parenting style. I find the child's confusion with what appears "to be" and what she "dually perceives" very moving.

CT: The mother thinks the kid-phrasing of "I don't want to be looked" is funny, and has no idea, at least consciously, that anything happened, or that "being looked (at)" has any particular resonance for the child.

NM: In the poem "No Blue Allowed," are the children surreptitiously studding the prison walls along fault lines with the blue-truth when

> The kids would hide tiny objects
> deep inside the branches—
>
> gems of blue Lifesavers here and there,
> camouflaged, glued to a bird's wing.

so, when the walls crumble, Lifesavers and a bird's wing will abet their escape?

CT: The mother instantly spots the blue, and the kids know it, and since she says nothing, the tension and animosity between them is covert, unacknowledged. There's no prison in this poem, but the children are stuck in a world still ruled by adults, so I guess you could see it that way. And its true that the mother is a somewhat shadowy figure, always there but not fully present. Adult life is complicated and dangerous, and the speaker knows this but hasn't yet dealt with it except to poke it to see what happens (in this case by putting blue on the Christmas tree when the mother has banned it).

NM: Yes, thank you, Chase for clarifying. This is a more realistic and kinder perspective of the mother, and of the children's' intention. And, yes—what can/ do children of any era know about the dangers and complexities of the adult experience, or of their own prisons?

CT: To bend this back around to meditation, though, it's strange how specific individual memories, whether real, or invented as they often are in poems, become like rocks in a river. They're there, but the river has no trouble flowing around them. Even a huge dam made of rocks has no effect on the character of the water itself. I don't know if I learned that from meditation or from writing poems. In any case, both efforts arise from a need to know what human consciousness is. Why do I need to know that? No idea!

NM: What an intriguing image on which to end this enlightening conversation. Thank you, Chase. It's been an exceptional "mind-to-mind transmission."

The Children's Prison
~ Chase Twichell

Everyone's born in one, a prison.
Some parents keep children in,
some let them out.
Even the ones kept in
get out someday.

The grownups change the story's ending.
The man, standing in the garden
with a cut-up potato—a neighbor—
told the child that the eyes
just erupting into pale fingers

would someday reach for her hand.
That turned out to be true.
But no one ever saw any potatoes.
The vines flowered, but by then
the girl was already gone.

Maverick
~ Chase Twichell

I spent my one allowed hour per week
of television with Dad. Maverick.

I'd completely forgotten about the line
Smooth as the handle on a gun,
though I'd sung all the rest by heart

for many years. Still sing, when alone.

Who is the tall, dark stranger there?
Maverick is the name

(though I misremembered it
as Maverick is *his* name).

Dad corrected papers as we watched
(Latin teacher).

We liked the riverboats,
poker games and six-shooters,
Natchez to New Orleans.

I knew what
living on jacks and queens meant,
and the rank of hands.

I wasn't really a tomboy.
I didn't want to be a boy.

I wanted to not be a girl.

Snapshot With Eyes Turned Away
~ Chase Twichell

Here's a nurse with a vial of candy pills
and a miniature stethoscope, one finger raised
to the camera: *I don't want to be looked.*

Mom still quotes me when she sees me
self-conscious in photographs:
You still don't want to be looked!

The photographer took the nurse
to his basement studio. The cowgirl too.

Also a mermaid with slinky dragging tail.

Mom was right upstairs, in his house,
when he moved aside the tail to get the shot.

No Blue Allowed
~ Chase Twichell

No blue allowed on the tree.

The kids would hide tiny objects
deep inside the branches—

gems of blue Lifesavers here and there,
camouflaged, glued to a bird's wing.

When Mom saw blue her eyes
would stop on it overlong,

but she'd say nothing.

Blue hit a cold note
among the fire-like reds and golds,
the Christmas golds and greens.

Mom's Party
~ Chase Twichell

Maria arranged dahlias in a vase
Mom thought was too tall for them.

The caterers passed tenderloin
with horseradish on toast, miniature crab cakes,
and asparagus wrapped in prosciutto.

Yellow caution tape outlined the doors
to the deck. No one fell. The ocean rose and fell.

The ladies said, *Isn't it just like Ann
to know about a band like this?
I must get their name.*

She was glimpsed among dahlias
and lilies, both presence and absence.

Most of the guests were octogenarians.
They arrived promptly at 5:30
and did not overstay.

No one left without having had
a word with Ann, silver mermaid

shawled in the last gleaming
sea of her element,
both presence and absence.

Mom's Red Convertible
~ Chase Twichell

Mom has three walkers.
Her favorite, her red convertible,
wobbles, and is being repaired.

The new one is not really red.
More like magenta. All wrong.
She's sending it back.

Then there's the drugstore model,
aluminum, folding, black, light—
the one that goes in the car.

The red convertible is the exact red
of her first bicycle,
which she wishes she still had.

Of all the walkers,
it's the only *elegant* one.
It has good bones, says Mom.

I picture the red convertible
back in its early days,
speedy and sleek.

I picture the red convertible
parked in a dark workshop,
waiting for someone to come fix it.

Animals Not Initials
~ Chase Twichell

The crematorium sent Mom's ashes
via UPS, which left them on the porch
with the mail. In the box,

a card taped to a plastic urn bore
her name in schoolgirl calligraphy.

A name on a stone. How soon
no one remembers the person.

Watering her flowers, Mom left
sepia footprints on the slate.

Painters of caves left handprints
the colors of charcoal, pulverized rock.
Also legs and horns, outlines of lives—

antelope, bison, and bear.
Come to me, crude animals.

Tell me where you are now.

A Philosophy of Poppies
~ Lee Upton

I think that all my early wavering and fruitless decisions,
and those walks in the rain
drenched in my blouse,
the fabric dimpling against my waist
(the blouse shrank)
led me to the first inklings
of my later philosophy.
In my basement apartment
grass poked through the linoleum by the south corner,
and each morning I made my way to my typing job
to an office where I often heard strangers
crying—a therapy session upstairs—
and by five I was out in the rain again
—and once more passing those poppies
at the side of an apartment building,
and flaring and fresh from tossing off
the crust of their first world,
while another day I was in
a dress and the cheap poplin thinned
against my skin in the rain—
it was so often raining—
but the dress easily dried,
floating weightless,
a little bit of near nothingness
I would struggle not to become—
and another time I was so tired
I fell asleep for twelve hours
in one of the first blouses I earned
enough to buy for myself
that spring: the color of light through
closed eyelids—the color called "poppy":

that petal-like touch of what I wanted to be:
if uncertain about almost everything
at least unwilling to lie—
while on Monday once again
I passed on my way to work
those living poppies—
raveled at the brim,
improvisers, the word for what they were
the exact word for what they did.

The Smallest Hummingbird
~ Michael Van Walleghen

I thought it was just a big cicada
or giant bumblebee at first …

a thumb-sized "something" anyway,
hovering with a blurred, manic intensity
over one very important flower, then
speeding off to hover over another one
even more important, close by …

It even flew backwards for a while—
then seemed to think better of it
and went leaping off with her nose
in the air like a miniature Pavlova

to explore a blowsy pink hyacinth
on the other side of the restaurant's
done-for, back-patio garden …

not unlike the farouche young wife
of the Dean of Liberal Arts
who just five minutes ago fled
the annual Government Grants
and Achievement Awards dinner

early, barefoot, and a little drunk,
with an alumnus Nobel Laureate
almost as old as I am …

leaving a few older faculty wives
who still remembered him,

fluttering
        like minor aristocracy
at some sweaty
             Winter Palace ball
on the eve of the Crimean War ...

As if she were an errant princess,
or sorority girl
           from an entirely
different era and graduating class—

who, after twirling splendidly
through every waltz with a certain Captain
Bobyshev of the imperial guard

simply disappears with him
hand in hand
           without a polite word
or goodbye
          in a brand new BMW—

a scandal that would realign
state borders and strain established
alliances for the next thirty years....

In the meantime,

           I've finished my martini
and wandered out onto the patio again
to watch an early moon rising
over the beautiful sixteenth hole
of the Lincolnshire Country Club—

white and thin as the consecrated
wafer a traitor might receive
before facing the firing squad ...

which at this point in history
seems to be a motorcycle gang
pop-popping and backfiring

on the close-by interstate
like Hussars or the imperial guard
shooting all at once into the sky—

or at the carefully folded
paper hummingbird the comedian
of the officer's mess, or someone

like myself in fact—my blindfold
having slipped down around my ears
and still waiting, without hope,

for some last-minute pardon—
might pin to his chest as a dare.

When Uncle Fernando Conjures Up a Dead-Bird Theory of Everything
~ Marc Vincenz

CHAPTER ONE
In Which Our Dead Bird Speaks of Epic Change in a Foreign Tongue

(I)
In your own myopic view you exist
only as part of your own narrative,
nonplussed by mass and those bundles
of positive energy. Deep in gin, you ask:

Are there really universal truths

when particles become fields and fields, not
underlining, but dragonflying on top of a deadpan description:
symbols based on the metaphor of a bird that dies
in the natural philosophy of its own groundbreaking design?

and with the ice clinking, unpeeling

the layers of this reality shows how restless
you are, even at this hour. For no matter how
silent or how softly something deadly moves,
even a bird squashed on a little-known path to Eden,

is anything truly at rest? and yes,

light is bending toward
all that gravity converging on something
resembling to a straight line. In this billionth
of a second are we just leaves floating

upon an endless Orinoco, Ganges or Amazon?

On the other hand, who cares what occurs
four billion years from now. What is it then
about immortality—that bizarre notion of newness,
the sharp pinch of loose fingers on loose skin

when there really are *no* words on this page.

(II)
and isn't every word mired in what already occurred. Being
is purely a trick of light caught in a blurring
of the here and that visual cortex weaving
in and out of the sky meeting a sea;

and upon its surface two bolts of lightning hurtling.

and didn't we arrive here in a cloud
of toxic gas amidst a whorl of radiation
our collective histories converging
upon something only visible in its own becoming?

You ponder the meaning of all that infinitude.

I have been told the best thing to do
is to stare into the smallest distance, deep
into a zero volume—
for there is no such thing as *needed*,

even in the excesses of a wild imagination.

Several times you've mentioned
your immutable sense of loss
watching those ancient footprints lead away
and how you feel somehow everything

needs to be made up.

In the Penal Colony
~ Marc Vincenz

after Kafka

Not from the gagged mouth—it knots and tangles in the larynx
and the chain simply groans: "Have done it.
    Have it etched to the bone."

It's all in the pointed nib of the writers' dark truth.
In an enlightened moment the Bewildered gasps alone—

he knows he is condemned, he shall be bound nude
by his feet, sprung by his neck, stretched from his hands.
    He is bound to intone.

Brushing his bristling tweed the Uniformed flips the switch.
Nobs and spokes gleam: his conscience bears witness to false teeth.

"No doubt, no doubt in guilt, but doubt your own compassion," he says.
"When in doubt, doubt blind faith." But then there's another
    voice within—

the sound of an erudite soul chanting praises to a virtuous god, the
    Uniformed
eats his hat, rejoices in the cast iron life ahead, rejoices in the words
    etched on his skin.

How you should love to squelch them beneath your boots like vermin:

Just   **Be**

a
good Citizen

Be   **Just**

And, as the boat leaves the island, you stare at an inner rust
and think: *perhaps it is time to repair the clock.*

Speech
~ Arthur Vogelsang

in hiding places in a house in the sixties
seventies and eighties I held a hopeful weird thought

that in two generations all Americans
would be one nice beige color

a secret thought of mine a private thought
that I secretly thought was fated, a sure thing

given the new mingling
and the species' appetite for intercourse

   *

as in that hopeful weird thought
I also thought there would be a craze for knives

that wiped out guns like tv wiped out radio
and thank god it's come true

the popular lovely new law that says if you get stopped
by a cop and don't have a big serrated knife on you

you're cuffed and incarcerated for a month
by the way look around two generations later

   *

and see the rainbow of colors yellow
brown pink (they don't call it white anymore)

red black (at least there's brown, a piece of my old
prediction) and everybody's got a terrific knife

it's much worse than the gun thing (bloodier and daily) (shredded flesh) it's so ugly I might change my mind

OK what about escalators and the surf and tomatoes
Could you speak about them a second? No.

New Glina
~ Diane Vreuls

You could tunnel standing straight up
and digging, so high were the snows
in that country when you were five.
At thirty below all the windows were
petalled in rime, but you could just make out
across the fields black rows of mine cars
frozen in ascent. In the barn the cow's white
breaths glazed the feed trough. Walk to
the outhouse you might never return
to thaw at her aproned chest.

Hotter than winter was cold,
summer flowered the stony fields where
we swam in a creek the color of Coca-Cola.
We stole from the kitchen garden,
fed the pigs and fowl, and wept when they
were slaughtered. Playing in mud or
sliding down slagheaps would get you
worse than a licking: Serbian sighs as
Stana boiled your clothes on the woodstove,
then forgave you with stifling hugs.

First the mines gave out,
then her smokehouse and drafty barn,
and finally Stana herself,
gone to rest in that graveyard
directly across the road,
a modest hill she guarded
from the porch of her tarpaper house,
beating her breast and keening
when a child was taken in.

When she was received
we prayed for her in a language
she never really learned.

Hers we knew.
By heart.

Osprey and Needlefish
~ Sidney Wade

The raptor
plunges

and clasps
in yellow talons

a thrashing
slender ribbon

of scale
and bone,

almost
too large

for its grasp.
They lisp

through
sunglare—

now up,
now down—

the fish
drowning

in air,
gasping

brute flesh,
until

the osprey
firms

control,
rights course,

the struggling
needlefish

a shuddering
keel

as they gain
altitude

and wheel
into the woods

where a brood
of wide-

mouthed heads
awaits

its lively
silver food

Shall Bear Upon His Shoulder in the Twilight
~ G. C. Waldrep

—Ezekiel 12:12

Reaching from history, that alpenglow, towards the dead whose clothes I wear
tracked from room to room, the prodigy house we've built
from the ambient low-fi hum—You pass your tongue through it. But what are you,
the woman in the checkout line kept asking (watched over by the tabloids,
themselves an extinction event, a deferred ecology). What makes you permeable
to axe. Shelter. Effigy. Tarot. I place my hand inside the box
& then I draw it out again. (The film students worship in ragged pairs.)
In the carrion-fields the insect eye unpicks the red thread, its tiny miracle-play:
Split the body to expose the toll. So you step out into the diversity retreat
the faith calls "Easter." Someone else's memory, the jeweled slime of the carp's
underbelly, its torsion & snap. We loot the house of its unmentionables.
Today I wear the hat of a man whose daughter I did not marry
& the dark brown shirt of another man whose daughter did not marry me.
Music sifts through the otherwise empty room reserved for what we call the future,
though it isn't that. Almost imperceptibly my organs break
from the picture plane, the finance sector, the matte radio whose sticky wave-fronts buy the body back.—That's what it wants. What it always wanted.

A Working Class Gyro
~ Charles Harper Webb

I'm right behind him in the cafeteria line. Full beard, granny glasses, shoulder-length brown hair with *Abbey Road*-style all-white shirt, coat, pants, and shoes, he picks the Dinkum Dog. I go with Humbo Jumbo Pie.
He squints at his "side" of slaw—"What's this, then?"—as he slides into the crowd, me close behind.
Two empty seats appear: kid-sized, but we sit down.
"Haddy Grimble, Randoob," I say, to let him know I know.
"Merry Chrustchove, old pal buddy," he replies.
I mumble, "How's Yoko?" If he takes offense, I'll claim I said, "How's go-go?" This seems a good plan at the time.
"Nobody's shot her. What more can you arsk?" he says, and laughs to let me know it's all okay.
"Any new songs in the works?"
Grinding his Dinkum Dog, he nods. "One called 'A Working Class Gyro.' Or 'Nero' or 'Zero.' *It's among me best,*" he says, the way he said, *The people in the cheap seats clap your hands. The rest of you, rattle your jewelry.*
The PA blasts "Ticket to Ride," played on kazoos.
"I tried to buy that tape and bloody burn it," he says. "The publisher hung on like a case o' crabs."
The *u* in *publisher* sounds like the *u* in *pudding*. I want to tell him how I imitated this to seem British, which my dad's parents were. I want to say that my first band, The Super Sports, never mastered the "She Loves You" harmonies, and that the only words I ever spoke to heart-shredding Teri Kronenberg were, "Did you see the Beatles on TV?"
I want to ask what happened between him and Paul, and tell him how, when my friend Jon and I stopped hanging out, it was like a marriage down in flames. I want to tell my dream where I tire-tooled Mark David Chapman's head, screaming, "'Imagine''s the greatest song I know," and the crazy bastard grinned.

But no, I need to keep things light: two average blokes, grabbing a bite.
"What's lobscouse like?" I say to show I know my Liverpool.
"Nothin' to write a gnome about," he quips as "Iron the Waldorf"
blasts from the P.A.
I grope for something smart to say: "I love the way you dressed your
Genghis Khan as Gandhi"? "A good song is a virus that turns dumping-
by-Trudi into making-out-with-Pam"?
Instead I say, "Nobody blames you for British Petroleum."
"One sea turtle's worth a million crapitalists," he sighs.

Water Composes on Our Moon
~ Dara Wier

say, if not that, in ordinary earthbound music, say, in words, say
in some "subtle relationship

among harmonious and not so harmonious pitch"
in keyboards and consequences

in any and all instruments
even instruments of the insurance industry for instance

privatizing gains, socializing losses
something whispered in your ear, something encircling us

beyond sense if sense is
what we mean when we let something enter us without opposition

taking what's mine, what used to be some one else's
letting go your place in line

to transforms one's self from one thing into another
for instance

to have grown up among girls for instance as one of them
and then to leave them and begin to be one of the boys

or to feel you do have a soul
and without fail you come to

you understand
you cannot give it to anyone else

Hendrick Van Buyten
~ David Wojahn

—Vermeer's baker

The flour on his hands—raising minute clouds around the painting
    he has straightened
on his bedroom wall, twenty-four inches square, bartered to settle
    a bill for three years of bread:
the bankrupt painter with his taste for the most luxuriant pigments,
    pricey resplendent ultramarine, leavened

& aglow with lapus lazuli. & his oversized, Popish brood, the nattering
    diapered crew he'd shove
from his studio, the door he'd bolt against them. In his canvases
    there are no children. The baker's
snowy fingerprints have pocked the gilded frame surrounding
    Mistress & Maid, now set aright.

Transfixed, he stares—lustrous pearls entwining the mistress's
    pallid neck, her teardrop
earring's incandescence, brushstrokes invisible as the laboring yeast
    ballooning his vats
of flour-spattered dough. The art, he knows, is to render
    the recipe exact.

His eyes move to her jacket's creamy chiaroscural folds,
    the ermine trim.
She has laid her quill down on a sheaf of paper, her letter stopped
    mid-sentence & set
upon a tablecloth so perfectly azure it seems to hum
    with a steady inner light.

Elongate hand against her chin, head in profile, slightly a-tilt.
    He senses her tension
though he cannot see her face, only the pock-marked visage
    of her maid, mouth slightly open,
her skin lined & umberous & umber too her rough woolen dress,
    so that the letter

she holds out to her mistress contrasts so violently with her drabness
    the paper seems to be a-blaze.
Bad news, surely, thinks the baker: the lover who is breaking it off,
    the lover lost at sea.
Or to cholera, smallpox, the bite of a rabid mastiff, musket ball
    from an harquebus, festering

in a gangrenous thigh. Beyond the time-stilled, flawless confines
    of this drawing room,
these figures within a flattened gilded square, lies only peril, the steady
    percussive drone of our transience,
insistent as the scrape of a scullery woman's broom across these
    cobblestones of fog-enshrouded Delft.

Or a knock upon the door of the newly widowed Catherina Vermeer,
    the house the baker walks before
each morning at dawn-light on his way to stoke his ovens. The creditors
    file in & the inventory commences.
A checklist made: blankets, cushions, beds, earthenware crockery
    "of little value."

A study of a young woman, in a turban "of the Turkish fashion,"
    a palette, a knobstick
with an ivory maul. & in the open wardrobe, a lemon-colored jacket
    with ermine trim, shabby now,

its silk in tatters. The notary turns to smooth it in his hands—no value here.
He sets it down

& strides on to the kitchen. His boot-spurs click across the patterned tiles.

Prayer for the Wild and Crazy Regret Club
~ Hisia Yü, translated by Steve Bradbury

It's rolled and ready to go
I just need for you to strike a match for me
But from first to last I can't get past your attention deficiency
But then again my eyes have been roving too
In the end if I do chance to meet you I shall
So want to meet you please you must explain how a body
On a dance floor becomes estranged by verbal translation

Please persuade me that nothingness remains worthy of my
Worthless confession especially in light of every taste of
Honey more and more I have the feeling I'm stealing
On those luscious wild and crazy gypsy nights

Stealing the pervasive effluence of those luscious gypsy nights those
Wild and crazy nights regretting I do sometimes
Indeed forget you
In those fleeting travelers inns filled with strange designs
Those guests who check out early with their pocket translators do not
    love
Their neighbors nearly enough and can never
Find the time to return their rooms
To the condition they were in when they arrived

You put your earphones in your ears and in the playlist we prepared
    for you
You listen to the playlist you prepared for yourself
How could I have known you had a complete
Account of musicals that simultaneously accounted for the fact
That when life turns tragic there is no soundtrack

How could I have not known how paltry people are when you have
No intention of watching over them how could you not have foreseen
 those
Deaths that shall befall us in such swift and effortless profusion they
Will annul spatial perspective
Surface and depth
Collapsing into one

How could I have not known
All this is just in lieu of
Those unspoken lines how paltry people are when you
Do watch over them and were you to
Descend this evening for shelter's sake

We shall not hold ourselves aloof
For it behooves us to prepare a table before you it behooves me to
 recommend
The smoked rack of rosemaried lamb with potato purée
O potato purée potato purée you are the perfect
Compliment for every entrée

We shall await your coming to anoint
Our heads with oil we shall lift our voices in
Praise you making such little sense that
We shall become canonical
How could you not have known how we yearn
To return to that evening we all lay down like lambs embracing
And slept

We shall hear you say I love you all
That evening you said I love your
Tactical diversions so love how you never say anything serious how you
Never stop kissing just like in French movies
You never stop hugging and kissing
Just like all those French movies

Your Mother Dancing on the Table (Fiesole 1966)
~ Cynthia Zarin

In the long low living room
after everyone has gone,
your mother in a sleeveless
shift dress made out of some stiff
turquoise material
is dancing on the table.

It is a cold night. She is
not wearing stockings. She has
kicked off her shoes. In her bare
feet, long arms aloft, she is
conducting Mozart, which
streams from the turntable

to the stereo speakers,
then eddies, waves lapping the
huge untidy room, where she
is just now beautifully
alone for one minute.
Upstairs you and your sister

are asleep. Your grandmother
is reading in the next room.
It is the year the Arno
flooded. Your grandmother's own
house is underwater.
Her bookmark is embossed with

a crescent moon C, her own
watermark. Her earrings are
diamond clips. Her feet are dry.

Her neighbors were rescued from
        their roofs and pulled from their
windows. What's that noise? you asked

            your sister. She is six, she
is two years older, she can
read; in her white nightgown she
is a dandelion. You
        are not asleep—really, it
is early evening, not night

            at all. You are playing a
game with counters, she has the
shoe and you have the hat, and
you run down the hall to fetch
        your grandmother, who puts
down her open book and in

            stocking feet walks downstairs with
you and your sister. The word
you use when you tell me this
story is accomplices,
        in the language that first
belonged to your mother and

            now we use between us. In
the living room at the foot
of the stairs your mother was
still dancing, her body a
        tuning fork, conducting
the music. Stop it! your sister

cried out, and tried to shield you
so you would not see. "Don't be
so puritanical," said
your mother, a word that your
        sister did not know but
in the language in which your

        mother spoke to her, she heard
a word she both did and did not
not know, a bad thing, and she
began to hit your mother on
        the legs, to make her come
down from the table, as the

        tide of sound roared under her.
Outrageous! your Grandmother,
said—she'd always known about
your mother and here was proof!
        Your black hair was damp from
your bath. Your light blue cotton

        pajamas were buttoned to
the neck. Your body was sleek
as a badger's, a body
to which nothing much had yet
        happened, the secret life
of the body that occurs,

        to us and in us in small
increments, fiercely, subtly,
as it did the afternoon

you told me this story—but
        even then you knew you
you'd never seen anything

    more beautiful than the sight
of your mother dancing on
the table, Mozart coursing
under her above
        the flooded city, through
the open shutters into

    the green twilight, as when the
angel said to Tobias:
see the fish flashing in the
river. Half a century
        later, six stories up,
blocks from the Hudson, you say

        to me, I missed you, I had
music on before people
came and I was dancing. Now
you ask me to listen to
        you and I do, and what
I hear is the sound of your

        mother's bare feet keeping time
as she danced on the table
the high notes her hands, quick stars
in quickened air, the music—
        the moment before she
                stopped and after it.

Ekiwah Adler-Beléndez • Kelli Russell Agodon • Sandra Alcosser • Meena Alexander • Pamela Alexander • Dick Allen • J. Bradford Anderson • Nathalie Anderson • Rae Armantrout • Simon Armitage • Juliana Baggott • Angela Ball • J. T. Barbarese • Amy Beeder • Robin Behn • Charles Bernstein • Linda Bierds • Michelle Bitting • Chantal Bizzini • Danielle Blau • Sally Bliumis-Dunn • Bruce Bond • Yves Bonnefoy • Marianne Boruch • Laure-Anne Bosselaar • David Bottoms • Steven Bradbury • Julie Bruck • Christopher Buckley • Joseph Campana • Rafael Campo • Hélène Cardona • José Manuel Cardona • Maxine Chernoff • Kelly Cherry • Alex Cigale • Patricia Clark • Andrei Codrescu • Andrea Cohen • Bruce Cohen • Peter Cole • Billy Collins • Martha Collins • Peter Cooley • Jake Crist • Cynthia Cruz • Jim Daniels • Lydia Davis • Kwame Dawes • Chard deNiord • Stephen Dobyns • Norman Dubie • Denise Duhamel • Stephen Dunn • Efe Duyan • Cynthia Schwartzberg Edlow • Elaine Equi • Mikhail Eremin • Marie Étienne • Sylva Fischerova • John FitzGerald • Keith Flynn • Luigi Fontanella • Stuart Friebert • Philip Fried • Jeff Friedman • Albert Goldbarth • Beckian Fritz Goldberg • Kathleen Graber • Paul Guest • Richard Gwyn • Marilyn Hacker • Rachel Hadas • Barbara Hamby • A. J. Hauner • Jennifer Michael Hecht • Bob Hicok • Sean Hill • Tony Hoagland • Cynthia Hogue • Paul Hoover • David Huddle • T. R. Hummer • Mark Irwin • Mark Jarman • Troy Jollimore • Pierre Joris • Marilyn Kallett • Christopher Kennedy • Yassir Khanjer • John Kinsella • Dore Kiesselbach • David Kirby • Karl Kirchwey • Jennifer L. Knox • Steve Kronen • Sydney Lea • David Lehman • Phillis Levin • Frannie Lindsay • Paul Lisicky • Timothy Liu • William Logan • Adrian C. Louis • Nathaniel Mackey • Amit Majmudar • Maurice Manning • Gail Mazur • J. D. McClatchy • Philip Metres • Elizabeth Metzger • Joseph Millar • Nancy Mitchell • Carol Muske-Dukes • Robert Nazarene • D. Nurkse • Jennifer O'Grady • William Olsen • Dzvinia Orlowsky • Gregory Orr • Kathleen Ossip • Alicia Ostriker • Michael Palma • Jay Parini • Linda Pastan • Molly Peacock • Joyce Peseroff • Christina Pugh • Lia Purpura • Lawrence Raab • Barbara Ras • Donald Revell • Susan Rich • Alberto Ríos • Max Ritvo • Hoyt Rogers • Ira Sadoff • Jerome Sala • Sherod Santos • Lloyd Schwartz • Alan Shapiro • Betsy Sholl • Jeffrey Skinner • Floyd Skloot • Tara Skurtu • Ron Slate • Tom Sleigh • Bruce Smith • Patricia Smith • R. T. Smith • Ron Smith • Katherine Soniat • Lisa Russ Spaar • Jane Springer • Page Hill Starzinger • Terese Svoboda • Brian Swann • Cole Swensen • Arthur Sze • Adam Tavel • Daniel Tobin • William Trowbridge • Chase Twichell • Lee Upton • Michael Van Walleghen • Marc Vincenz • Arthur Vogelsang • Diane Vreuls • Sidney Wade • G. C. Waldrep • Charles Harper Webb • Dara Wier • David Wojahn • Hisia Yü • Cynthia Zarin

Contributors' Biographies

Ekiwah Adler-Belendez is from Amatlan, Mexico, a small village an hour from Mexico City. The son of a North American father and a Mexican mother, Ekiwah is a poetic prodigy whose powerful verses have mesmerized Mexico's literary scene. Ekiwah is the author of three volumes of poetry: *Soy* (I Am); *Palabras Inagotables*, (Never-ending Words); *Weaver* (2003), his first book in English; and *The Coyote's Trace*, which features an introduction by Mary Oliver. Ekiwah lives in Massachusetts, has dual citizenship and is bilingual.

Kelli Russell Agodon is an award-winning poet, writer, and editor. She's the author of six books, most recently *Hourglass Museum* (Finalist for the Washington State Book Award in Poetry & the Julie Suk Poetry Prize) & *The Daily Poet: Day-By-Day Prompts For Your Writing Practice*. She is the co-founder of Two Sylvias Press, where she works as an editor and book cover designer. Her work has appeared in magazines such as *The Atlantic, New England Review*, and *O, The Oprah Magazine*. Kelli is also the Co-Director of the Poets on the Coast writing retreat as well as an avid paddleboarder, mountain biker, and hiker. She lives in a sleepy seaside town a ferry ride away from Seattle. agodon.com / twosylviaspress.com

Sandra Alcosser's poems have appeared in *The New Yorker, The New York Times, Paris Review, Ploughshares, Poetry,* and the *Pushcart Prize Anthology*. Her books of poetry, *A Fish to Feed All Hunger* and *Except by Nature* received the highest honors from National Poetry Series, Academy of American Poets and Associated Writing Programs. She received two individual artist fellowships from NEA and served as National Endowment for the Arts' Conservation Poet for the Wildlife Conservation Society and Poets House, New York, as well as Montana's first poet laureate and recipient of the Merriam Award for Distinguished Contribution to Montana Literature She founded and directs SDSU's MFA each fall and serves on the MFA faculty of Pacific University.

Meena Alexander, described in *The Statesman* (India) as "undoubtedly one of the finest poets in contemporary times," has new work forthcoming in 2018: her eighth book of poetry, *Atmospheric Embroidery* (TriQuarterly Books/Northwestern U. Press), and a volume she edited: *Name me a Word: Indian Writers Reflect on Writing* (Yale U. Press). She is Distinguished Professor of English at The Graduate Center/Hunter College, City University of New York. meenaalexander.com

Pamela Alexander is the author of four collections of poetry, most recently *Slow Fire* (Ausable/Copper Canyon). Her poems have been featured on the websites of National Public Radio and the American Academy of Poets and appear in many anthologies. On the writing faculty at M.I.T. and Oberlin College for many years, she now writes nonfiction and poetry while traveling the continent in an RV with her cat. Her essays have appeared in *Cimarron Review* and *Denver Quarterly*. She is on the editorial board of *FIELD*.

Dick Allen has had poems in the nation's premier journals including *Poetry, The New Yorker, The Atlantic, The Hudson Review, New Republic, American Scholar,* and *Ploughshares,* as well as in scores of anthologies. He has nine poetry collections and won numerous awards including a Pushcart Prize, the Robert Frost prize, fellowships from the National Endowment for the Arts and Ingram Merrill Poetry Foundation, and the *New Criterion* Poetry Book Award for *This Shadowy Place* (St. Augustine's Press, 2014). His poems have been included in six *Best American Poetry* and have been featured on *Poetry Daily*, Garrison Keillor's *Writer's Almanac* and in Ted Kooser's *American Life in Poetry*, as well as on *Tricycle*. Allen was the Connecticut State Poet Laureate 2010–2015. His newest collection, *Zen Master Poems*, is from the noted Buddhist publishing house Wisdom, Inc. (Simon & Schuster, 2016).

J. Bradford Anderson is a teacher and translator living in New York City. Anderson was the lead translator of Alexander von Humboldt's *Political Essay on the Island of Cuba.* Anderson's translations of Chantal Bizzini's poetry have appeared in the Backwoods Broadsides series, *Two*

Lines: A Journal of Translation, and *Esopus Magazine.* He published a collection of Bizzini's poetry, *Disenchanted City,* with Black Widow Press in 2015.

Nathalie Anderson is the author of three books of poetry, *Following Fred Astaire, Crawlers* and *Quiver,* and libretti for four operas. Her poems have appeared in such journals as *Atlanta Review, DoubleTake, Natural Bridge, The New Yorker,* and *The Recorder.* In 2017, Word Works will publish her new book, *Stain,* and Muddy Ford Press will publish her chapbook *Held and Firmly Bound.* She serves as Poet in Residence at the Rosenbach Museum and Library, and she teaches at Swarthmore College, where she is a Professor in the Department of English Literature and directs the Program in Creative Writing.

Rae Armantrout's new and selected poems, *Partly,* is coming out from Wesleyan in the fall of 2016. She has published eleven books of poetry and has also been featured in a number of major anthologies. Her book of poems *Versed* was awarded the 2009 National Book Critics Circle Award and the 2010 Pulitzer Prize for Poetry. Armantrout's most recent collection is *Itself.*

Simon Armitage is the current Professor of Poetry at Oxford University.

Juliana Baggot is the author of over twenty books, including two *New York Times* Notable Books of the Year, *Pure* and *Harriet Wolf's Seventh Book of Wonders.* Her poems have appeared in *Best American Poetry, Poetry,* and *APR.* Her fourth collection of poems, *Instructions, Abject & Fuming,* will be published this year. She teaches screenwriting at Florida State University's College of Motion Picture Arts and holds the Jenks Chair of Contemporary American Letters at the College of the Holy Cross.

Angela Ball teaches in the Center for Writers at the University of Southern Mississippi. Her sixth book of poems, *Talking Pillow,* will appear in Fall 2017 from the University of Pittsburgh Press.

J. T. Barbarese has published five books of poems; his most recent, *Sweet Spot* (Northwestern University Press, 2012). His poems and translations have appeared in *The Atlantic, Boulevard, Poetry, The New Yorker* and *The Times Literary Supplement,* and his literary journalism in *Tri-Quarterly, boundary 2, The Sewanee Review, Studies in English Literature,* and *The Journal of Modern Literature.* Since 2008 he has been the editor of *StoryQuarterly.*

Amy Beeder is the author of *Burn the Field* and *Now Make An Altar.* A recipient of a 2015 NEA Fellowship in Poetry, a "Discovery"/*The Nation* Award, the Witness Writers Award, and others, she has worked as a creative writer instructor, freelance reporter, political asylum specialist, high-school teacher in West Africa, and an election and human rights observer in Haiti and Suriname.

Robin Behn directs the MFA Program at the University of Alabama. She is the author of four books of poems, most recently *The Yellow House.* Rcent projects include the libretto for the opera *Freedom and Fire! A Civil War Story* and a textbook for high school and undergraduate writers, *Once Upon a Time in the Twenty-First Century: Unexpected Exercises in Creative Writing,* from The University of Alabama Press.

Charles Bernstein's most recent book is *Pitch of Poetry,* essays from the University of Chicago Press. UCP also published his most recent collection of poems, *Recalculating.* He teaches at the University of Pennsylvania.

Linda Bierds is the author of nine volumes of poetry, most recently *Roget's Illusion,* which was longlisted for the 2014 National Book Award. Her work appears regularly in *The Atlantic.* She has won several major awards and grants including the Guggenheim and the "genius" grant from the MacArthur Foundation.

Michelle Bitting's latest collection is *The Couple Who Fell to Earth* (C & R Press, 2016), named to *Kirkus Reviews'* Best Books of 2016.

She has poems in *APR, Prairie Schooner, Narrative, Vinyl, Plume, Diode, Nimrod, The Paris-American, Fjords* and others, and on *Poetry Daily* and *Verse Daily*. Her book *Good Friday Kiss* won the DeNovo First Book Award, and *Notes to the Beloved* (C & R Press) won the Sacramento Poetry Center Book Award. She has won the Beyond Baroque Foundation, Virginia Brendemuehl, and *Glimmer Train* poetry contests, has taught poetry in the UCLA Extension Writer's Program, at Twin Towers prison, and for ten years has been an active California Poet in the Schools. She holds an MFA in Poetry from Pacific University and is completing a PhD in Mythological Studies at Pacifica Graduate Institute. michellebitting.com

Chantal Bizzini is a French poet, translator, photographer, and collage artist, who lives in Paris. She has published poetry and translations in *Po&sie, Europe, Poésie 2005, Action Poétique, Le Mâche-Laurier, Rehauts, Public Republic,* and *Siècle 21,* among other international literary journals. Her own poetry has been translated into English, Italian, Spanish, and Greek. Her first volume of poetry, *Boulevard Magenta,* was published in 2015 by le bousquet-la barthe éditions. Her current project involves a series of meditations on photo-illustrated books, including *The Bridge* by Hart Crane and Walker Evans; Rodenbach's *Bruges-la-Morte,* Brassaï's *Paris la nuit,* Walker Evans's *Many Are Called,* and Sebald's *Austerlitz.* In 2015, her book *Disenchanted City,* translated in English by Marilyn Kallet, J. Bradford Anderson and Darren Jackson, was published in a bilingual edition by Black Widow Press.

Danielle Blau's *Rhyme and Reason: Poets and Philosophers on the Questions that Matter* is forthcoming from W. W. Norton. Her collection *mere eye* was selected for a Poetry Society of America Chapbook Award and published in 2013, and she won the 2015 multi-genre *Narrative 30 Below Contest* for poetry. Poems, short stories, articles, and interviews by Blau can be found in such publications as *The Atlantic* online, *The Baffler, Black Clock, Harvard Review, The Literary Review, Narrative Magazine, The New Yorker*'s book blog, *Paris Review, Ploughshares, Plume, The Saint Ann's Review, The Wolf,* and the Argos Books poetry anthology *Why I Am Not a Painter*. A graduate of Brown with an honors degree in philosophy, and of NYU with an MFA in poetry, she curates and hosts the monthly Gavagai Music + Reading Series, and teaches at Hunter College.

Sally Bliumis-Dunn teaches Modern Poetry at Manhattanville College and the Palm Beach Poetry Festival. Her poems have appeared in *New Ohio Review, Paris Review, Prairie Schooner, Poetry London, The Bellevue Literary Review, The New York Times, PBS NewsHour, Terrain, The Writer's Almanac,* The Academy of American Poets' Poem-a-day, and Ted Kooser's newspaper column, among others. In 2002, she was a finalist for the Nimrod/Hardman Pablo Neruda Prize. Her third book, *Echolocation,* is seeking a publishing home.

Bruce Bond is the author of sixteen books including, most recently, *Immanent Distance: Poetry and the Metaphysics of the Near at Hand* (University of Michigan Press, 2015), *For the Lost Cathedral* (LSU Press, 2015), *The Other Sky* (Etruscan Press, 2015), *Black Anthem* (Tampa Review Prize, University of Tampa Press, 2016), and *Gold Bee* (Crab Orchard Open Competition Award, Southern Illinois U. Press, 2016).

Before his death in July of 2016, **Yves Bonnefoy** had published eleven major collections of verse, several books of tales, and numerous studies of literature and art. Recognized as the greatest French poet of the last fifty years, his work has been translated into scores of languages. He himself was a celebrated translator of Shakespeare, Yeats, Keats, and Leopardi. He received the European Prize for Poetry (2006) and the Kafka Prize (2007), among many other honors. His latest anthology in English, *Second Simplicity: New Poetry and Prose 1991–2011,* was published by Yale University Press in 2012. *The Yves Bonnefoy Reader,* a new anthology in two volumes, will appear at Carcanet Press in 2017.

Marianne Boruch's nine poetry collections include the recent *Eventually One Dreams the Real Thing; Cadaver, Speak;* and *The Book of Hours,* a Kingsley-Tufts Poetry Award winner. She's written a memoir

(*The Glimpse Traveler*), and two essay collections, a third due out from Michigan in 2017. A former Guggenheim and NEA Fellow, she's been a visiting artist at two national parks (Denali and Isle Royale) and at the American Academy in Rome. Her poems have appeared in *The New Yorker, APR, Poetry*, the *NYRB, Field*, and elsewhere. She teaches in the MFA Programs at Purdue University and at Warren Wilson College.

Laure-Anne Bosselaar is the author of *The Hour Between Dog and Wolf, Small Gods of Grief*, winner of the Isabella Gardner Prize; and *A New Hunger*, selected as a Notable Book by the American Library Association. The editor of four anthologies, and the recipient of a Pushcart Prize, she teaches at the Solstice Low Residency MFA Program at Pine Manor College. Her next book will be published by Four Way Books in spring 2019.

David Bottoms' first book, *Shooting Rats at the Bibb County Dump* (William Morrow, 1980), was chosen by Robert Penn Warren as winner of the 1979 Walt Whitman Award of the Academy of American Poets. His poems have appeared widely in magazines such as *The Atlantic, The New Yorker, Harper's, Poetry*, and *Paris Review*, as well as in sixty anthologies and textbooks. He is the author of seven other books of poetry, two novels, and a book of essays and interviews. His most recent book of poems is *We Almost Disappear* (Copper Canyon, 2011).

Steve Bradbury translates the work of contemporary poets writing in Chinese. His translation of Hsia Yü's *Salsa* (Zephyr Press, 2014) was short-listed for the Lucien Stryk Prize. His current project, a translation of Hsia Yü's Poems, *Sixty of Them* (2011), just received an NEA Literature Translation Fellowship. He lives in Ft. White, Florida.

Julie Bruck is the author of three books of poetry, most recently *Monkey Ranch* (Brick Books, 2012). Her work has appeared in *Ms., Ploughshares, Numero Cinq, The New Yorker*, and many other journals and magazines. She was the recipient of Canada's 2012 Governor General's Literary Award for Poetry.

Christopher Buckley's *Star Journal: Selected Poems* is published by the U. of Pittsburgh Press, 2016. His 20th book of poetry, *Back Room at the Philosophers' Club*, won the 2015 Lascaux Prize in Poetry from the *Lascaux Review*. Among several critical collections and anthologies he has edited: *Bear Flag Republic: Prose Poems and Poetics from California*, 2008, and *One for the Money: The Sentence as a Poetic Form*, from Lynx House Press, 2012, both with Gary Young. He has also edited *On the Poetry of Philip Levine: Stranger to Nothing*, U. of Michigan Press, 1991, and *Messenger to the Stars: a Luis Omar Salinas New Selected Poems & Reader*. *Chaos Theory* is forthcoming in 2017 from Plume Editions.

Joseph Campana is a poet, arts writer, and scholar of Renaissance literature. He is the author of *The Book of Faces* (Graywolf, 2005) and *Natural Selections* (2012), winner of the Iowa Poetry Prize. His poems appear in *Slate, Kenyon Review, Poetry, Conjunctions, Colorado Review*, and many other venues. His poems have received prizes from the *Southwest Review* and *Prairie Schooner*. He has received grants from the National Endowment for the Arts, the Houston Arts Alliance, and the Bread Loaf Writers' Conference. His third collection, from which this poem is drawn, *The Book of Life*, is forthcoming from Tupelo Press.

Rafael Campo teaches and practices internal medicine at Harvard Medical School and Beth Israel Deaconess Medical Center in Boston. He is also on the faculty of Lesley University's Creative Writing MFA Program. He received a Guggenheim fellowship, a National Poetry Series award, and a Lambda Literary Award for his poetry; *The Enemy* (DUP, 2007) won the Sheila Motton Book Award from the New England Poetry Club. He has also won the Hippocrates Open International Prize for verse on a medical theme. His work has appeared in *The Nation, New Republic, The New York Times Magazine, Paris Review, POEM* (UK), *Poetry, The Poetry Review* (UK), Slate.com, *Yale Review*, and elsewhere. A volume of his new and selected poems is due out in 2017

Hélène Cardona's most recent books include *Life in Suspension* and *Dreaming My Animal Selves* (both from Salmon Poetry); and the translations *Beyond Elsewhere* (Gabriel Arnou-Laujeac, White Pine Press), winner of a Hemingway Grant; *Ce que nous portons* (Dorianne Laux, Éditions du Cygne); and *Walt Whitman's Civil War Writings* for WhitmanWeb. She holds a Master's in American Literature from the Sorbonne, worked as a translator/interpreter for the Canadian Embassy in Paris, and taught at Hamilton College and Loyola Marymount University. Publications include *World Literature Today, Washington Square Review, Poetry International, Dublin Review of Books, Hayden's Ferry Review, The Brooklyn Rail, Asymptote,* and *The Warwick Review.*

José Manuel Cardona is a poet from Ibiza, Spain. He is the author of *El Vendimiador* (Atzavara, 1953); *Poemas a Circe* (Adonais, 1959); and *The Birnam Wood* (Consell Insular d'Eivissa, 2007). He co-edited several literary journals, wrote for many publications and participated in the II Congreso de Poesía in Salamanca. He wrote his thesis on the Mexican revolution at the Instituto de Cultura Hispánica de Madrid. The Franco regime forced him into exile in France. He is an attorney (University of Barcelona) and holds PhDs in Literature and Humanities (University of Nancy), and Political Sciences and Economy (IHEI, Geneva). He worked for the UN most of his life, in Geneva, Paris, Rome, Vienna, Belgrade, Sofia, Kiev, Tblisi, Moscow, St. Petersburg and Panama, among many places.

Maxine Chernoff chairs the Creative Writing Program at SFSU and is former editor of New American Writing. She has published 14 books of poetry and is the winner of a poetry NEA in 2013 and of the 2009 PEN Translation award for her co-translation of the German poet Friedrich Hoelderlin. Her most recent book of poems is *Here* (Counterpath, 2014), finalist for the Northern California Book Award.

Kelly Cherry has published twenty-four books, ten chapbooks, and two translations. Her twenty-fifth book—and tenth poetry book—*Quartet for J. Robert Oppenheimer: A Poem,* comes out in February 2017. A book of short-shorts and flash fiction is due out in the fall. Groundhog Poetry Press will publish another poetry book in 2018.

She is Eudora Welty Professor Emerita of English and Evjue-Bascom Professor Emerita in the Humanities at University of Wisconsin–Madison and served as Visiting Eminent Scholar 1999–2004 at the University of Alabama. She is a former Poet Laureate of Virginia and an Emeritus Member of the electorate of Poets Corner, Cathedral Church of St. John the Divine, NYC. Awards include grants from NEA, USIA, Rockefeller, Bradley Lifetime Award, Weinstein Poetry Award, Lifetime Achievement Award from UNC–G, publications in prize anthologies, and others.

Alex Cigale (b. 1963) is a poet and translator. His own poems in English appear in *Colorado Review, The Common Online*, and *The Literary Review*, and his translations in *Kenyon Review Online, Modern Poetry in Translation, New England Review, PEN America, TriQuarterly*, and *World Literature in Translation*. In 2015, he was awarded an NEA Literary Translation Fellowship for his work on Mikhail Eremin, and he guest-edited the Spring 2015 Russia Issue of the *Atlanta Review*, writing about it in *Best American Poetry*. His first book, *Russian Absurd: Daniil Kharms, Selected Writings*, is just out in the Northwestern University Press World Classics series. He has previously contributed translations of Abdllaev, Aigi, Ulanov, and Ulzytuev to *Plume*, and an interview with *Plume*'s editor, Daniel Lawless, to the *Asymptote* blog. He is *Plume*'s Contributing Editor for Translations.

Patricia Clark is a professor in the Writing Department and also the poet-in-residence at Grand Valley State University in Michigan Her poetry has appeared in magazines such as *The Atlantic, Poetry, Slate, New England Review, North American Review, Pennsylvania Review, Black Warrior Review*, and *Seattle Review*. She is the recipient of a Creative Artist Grant from ArtServe Michigan for 2003. Her book of poems *North of Wondering* won the first book competition sponsored by Women in Literature, Inc. Patricia has also co-edited an anthology of contemporary women writers, *Worlds in Our Words*. Her most recent book of poems is *Sunday Rising* (2013).

Born in Sibiu, Romania, **Andrei Codrescu** explores politics and society as a poet, novelist, essayist and film-maker. Widely known as a commentator for NPR's *All Things Considered,* he returned to his native Romania in 1989 to cover the collapse of the dictatorship for NPR and ABC News. He has written over forty books, including *The Posthuman Dada Guide: Tzara and Lenin Play Chess* (Princeton University Press, 2009), and is a winner of the Peabody Award and the Ovidius Prize. His poetry collection *So Recently Rent a World* (Coffee House Press, 2012) was a National Book Award nominee. His latest book of poems is *The Art of Forgetting.* He is a MacCurdy Professor Emeritus of literature at Louisiana State University in Baton Rouge. @acodrescu on Twitter.

Andrea Cohen's poems have appeared in *The New Yorker, The Atlantic, Poetry, Threepenny Review,* and elsewhere. Her fifth poetry collection, *Unfathoming,* is forthcoming from Four Way Books. Other recent collections include *Furs Not Mine* and *Kentucky Derby.* She directs the Writers House at Merrimack College and the Blacksmith House Poetry Series in Cambridge, MA.

Bruce Cohen has published five volumes of poetry: *Disloyal Yo-Yo* (Dream Horse Press), which was awarded the 2007 Orphic Poetry Prize, and *Swerve, Placebo Junkies Conspiring with the Half-Asleep* and *No Soap, Radio!* (all from Black Lawrence Press). His latest book, *Imminent Disappearances, Impossible Numbers & Panoramic X-Rays,* won the 2015 Green Rose Prize (New Issues Press, 2016). His poems have appeared in literary periodicals including *AGNI, Georgia Review, Gettysburg Review, Harvard Review, The New Yorker, Ploughshares, Poetry* and *Southern Review,* and featured on *Poetry Daily, Verse Daily,* & the Academy of American Poets Poem-A-Day. He teaches at the University of Connecticut.

Peter Cole's recent books of poems include *The Invention of Influence* (New Directions) and *The Poetry of Kabbalah: Mystical Verse from the Jewish Tradition* (Yale). In the spring of 2017 FSG will publish *Hymns & Qualms: New and Selected Poems and Translations.* A 2007 MacArthur Fellow, Cole divides his time between Jerusalem and New Haven.

Billy Collins' latest collection of poems is *The Rain in Portugal* (Random House, 2016). He is a former distinguished professor at Lehman College (CUNY), and he served as U.S. Poet Laureate (2001–2003). Last year, he was inducted into the American Academy of Arts and Letters.

Martha Collins' eighth book of poems, *Admit One: An American Scrapbook*, was published by Pittsburgh in 2016. Collins is also the author of seven earlier books of poetry, most recently *Day Unto Day, White Papers*, and *Blue Front*, and co-translator of four collections of Vietnamese poetry. She is editor-at-large for *FIELD* magazine and an editor for the Oberlin College Press.

Peter Cooley's latest book of poetry is *Night Bus to the Afterlife*. Recent poems have appeared in *Southern Review, The Hopkins Review, The Other Journal*, and *Conte*. He is Senior Mellon Professor in the Humanities and Director of Creative Writing at Tulane, and Louisiana Poet Laureate. Carnegie Mellon will publish his new book *World without Finishing* in 2017.

Jake Crist lives in Columbus, Ohio, where he works as a supervisor of a homeless shelter. His poems have appeared in *Anglican Theological Review, Boulevard, Rattle*, and *Shenandoah*, and he has been the recipient of a fellowship from the MacDowell Colony.

Cynthia Cruz is the author of four collections of poems: *Ruin* (Alice James Books, 2006), *The Glimmering Room* (Four Way Books, 2012), *Wunderkammer*, (Four Way, 2014), and *How the End Begins* (Four Way, 2016). Her essays and art writings have been published in *The Los Angeles Review of Books, APR, Guernica*, and *The Rumpus*. She is at work on two poetry anthologies: one of Latina poets, and the other of female poets around the issue of consumption and nourishment. A regular contributor for the art journal *Hyperallergic*, she is writing a collection of essays on language and iterations of silence.

Jim Daniels' next books of poems, *Rowing Inland*, Wayne State University Press, and *Street Calligraphy*, Steel Toe Books, will both be published in 2017. His fifth book of short fiction, *Eight Mile High*, was published by Michigan State University Press in 2014. "The End of Blessings," the fourth short film he has written and produced, appeared in numerous film festivals in 2016. A native of Detroit, Daniels is a graduate of Alma College and Bowling Green State University. He is the Thomas Stockham University Professor of English at Carnegie Mellon University.

Lydia Davis is the author of one novel and many collections of stories, including most recently *Can't and Won't* (FSG, 2014). She has won awards for her translations of works from the French, among them Flaubert's *Madame Bovary* (Viking Penguin, 2010) and Proust's *Swann's Way* (2002), and in 2013, she received the Man Booker International Prize for her fiction.

Kwame Dawes is the author of twenty books of poetry and numerous other books of fiction, criticism, and essays. He has edited over a dozen anthologies. His most recent collection, *Speak from Here to There*, a co-written collection of verse with Australian poet John Kinsella, appeared in 2016. In 2017 a major collection, *City of Bones: A Testament* (Northwestern University Press) will appear along with *A Bloom of Stones: A Tri-lingual anthology of Haitian poems after the Earthquake*, which he edited. A Spanish-language collection of his poems, titled *Vuelo*, will appear in Mexico in 2017. He is Glenna Luschei Editor of *Prairie Schooner* and teaches at the University of Nebraska and the Pacific MFA Program. He is Director of the African Poetry Book Fund and Artistic Director of the Calabash International Literary Festival.

Chard deNiord is the Poet Laureate of Vermont and author of five books of poetry, including *Interstate* (University of Pittsburgh Press, 2015), *The Double Truth* (University of Pittsburgh Press, 2011), and *Night Mowing* (University of Pittsburgh Press, 2005). He teaches English and Creative Writing at Providence College, where he is a Professor of English and Creative Writing. His book of essays and interviews with American poets Galway Kinnell, Donald Hall. Maxine Kumin, Jack Gilbert, Ruth Stone, Lucille Clifton and Robert Bly, titled *Sad Friends, Drowned Lovers, Stapled Songs: Conversations and Reflections on 20th-Century American Poets*, was published by Marick Press in 2011. He is the co-founder and former program director of the New England College MFA Program in Poetry and a trustee of the Ruth Stone Trust. He lives in Westminster West, Vermont, with his wife Liz.

Stephen Dobyns is the author of forty books: fourteen books of poems, two books of essays on poetry, one book of short stories and twenty-three novels. His most recent book of poems is *The Day's Last Light Reddens the Leaves of the Copper Beech*, published by BOA Editions, Ltd. in 2016. His most recent novel is *Saratoga Payback*, published by Blue Rider/Penguin in 2017. He lives in Westerly, RI.

Norman Dubie is the author of twenty-five books of poetry, most recently *Quotations of Bone* (2015), winner of the 2016 International Griffin Poetry Prize. His other books of poetry include *The Volcano* (2010), *The Insomniac Liar of Topo* (2007), *Ordinary Mornings of a Coliseum* (2004), and *The Mercy Seat* (2001), all from Copper Canyon. He is the recipient of the Bess Hokin Prize from the Poetry Foundation, the PEN Center USA Literary Award for Poetry in 2002, and fellowships and grants from the Ingram Merrill Foundation, the John Simon Guggenheim Memorial Foundation, and the National Endowment for the Arts. He lives and teaches in Tempe, Arizona.

Denise Duhamel's most recent book of poetry, *Blowout* (University of Pittsburgh Press, 2013), was a finalist for the National Book Critics Circle Award. Her other titles include *Ka-Ching!* (Pittsburgh, 2009), *Two and Two* (Pittsburgh, 2005), *Queen for a Day: Selected and New Poems* (Pittsburgh, 2001), *The Star-Spangled Banner* (winner of the Crab Orchard Award, SIU Press, 1999) and *Kinky* (Orchises Press, 1997). Her work with Maureen Seaton was published in *CAPRICE* (Collaborations: Collected, Uncollected, and New) by Sibling Rivalry

Press in 2015. The recipient of fellowships from the Guggenhiem Foundation and the National Endowment for the Arts, Duhamel is a professor at Florida International University in Miami.

Stephen Dunn's nineteenth collection of poems, *Whereas*, has just been published by W. W. Norton. Recipient of the 2001 Pulitzer Prize, he lives in Frostburg, Maryland.

Efe Duyan (b. 1981, İstanbul, Turkey), teaches history of architecture at Mimar Sinan Fine Arts University. His poems have been translated into many languages. His translations include poetry collections of Radu Vancu (Romania) and Matthias Göritz (Germany). He edited a comtemporary poetry anthology, *Bir Benden Bir O'ndan* (2010) and is on the editorial board of the literature magazine *Istanbul Offline*. His critical essay "The Construction of Characters in Nâzım Hikmet's Poetry" was published in 2008. His poetry collections are *Sıkça Sorulan Sorular* (Frequently Asked Questions, 2016), *Tek Şiirlik Aşklar* (One Poem Stands, 2012) and *Takas* (Barter, 2006).

Cynthia Schwartzberg Edlow's poetry collection is *The Day Judge Spencer Learned the Power of Metaphor* (Salmon Poetry, 2012). Her chapbook is *Old School Superhero Loves a Good Wristwatch* (Dancing Girl Press, 2014). Her awards include the Red Hen Press Poetry Award, *Tusculum Review* Poetry Prize, *Willow Review* Prize, a Beullah Rose/ *Smartish Pace* Poetry Prize and three Pushcart Prize nominations, two from the Pushcart Prize Board of Contributing Editors. Her poetry has appeared widely, including *APR, Barrow Street, Cimarron Review, Folio, Fourteen Hills, Gulf Coast, The Los Angeles Review, Plume, Smartish Pace, Tahoma Literary Review,* and *The Texas Review*. Poems have been featured in the anthologies *Even the Daybreak: 35 Years of Salmon Poetry, Drawn to Marvel, Emily Dickinson Awards Anthology,* and *Not A Muse*. Her forthcoming poetry collection is *Horn Section All Day Every Day*.

Elaine Equi's books include *Ripple Effect: New & Selected Poems, Click and Clone,* and, most recently, *Sentences and Rain,* all from Coffee

House Press. She lives in New York City and teaches at New York University and in the MFA program at The New School.

Mikhail Eremin (b. 1936, in the Caucasus) participated in one of the first unofficial post-war poetry groups, the so-called "philological school" of the late 1950s. His books, *Poems* (1–6), were published by Pushkinskii Fond. Joseph Brodsky wrote this of him: "Eremin is an unreconstructed minimalist. Poetry in essence consists precisely in the concentration of language: a small quantity of lines surrounded by a mass of empty space. Eremin elevates this concentration to a principle: as though it is not simply language but poetry itself that crystallizes into verse.... Most remarkable is that all of it has been written for oneself, out of one's own conception of the mother tongue. Eremin's poetry may rightfully be called Futurist in the sense that, to this type of poetry, the future belongs." His *Selected Poems* is available in the English translation of J. Kates. Selection of poems in Alex Cigale's translations have appeared in *Asymptote, Atlana Review, Plume* 63 and are forthcoming in *Eleven Eleven, Two Lines*, and *Words Without Borders*.

Marie Étienne is the author of ten collections of poems, eight novels, short story collections and books of nonfiction prose, and two books on theater. She spent her childhood in Indochina, in what is now Vietnam, during the Second World War. The sequence published in *Plume 5* is from *Dormans* (Flammarion, 2006). *Roi des Cent Cavaliers/ King of a Hundred Horsemen*, which was translated by Marilyn Hacker and published by FSG in 2008, received the PEN Award for Poetry in Translation in 2009. She lives in Paris.

Sylva Fischerová is one of the most formidable Czech poets of her generation. Daughter of a non-Marxist philosopher whose work was banned under the communist régime, she is a distinguished classicist who teaches at Charles University in Prague. She has published nine volumes of poetry in Czech, and her poetry has been translated and published in numerous languages. Two earlier selections of her poems in English translation were published by Bloodaxe Books (*The Tremor* *of Racehorses*, 1990; *The Swing in the Middle of Chaos*, 2010). *Stomach of the Soul*, a bilingual collection of her poems in Czech and English, translated by the author with Stuart Friebert and Andrew J. Hauner, was published by Calypso Editions, USA, in 2014. She also writes prose, essays, and books for children.

John FitzGerald is a poet, writer, editor, and attorney for the disabled. He is author of four books, most recently *Favorite Bedtime Stories* and *The Mind* (both from Salmon Poetry). Other works include *Primate*, a novel and screenplay, and the non-fiction *For All I Know*. Other publications include *Human and Inhuman Monstrous Poems* (Everyman), *Even the Daybreak* (Salmon Poetry), *Poetry: Reading it, Writing it, Publishing it* (Salmon Poetry), *Dogs Singing: A Tribute Anthology* (Salmon Poetry), *From the Four-Chambered Heart: In Tribute to Anais Nin* (Sybaritic Press), *The Warwick Review*, and *World Literature Today*.

Keith Flynn is the award-winning author of seven books, including poetry *The Golden Ratio* (Iris Press, 2007) and *Colony Collapse Disorder* (Wings Press, 2013), and essays, *The Rhythm Method, Razzmatazz and Memory: How To Make Your Poetry Swing* (Writer's Digest Books, 2007). His latest book is a collaboration with photographer Charter Weeks, *Prosperity Gospel: Portraits of the Great Recession*. He was lyricist and lead singer for the rock band The Crystal Zoo 1984–1999. He tours with The Holy Men. His poetry and essays have appeared in journals and anthologies around the world. He has been awarded the Sandburg Prize, a 2013 NC Literary Fellowship, the ASCAP Emerging Songwriter Prize, the Paumanok Poetry Award, and was twice named Gilbert-Chappell Distinguished Poet for NC. He is the founder and managing editor of *The Asheville Poetry Review*: ashevillepoetryreview.com. keithflynn.net

Luigi Fontanella studied at the University of Rome, La Sapienza (Laurea in Lettere), and at Harvard University (PhD in Romance Languages and Literatures). He was a Fulbright Fellow at Princeton University, 1976–1978. He is Professor of Italian in the Dept. of European Languages, Literatures, and Cultures, at Stony Brook

University. Fontanella is Founder and President of IPA (Italian Poetry in America). and the editor of *Gradiva* and Gradiva Publications, which was recently awarded the Prize for Translation by the Ministero dei Beni Culturali and the Catullus Prize. He has given lectures and seminars in more than seventy universities. His poetry has been included in twenty-five anthologies. He has published thirty books (fourteen collections of poetry; thirteen volumes of criticism, three books of narrative), and ninety scholarly articles. In 2005 President Carlo Azeglio Ciampi nominated him Cavaliere della Repubblica Italiana.

Stuart Friebert's *Floating Heart* won the Ohioana Poetry Award for 2015. His new book, *On the Bottom*, is just out (Iris Press), as is his tenth collection of translations, *Be Quiet: Selected Poems of Kuno Raeber* (Tiger Bark Press).

Philip Fried's seventh book of poetry, *Squaring the Circle*, is forthcoming from Salmon early in 2017. His previous book, *Interrogating Water* (Salmon, 2014), which focuses on the national security state and its shadow wars, was praised by *The Guardian* for "the valor and vision of its protest." philiphfried.com

Jeff Friedman's seventh book—a collection of prose poems—is forthcoming from Plume Editions. His poems, mini-stories and translations have appeared in *APR, Poetry, New England Review, Antioch Review, Poetry International, Plume, Hotel Amerika, Flash Fiction Funny, AGNI Online, New Flash Fiction Review, New Republic* and numerous other literary magazines. Dzvinia Orlowsky's and his translation of *Memorials* by Polish poet Mieczslaw Jastrun was published by Lavender Ink/Dialogos in August 2014. Friedman and Orlowsky were awarded an NEA Literature Translation Fellowship for 2016. Nati Zohar and Friedman's book of translations, *Two Gardens: Modern Hebrew Poems of the Bible*, was published by Singing Bone Press in 2016.

Albert Goldbarth has published more than 30 collections of poetry and essays. He won the National Book Critics Circle Award in both

1991 and 2001 and is the only poet to have received this honor twice. His forthcoming book of essays, *The Adventures of Form and Content*, will be released in 2017 by Graywolf Press.

Beckian Fritz Goldberg is the author of seven books of poetry, *Body Betrayer* (Cleveland State University Press, 1991), *In the Badlands of Desire* (CSU, l993), *Never Be the Horse*, winner of the University of Akron Poetry Prize (U. of Akron Press, 1999), *Twentieth-Century Children*, winner of the *Indiana Review* chapbook prize (Graphic Design Press, 1999), *Lie Awake Lake*, winner of the 2004 FIELD Poetry Prize (Oberlin College Press, 2005), *The Book of Accident* (U. of Akron Press, 2006), *Reliquary Fever: New and Selected Poems* (New Issues Press, 2010), and *Egypt From Space* (Oberlin, 2013). She has won the Theodore Roethke Poetry Prize from *Poetry Northwest*, the *Gettysburg Review* Annual Poetry Prize, two Arizona Commission on the Arts Poetry Fellowships, and two Pushcart Prizes. Her work has appeared in anthologies such as *American Alphabets: 25 Contemporary Poets* and *Best American Poetry*, and in journals including *APR, FIELD, The Gettysburg Review, Harper's, The Iowa Review, Michigan Quarterly Review* and *Gulf Coast*. She lives in Arizona.

Kathleen Graber is the author of two collections of poetry, *The Eternal City* (2010) and *Correspondence* (2006). She is an Associate Professor of English at Virginia Commonwealth University.

Paul Guest is the author of three collections of poetry and one memoir. His poems have appeared in *Poetry, Paris Review, Southern Review, Kenyon Review, Tin House*, and elsewhere. A Guggenheim Fellow and Whiting Award winner, he teaches in the Creative Writing Program at the University of Virginia.

Richard Gwyn is a poet, novelist and translator who grew up in Breconshire, Wales, and studied anthropology at the LSE and then in countless bars, roadhouse cafés, dosshouses and A & E departments across Europe. He returned to his homeland in 1990 and completed a

PhD in Linguistics at Cardiff University, where he is Professor in English Literature. His books include *The Colour of a Dog Running Away, Deep Hanging Out, Sad Giraffe Café,* and *The Vagabond's Breakfast.* He has spent the last four years preparing and translating a major anthology of contemporary Latin American poetry, *The Other Tiger* (Seren, 2016).

Marilyn Hacker is the author of thirteen books of poems, including *A Stranger's Mirror* (W. W. Norton, 2015), *Names* (W. W. Norton, 2010) and *Desesperanto* (W. W. Norton, 2003), an essay collection, *Unauthorized Voices* (Michigan, 2010), and fourteen collections of translations of French and Francophone poets including Emmanuel Moses, Marie Etienne, Vénus Khoury-Ghata, Habib Tengour and Rachida Madani. *DiaspoRenga,* a collaborative sequence written with the Palestinian-American poet Deema Shehabi, was published by Holland Park Press in 2014. Her translations of contemporary Arabic poetry and prose have appeared in *Words Without Borders, AGNI, Critical Muslim,* and *A Public Space.* She lives in Paris.

Rachel Hadas is Board of Governors Professor of English at Rutgers-Newark. Her book of prose, *Talking to the Dead,* was published in 2015 by Spuyten Duyvil Press; a new book of poems, *Questions in the Vestibule,* was published in April 2016 by Northwestern University Press. Her translations of Euripides' plays *Iphigenia in Aulis* and *Iphigenia among the Taurians* will also be published by Northwestern.

Barbara Hamby is the author of five books of poems, most recently *On the Street of Divine Love: New and Selected Poems* (2014) published by the University of Pittsburgh Press, which also published *Babel* (2004) and *All-Night Lingo Tango* (2009). She was a 2010 Guggenheim fellow in Poetry and her book of short stories, *Lester Higata's 20th Century,* won the 2010 Iowa Short Fiction Award. Her poems have appeared in many magazines, including *The New Yorker, Poetry, APR, Ploughshares,* and *Yale Review.* She has also edited an anthology of poems, *Seriously Funny* (Georgia, 2009), with her husband David Kirby. She teaches at Florida State University where she is Distinguished University Scholar.

Andrew J. Hauner was born in New York to Czech émigrés; having studied Romance Philology at Charles University in Prague, he lives in New York and translates and writes both literary and academic texts.

Jennifer Michael Hecht's most recent poetry book is *Who Said* (Copper Canyon, 2013). Her poetry appears in *The New Yorker, Poetry, The New York Times*, and *Kenyon Review*. Her first poetry book, *The Next Ancient World* (Tupelo, 2001) won the Poetry Society of America's Norma Farber award. Her second, *Funny*, won the Felix Pollack award from Wisconsin. She writes reviews for *American Poets*, the journal of the Academy of American Poets. Hecht also writes history and philosophy. She holds a PhD from Columbia University (1995) in the History of Science and European Cultural History. She wrote *Doubt: A History* (HarperOne, 2003), a history of unbelief; *The End of the Soul* (Columbia, 2003), which won Phi Beta Kappa's Ralph Waldo Emerson Award in Intellectual History; and *Stay* (Yale, 2013), a history of suicide and the arguments against it. She is writing *The Wonder Paradox*, a prose book on poetry and our modern life (FSG).

Bob Hicok's latest book, *Elegy Owed* (Copper Canyon, 2013), was a finalist for the National Book Critics Circle Award. *Sex & Love &* was published by Copper Canyon in 2016.

Born and raised in Milledgeville, Georgia, **Sean Hill** is the author of *Dangerous Goods*, awarded the Minnesota Book Award in Poetry, (Milkweed Editions, 2014) and *Blood Ties & Brown Liquor*, named one of the Ten Books All Georgians Should Read in 2015 by the Georgia Center for the Book, (UGA Press, 2008). His awards include fellowships from Cave Canem, the Region 2 Arts Council, the Bush Foundation, Minnesota State Arts Board, The Jerome Foundation, The MacDowell Colony, the University of Wisconsin, a Stegner Fellowship from Stanford University, and a Creative Writing Fellowship from the National Endowment for the Arts. His poems have appeared in *Callaloo, Harvard Review, Oxford American, Poetry, Tin House* and elsewhere, and in anthologies including *Black Nature* and *Villanelles*.

Hill is a consulting editor at Broadsided Press and an assistant professor in the Creative Writing Program at UA–Fairbanks.

Tony Hoagland's most recent book of poems, *Application for Release from the Dream*, was published by Graywolf Press in 2015. His next collection, *Proof of Life*, is scheduled for 2018. He has published two collections of essays about poetry. and he has poems forthcoming in *Paris Review, Ploughshares, APR*, and *Prairie Schooner*. He teaches at U of H in Houston.

Cynthia Hogue has nine collections of poetry, most recently *Revenance* (2014) and the about-to-be-published *In June the Labyrinth*. She has two collections of translations (with Sylvain Gallais), including *Joan Darc* by Nathalie Quintane (La Presse, 2017). Her poems and translations have appeared recently in *Field, Poetry International, Crazyhorse, Prairie Schooner, Kestrel*, and *Best American Poetry 2016*. She holds the Maxine and Jonathan Marshall Chair in Modern and Contemporary Poetry at Arizona State University.

Paul Hoover has fifteen books of poetry including *Desolation: Souvenir* (Omnidawn, 2012) and *Sonnet 56* (Les Figues, 2009). His translations include, with Maxine Chernoff, *Selected Poems of Friedrich Hölderlin* (Omnidawn, 2008); with Nguyen Do, *Black Dog, Black Night: An Anthology of Contemporary Vietnamese Poetry* (Milkweed, 2008); and with Maria Baranda, *The Complete Poems of San Juan de la Cruz* (Milkweed, 2017). He also has two volumes in the Spanish translation of Maria Baranda: *En el idioma y en la tierra* (Conaculta, Mexico City, 2012) and *La intención y su materia* (Monte Avila Editores, 2012). He lives in Mill Valley, CA, and teaches in the Creative Writing Department at San Francisco State University.

David Huddle is from Ivanhoe, Virginia, and he taught at the University of Vermont for 38 years. His fiction, poetry, and essays have appeared in *The American Scholar, Esquire, The New Yorker, Harper's, Shenandoah*, and *Georgia Review*. In 2012 his novel *Nothing Can Make*

Me Do This won the Library of Virginia Award for Fiction, and his collection *Black Snake at the Family Reunion* won the 2013 Pen New England Award for Poetry. His most recent books are *Dream Sender*, a poetry collection published in 2015 by LSU Press, and a novel, *My Immaculate Assassin*, published in September 2016 by Tupelo Press.

T. R. Hummer's twelfth book of poems, *Eon*—which completes a three-book project ten years in the making—will appear from LSU Press in 2018.

Mark Irwin's eighth collection of poetry, *American Urn: New & Selected Poems (1987–2014)* was published in 2015. *A Passion According to Green* will appear from New Issues in spring of 2017. He has also translated two volumes of poetry. Awards include *The Nation*/ Discovery Award, two Colorado Book Awards, four Pushcart Prizes, the James Wright Poetry Award, and fellowships from the Fulbright, Lilly, NEA, and Wurlitzer Foundations. He is an associate professor in the PhD in Creative Writing & Literature Program at the University of Southern California and lives in Los Angeles and Colorado.

Mark Jarman is the author of eleven books of poetry, the most recent of which is *The Heronry* (Sarabande Books, 2017). He has also published two collections of his prose, *The Secret of Poetry* (Story Line Press, 2000) and *Body and Soul: Essays on Poetry* (University of Michigan Press, 2001). He is Centennial Professor of English at Vanderbilt University.

Troy Jollimore's most recent collection of poetry, *Syllabus of Errors*, was one of the *New York Times* ten best poetry books of 2015. His other poetry books are *Tom Thomson in Purgatory* (2006), which won the National Book Critics Circle Award, and *At Lake Scugog* (2011). His poems have appeared in publications including *The New Yorker, Poetry, The Believer, McSweeney's*, and *Subtropics*. He has been an External Faculty Fellow at the Stanford Humanities Center, the Stanley P. Young Poetry Fellow at the Bread Loaf Writers' Conference, and a Guggenheim fellow.

Pierre Joris most recently published *The Agony of I. B.* (a play commissioned & produced in June 2016 by the Théatre National du Luxembourg; Editions PHI); *An American Suite* (early poems; inpatient press 2016); *Barzakh: Poems 2000–2012* (Black Widow Press 2014); & *Breathturn into Timestead: The Collected Later Poetry of Paul Celan* (FSG 2014). When not on the road, he lives in Sorrentinostan, a.k.a. Bay Ridge, Brooklyn, with his wife, multimedia performance artist and writer Nicole Peyrafitte.

Marilyn Kallet has published seventeen books, including *The Love That Moves Me*, poetry from Black Widow Press. She has translated Eluard's *Last Love Poems*, Péret's *The Big Game*, and has recently co-edited and co-translated Chantal Bizzini's *Disenchanted City* (with J. Bradford Anderson and Darren Jackson.) She is Nancy Moore Goslee Professor at the University of Tennessee–Knoxville, and she also teaches poetry workshops for VCCA–France in Auvillar. She has performed her poems on campuses and in theaters across the U.S. and in France and Poland, as a guest of the U.S. Embassy.

Christopher Kennedy is the author of *Ennui Prophet* (BOA Editions), *Encouragement for a Man Falling to His Death* (BOA Editions), which received the Isabella Gardner Poetry Award in 2007, *Trouble with the Machine* (Low Fidelity Press), and *Nietzsche's Horse* (Mitki/Mitki Press). His work has appeared in many print and online journals and magazines, including *Plume, New York Tyrant, Ninth Letter, Wigleaf, The Threepenny Review, Mississippi Review, Ploughshares*, and *McSweeney's*. In 2011, he was awarded an NEA Fellowship for Poetry. He is a professor of English at Syracuse University where he directs the MFA Program in Creative Writing.

Yasser Khanjer was born in 1977 in the village of Majdal Shams in the occupied Golan Heights. He was imprisoned from 1997 till 2005 by the Israeli authorities, on charges of resisting the occupation. His first collection of poems, *Freedom Bird*, was published in Beirut during his incarceration : a fourth will be published in Milan in 2017.

John Kinsella's new collection of poetry is *Firebreaks* (W. W. Norton, 2016). He is a Fellow of Churchill College, Cambridge University, and Professor of Literature and Sustainability at Curtin University.

Dore Kiesselbach is an Oberlin College, Iowa Writers' Workshop, and New York University School of Law graduate. His first collection, *Salt Pier* (2102), received the Agnes Lynch Starrett Prize and appeared in the Pitt Poetry Series. Other honors include the Poetry Society of America's Robert H. Winner Memorial Award, an Artist Initiative grant from the Minnesota State Arts Board, a U.S. Department of Education Jacob Javits Fellowship in creative writing, a National Endowment for the Humanities Younger Scholar Award, and Britain's Bridport International Writing Prize in poetry. His second collection, *Albatross*, is forthcoming from Pittsburgh this fall.

David Kirby's collection *The House on Boulevard St.: New and Selected Poems* was a finalist for the National Book Award in 2007. Kirby is the author of *Little Richard: The Birth of Rock 'n' Roll*, which the *Times Literary Supplement of London* called "a hymn of praise to the emancipatory power of nonsense." His new poetry collection from LSU Press is *Get Up, Please*. davidkirby.com.

Karl Kirchwey's seventh book, *Stumbling Blocks: Roman Poems*, will be published in fall 2017 by TriQuarterly/Northwestern University Press. He is working on translations of the Italian poet Giovanni Giudici (1924–2011). His translation of Paul Verlaine's first book is *Poems Under Saturn* (Princeton University Press, 2011). A Professor of English and Creative Writing at Boston University, he was Andrew Heiskell Arts Director at the American Academy in Rome (2010–2013) and for many years directed and taught in the Creative Writing Program at Bryn Mawr College. He received the 2015 Classics Conclave Cato Prize for Poetry from the Institute for Digital Archeology.

Jennifer L. Knox is the author of four books of poems. Her work has appeared four times in *The Best American Poetry* series as well as in

The New York Times, The New Yorker, and *APR. The New York Times Book Review* said her new book, *Days of Shame and Failure,* "hits, with deceptive ease, all the poetic marks a reader could want: intellectual curiosity, emotional impact, beautiful language, surprising revelation and arresting imagery." Jennifer is a 2017 Iowa Arts Council Fellow and the curator of the Iowa Bird of Mouth project. She teaches at Iowa State University.

Steve Kronen's collections are *Splendor* (BOA), and *Empirical Evidence* (University of Georgia). His work has appeared in *New Republic, Paris Review, Yale Review, New Statesman, American Scholar, APR, Poetry,* and *Little Star.* His awards include an NEA, three Florida Individual Artist fellowships, and the Boatwright Prize for Poetry from *Shenandoah.* He recently completed two manuscripts, *Gimme That. Don't Smite Me,* and a collection of translations/versions, *Cain on the Moon.* stevekronen.com

Sydney Lea's twelfth poetry collection is *No Doubt the Nameless* (Four Way Books, 2015). His fourth volume of personal essay, *What's the Story? Reflections on a Life Grown Long* appeared from Green Writers Press in 2016. Founder and longtime editor of *New England Review,* he was Poet Laureate of Vermont from 2011 to 2015.

David Lehman is the author of nine books of poetry, including *Poems in the Manner Of,* which Scribner will publish in March 2017. His *New and Selected Poems* appeared from Scribner in 2013. The most recent of Lehman's eight books of nonfiction are *Sinatra's Century: One Hundred Notes on the Man and His World* (HarperCollins) and *The State of the Art: A Chronicle of American Poetry, 1988–2014* (University of Pittsburgh Press), both published in 2015. Lehman is the editor of *The Oxford Book of American Poetry* and series editor of *The Best American Poetry,* which he launched in 1988. He teaches in the graduate writing program of the New School in New York City.

Phillis Levin's fifth collection, *Mr. Memory & Other Poems,* was published by Penguin in 2016. She is the author of four other collections, *Temples and Fields* (U. of Georgia Press, 1988), *The Afterimage* (Copper Beech Press, 1995), *Mercury* (Penguin, 2001), and *May Day* (Penguin, 2008), and is editor of *The Penguin Book of the Sonnet* (2001). Her honors include the PSA Norma Farber First Book Award, a Fulbright Scholar Award to Slovenia, the Amy Lowell Poetry Travelling Scholarship, and fellowships from the Guggenheim Foundation, the Bogliasco Foundation, and the National Endowment for the Arts. Her work has appeared in *Poetry, The New Yorker, Paris Review, AGNI, The Atlantic, Southwest Review, Yale Review, New Republic, Literary Imagination, Kenyon Review*, and *The Best American Poetry*. She teaches at Hofstra University and lives in New York City.

Frannie Lindsay's fifth poetry volume is *If Mercy* (Word Works, 2016). Her previous volumes have all won press prizes. She has held fellowships from the National Endowment for the Arts and the Massachusetts Cultural Council. Her work has appeared in *The Atlantic, APR, Yale Review, Georgia Review, Field, Crazyhorse, Harvard Review, Salamander*, and many others. She was awarded the 2008 *Missouri Review* prize in poetry, and one of her poems appears in *Best American Poetry 2014*. It has also been featured in Ted Kooser's syndicated column, *American Life in Poetry*, on Garrison Keillor's *Writer's Almanac*, and on *Poetry Daily*. She is also a classical pianist, and is active in greyhound rescue.

Paul Lisicky is the author of five books: *The Narrow Door* (a *New York Times* Editors' Choice), *Unbuilt Projects, The Burning House, Famous Builder*, and *Lawnboy*. His work has appeared in *The New York Times, The Atlantic, Conjunctions, Fence, The Offing, Ploughshares, Tin House*, and elsewhere. He has received fellowships from the Guggenheim Foundation, the National Endowment for the Arts, and the Fine Arts Work Center in Provincetown, among others. He teaches in the MFA Program at Rutgers University-Camden.

Timothy Liu's most recent book of poems is *Don't Go Back To Sleep*. For his upcoming sabbatical, he will be retracing the Mormon trail. timothyliu.net

William Logan's most recent book of poetry is *Madame X* (Penguin, 2011). A volume of new poems, *Rift of Light*, will be out in 2017. He has published ten books of poetry and six of essays and reviews. *The Undiscovered Country* won the National Book Critics Circle Award in Criticism. He teaches at the University of Florida and lives in Gainesville, Florida, and Cambridge, England.

Adrian C. Louis grew up in northern Nevada and is an enrolled member of the Lovelock Paiute Tribe. From 1984 to 1997, Louis taught at Oglala Lakota College on the Pine Ridge Reservation in SD. He recently retired as Professor of English at Southwest Minnesota State. Pleiades Press published his latest book of poems, *Random Exorcisms*, in 2016. More info at Adrian-C-Louis.com

Nathaniel Mackey is the author of six books of poetry, the most recent of which is *Blue Fasa* (New Directions, 2015); an ongoing prose work, *From a Broken Bottle Traces of Perfume Still Emanate*, whose fifth and most recent volume is *Late Arcade* (New Directions, 2017); and two books of criticism, the most recent of which is *Paracritical Hinge: Essays, Talks, Notes, Interviews* (University of Wisconsin Press, 2005). *Strick: Song of the Andoumboulou 16-25*, a CD of poems read with musical accompaniment (Royal Hartigan, percussion; Hafez Modirzadeh, reeds and flutes), was released in 1995 by Spoken Engine Company. He is the editor of the literary magazine *Hambone* and co-editor, with Art Lange, of the anthology *Moment's Notice: Jazz in Poetry and Prose* (Coffee House Press, 1993). His awards include the National Book Award for poetry, the Stephen Henderson Award from the African American Literature and Culture Society, a Guggenheim Fellowship, the Ruth Lilly Poetry Prize, and the Bollingen Prize for American Poetry. He is Reynolds Price Professor of English at Duke University.

Amit Majmudar is a novelist, essayist, diagnostic nuclear radiologist, and the first Poet Laureate of Ohio. His latest collection is *Dothead* (Knopf, 2016). His forthcoming book is a verse translation of the Bhagavad-Gita, *Godsong* (Knopf, 2018).

Maurice Manning's sixth book of poems is *One Man's Dark* (Copper Canyon, 2017). Manning's first book, Lawrence Booth's *Book of Visions* was selected by W. S. Merwin for the Yale Series of Younger Poets. His fourth book, *The Common Man*, was a finalist for the Pulitzer Prize. Manning teaches at Transylvania University and in the MFA Program for Writers at Warren Wilson College. He and his family live on a small farm in Kentucky.

Gail Mazur's seventh collection, *Forbidden City*, was published by University of Chicago Press in 2016. *They Can't Take That Away from Me* was a finalist for the National Book Award, and *Zeppo's First Wife* was awarded the Massachusetts Book Prize. A member of the Fine Arts Work Center in Provincetown Writing Committee, she is the founder of the Blacksmith House Poetry Series in Cambridge, Massachusetts, and long-time Senior Writer in Residence at Emerson College She is Visiting Faculty in Boston University's Creative Writing Program.

J. D. McClatchy is the author of eight collections of poems, most recently *Plundered Hearts: New and Selected Poems* (Knopf, 2014). He has also written four volumes of prose, including *Sweet Theft: A Poet's Commonplace Book* (Counterpoint, 2016), and edited dozens of other books; the latest a new selection of Howard Moss's poems from Sheep Meadow Press this spring. In addition, he has written eighteen librettos that have been performed in leading opera houses around the world. He teaches at Yale and serves as editor of *Yale Review*.

Philip Metres is the author of *Pictures at an Exhibition* (2016), *Sand Opera* (2015), *I Burned at the Feast: Selected Poems of Arseny Tarkovsky* (2015), *A Concordance of Leaves* (2013), *To See the Earth* (2008) and others. He has won a Lannan fellowship, two NEAs, six Ohio Arts Council Grants, the Hunt Prize for Excellence in Journalism, Arts & Letters, the Beatrice Hawley Award, two Arab American Book Awards, the Watson Fellowship, the Creative Workforce Fellowship, the Cleveland Arts Prize, and a PEN/Heim Translation Fund grant. He is professor of English at John Carroll University in Cleveland. philipmetres.com

Elizabeth Metzger is the Poetry Editor of the *Los Angeles Review of Books Quarterly Journal*. She won the 2013 *Narrative* Poetry Contest and was listed as one of *Narrative*'s 30 Under 30. Her poetry has recently appeared in *The New Yorker, Kenyon Review Online, BOMB, Yale Review, Guernica,* and *Best New Poets 2015*. Her essays and reviews appear in *PN Review*, the *Southwest Review*, and *Boston Review*. Her debut collection, *The Spirit Papers*, won the 2016 Juniper Prize (U. of Massachusetts Press, 2017). Her chapbook *The Nutshell Studies of Unexplained Death* will be published by Horsethief Books in 2017. She has taught writing at Columbia University, where she received her MFA.

Joseph Millar's third collection, *Blue Rust*, was published by Carnegie-Mellon in 2012. A fourth collection, *Kingdom*, is due out in 2017 from the same publisher. His poems have won fellowships from the Guggenheim Foundation (2012), the NEA (2002), and a Pushcart Prize. Millar teaches in Pacific University's MFA program and spends his time between Raleigh, NC, and Richmond, CA.

Nancy Mitchell is a 2012 Pushcart Prize winner and the author of *The Near Surround* (Four Way Books, 2002) and *Grief Hut* (Cervena Barva Press, 2009). Her recent poems appear, or will soon appear, in *Poetry Daily, AGNI, Washington Square Review, Green Mountains Review, Tar River Poetry, Columbia College Literary Review,* and *Thrush,* among others. Mitchell teaches at Salisbury University and serves as the Associate Editor of Special Features for *Plume*.

Carol Muske-Dukes is the author of 8 books of poems, four novels, two essay collections & has co-edited anthologies. Her books have been *New York Times* Most Notable Books & she has received the Castagnola Award, Dylan Thomas prize, six Pushcarts, Guggenheim, and the Barnes & Noble Writer for Writers award. She was California Poet Laureate 2008–2011, poetry columnist for the *LA Times*—also writes for the *New York Times* and *The New Yorker*. She is professor of English/Creative Writing at the University of Southern California, where she founded the PhD Program in Creative Writing/Literature.

She is making a film, with others, based on the ancient Greek poet Sappho as a time traveler. carolmuskedukes.com

Robert Nazarene is the founding editor of *The American Journal of Poetry*, theamericanjournalofpoetry.com. In 2006, as editor-in-chief and publisher of *MARGIE*, he published the winning volume for the National Book Critics Circle Award in poetry: *Tom Thomson in Purgatory*, by Troy Jollimore. He is the author of two collections of poems, *CHURCH* (2006) and *Empire de la Mort*, (2017). He was educated at The McDonough School of Business at Georgetown University—barely.

D. Nurkse is the author of ten poetry collections, most recently *A Night in Brooklyn*, which Knopf will reissue in paperback in 2016. He's the recipient of a Literature Award from the American Academy of Arts and Letters.

Jennifer O'Grady is a poet and playwright. Her first book, *White*, won the Mid-List Press First Series Award for Poetry and a Greenwall Fund grant from The Academy of American Poets. Her poems have appeared in numerous places including *Harper's, The Writer's Almanac, Poetry, Yale Review, Kenyon Review, Georgia Review, Poetry Daily*, and *New Republic*. Her plays have been produced and selected for *The Best Ten-Minute Plays 2017, The Best Women's Stage Monologues 2017, The Best Ten-Minute Plays 2016*, and *The Best Women's Stage Monologues 2014* (all Smith and Kraus) as well as *Best Contemporary Monologues for Women 18–35* (Applause). She lives near New York City with her husband, son, and daughter. A new collection of poetry, *Exclusions and Limitations*, is seeking a publisher. jenniferogrady.net

William Olsen has published five collections of poetry, including *Sand Theory*. A new collection, *TechnoRage*, will be released this year. He lives in Kalamazoo.

Dzvinia Orlowsky is the author of five collections of poetry from Carnegie Mellon University Press, including *A Handful of Bees*, reprinted in 2009 as a Carnegie Mellon Classic Contemporary; *Convertible Night, Flurry of Stones*, recipient of a 2010 Sheila Motton Book Award; and her most recent, *Silvertone*. Her translation from Ukrainian of Alexander Dovzhenko's novella, *The Enchanted Desna*, was published by House Between Water in 2006; and Jeff Friedman's and her translation of *Memorials* by Polish poet Mieczyslaw Jastrun was published by Dialogos in 2014. She is a Founding Editor of Four Way Books, a recipient of a Pushcart Prize, a Massachusetts Cultural Council poetry grant, and recipient with Jeff Friedman of a 2016 NEA Translation Grant. She teaches at the Solstice Low-Residency MFA for Creative Writing Program of Pine Manor College; as Special Lecturer in Creative Writing at Providence College; and serves as Editor for Poetry in Translation for *Solstice Literary Magazine*.

Gregory Orr's most recent collection is *River Inside the River* (W. W. Norton, 2013). His prose text *A Primer for Poets and Readers of Poetry* will appear next year from W. W. Norton.

Kathleen Ossip is the author of *The Do-Over*, a *New York Times* Editors' Choice; *The Cold War*, which was one of *Publishers Weekly*'s best books of 2011; *The Search Engine*, selected by Derek Walcott for the *APR*/Honickman First Book Prize; and *Cinephrastics*, a chapbook of movie poems. Her poems have appeared in *Best American Poetry, Best American Magazine Writing*, the *Washington Post, Paris Review, Poetry, The Believer, A Public Space*, and *Poetry Review* (London). She teaches at The New School in New York, and she is the editor of the poetry review website *SCOUT*. She has received a fellowship from the New York Foundation for the Arts, and she is a 2016–2017 Fellow at the Radcliffe Institute for Advanced Study, Harvard University.

Alicia Ostriker is a poet and critic. Her thirteenth poetry collection, *The Book of Seventy*, received the 2009 National Jewish Book Award for Poetry; *The Book of Life: Selected Jewish Poems 1979–2011* received a Paterson Lifetime Achievement Award in 2013. She has also received awards from the Poetry Society of America, the San Francisco Poetry

Center, the Guggenheim foundation and the Rockefeller Foundation among others. Her most recent book of poems is *The Old Woman, the Tulip, and the Dog.* As a critic, Ostriker is the author of *Stealing the Language: the Emergence of Women's Poetry in America*, and has published several other books on poetry and on the Bible. She is Professor Emerita of Rutgers University, lives in Princeton, NJ, and NYC, and teaches in the Low-Residency MFA Program of Drew University.

Michael Palma is an Italian-American author and translator who lives in Vermont. His poetry collections in English include *The Egg Shape* (Archival Press, 1972), *A Fortune in Gold* (Gradiva, 2000) and *Begin in Gladness* (Star Cloud Press, 2011). His many translations of modern Italian poets include the prize-winning volumes of Guido Gozzano, *The Man I Pretend To Be*, and Diego Valeri, *My Name on the Wind*, both published by Princeton University Press. He has contributed translations to Luciano Erba's *The Metaphysical Streetcar Conductor* (Gradiva, 1998) and Alfredo de Palchi's *Addictive Aversions* (Xenos Books, 1999) and *Paradigm* (Chelsea Editions, 2013). His rhymed translation of Dante's *Inferno* was published by W. W. Norton in 2002 and reissued as a Norton Critical Edition in 2007.

Jay Parini, a poet and novelist, teaches at Middlebury College. His most recent book is *New and Collected Poems, 1975–2015* (Beacon Press). His novels include *The Last Station* and *Benjamin's Crossing*. He has written biographies of Steinbeck, Frost, Faulkner, and Gore Vidal.

Linda Pastan's fourteenth book, *Insomnia*, has recently been published by W. W. Norton. She is a former Poet Laureate of Maryland, and in 2003 she won the Ruth Lily Prize for lifetime achievement.

Molly Peacock is the author of seven volumes of poetry, including *The Analyst* as well as *The Second Blush* and *Cornucopia* (all from W. W. Norton). Her poetry is widely anthologized, appearing in *The Oxford Book of American Poetry* as well as in leading literary journals such as *Poetry* and *The TLS*. She is the co-editor of *Poetry in Motion: 100*

Poems from the Subways and Buses and the Series Editor for *The Best Canadian Poetry in English*. She is also the author of the best-selling *The Paper Garden: Mrs. Delany Begins Her Life's Work at 72*, a biography and meditation on late-life creativity. Recently she has worked with illustrator Kara Kosaka on *Alphabetique: 26 Characteristic Fictions*.

Joyce Peseroff's fifth book of poems, *Know Thyself*, was named a "must-read" by the 2016 Massachusetts Book Awards. She is the author of *The Hardness Scale, A Dog in the Lifeboat, Mortal Education*, and *Eastern Mountain Time*. She edited *Robert Bly: When Sleepers Awake, The Ploughshares Poetry Reader*, and *Simply Lasting: Writers on Jane Kenyon*. She was Distinguished Lecturer at the University of Massachusetts, Boston, where she directed the MFA Program for its first four years, and blogs on writing and literature at joycepeseroff.com.

Christina Pugh is the author of four books of poems, including *Perception* (Four Way Books, 2017) and *Grains of the Voice* (Northwestern University Press, 2013). Her poems have appeared in T*he Atlantic, Poetry, Ploughshares, Kenyon Review*, and many other periodicals. She was awarded a Guggenheim fellowship in poetry for 2015–2016 and a Bogliasco Foundation fellowship in 2016. Her previous awards have included the Lucille Medwick Award from the Poetry Society of America, a poetry fellowship from the Illinois Arts Council, and the Grolier Poetry Prize. She is a professor in the Program for Writers at the University of Illinois at Chicago, and consulting editor for *Poetry*.

Lia Purpura is the author of four books of poems, *It Shouldn't Have Been Beautiful* (Penguin/Viking, 2015), *King Baby, Stone Sky Lifting, The Brighter the Veil*; three books of essays (*Rough Likeness, On Looking, Increase*), and one book of translations (*Poems of Grzegorz Musial: Berliner Tagebuch and Taste of Ash*). She has received a Guggenheim Fellowship, an NEA Fellowship, a Fulbright Foundation Fellowship (Translation, Warsaw, Poland), three Pushcart Prizes, a grant from the Maryland State Arts Council, and multiple residencies and fellowships at the MacDowell Colony. Her poems and essays appear in *AGNI*,

Ecotone, FIELD, Georgia Review, Orion, New Republic, The New Yorker, Paris Review, Parnassus: Poetry in Review, Ploughshares, The Southern Review and many other magazines and anthologies.

Lawrence Raab's collection of poems, *What We Don't Know About Each Other*, won the National Poetry Series and was a Finalist for the 1993 National Book Award. Recent books include *The Probable World, Visible Signs: New & Selected Poems,* and *The History of Forgetting.* His newest collection is *Mistaking Each Other for Ghosts* (Tupelo, 2015), which was nominated for the National Book Award, and named one of the ten best poetry books of 2015 by the *New York Times.*

Barbara Ras was born in New Bedford, Massachusetts, and has lived in Costa Rica, Colombia, California, and Texas. She is the author of *The Last Skin* (2010), winner of the best poetry award from the Texas Institute of Letters; *One Hidden Stuff* (2006); and *Bite Every Sorrow* (1998), which was selected by C.K. Williams for the Walt Whitman Award. Ras is the recipient of numerous awards including the Kate Tufts Discovery Award and a Guggenheim fellowship. She has taught at the Warren Wilson MFA Program for Writers. She directs the Trinity University Press in San Antonio, Texas.

Donald Revell is the author of more than a dozen collections of poetry, most recently of *Drought-Adapted Vine* (Alice James Books, 2015). A former Fellow of the Guggenheim and Ingram Merrill Foundations, he has twice been awarded fellowships from the NEA. His other honors include the Academy of American Poets' Lenore Marshall Prize and three awards in Poetry and Translation from PEN USA. Revell is a Professor of English at the University of Nevada, Las Vegas/Black Mountain Institute.

Susan Rich is the author of four poetry collections including *Cloud Pharmacy, The Alchemist's Kitchen, Cures Include Travel,* and *The Cartographer's Tongue: Poems of the World* (White Pine). She is co-editor of *The Strangest of Theatres: Poets Crossing Borders,* and she has received awards from *The Times Literary Supplement,* Peace Corps Writers, PEN USA, Fulbright Foundation and Washington State Book Awards. Rich's poems have appeared in *Harvard Review, New England Review,* and elsewhere. Her work has been translated into Slovenian and Swedish.

Alberto Alvaro Ríos is the author of poetry books *A Small Story About the Sky* (2015), *The Dangerous Shirt* (2009), *The Theater of Night* (2006) and *The Smallest Muscle in the Human Body* (2002), nominated for the National Book Award, all from Copper Canyon; *Teodora Luna's Two Kisses* (W. W. Norton, 1990); *The Lime Orchard Woman* (1988), *Five Indiscretions* (1985) and *Whispering to Fool the Wind* (1982), which won the 1981 Walt Whitman Award, from Sheep Meadow Press. Other books include *Capirotada: A Nogales Memoir* (University of New Mexico Press, 1999), *The Curtain of Trees: Stories* (U. of New Mexico Press, 1999), *Pig Cookies and Other Stories* (Chronicle Books, 1995), and *The Iguana Killer: Twelve Stories of the Heart* (Blue Moon and Confluence Press, 1984), which won the Western States Book Award.

Max Ritvo (1990–2016) wrote *Four Reincarnations* (Milkweed, 2016) in New York and Los Angeles over the course of a long battle with cancer. He is also the author of the chapbook *Aeons,* chosen by Jean Valentine to receive the Poetry Society of America Chapbook Fellowship in 2014. Ritvo's poetry has appeared in *The New Yorker, Poetry,* and the *Boston Review,* and as a Poem-a-Day for Poets.org. His prose and interviews have appeared in publications such as *Lit Hub, Huffington Post,* and the *Los Angeles Review of Books.* He finished writing the poem "First Snowfall" on August 16, just a week before his death.

Hoyt Rogers is the author of a collection of poetry, *Witnesses,* and a volume of criticism, *The Poetics of Inconstancy.* His poems, stories, and essays have appeared in many periodicals. He has published dozens of French, German, Italian, and Spanish translations, including the *Selected Poems of Borges* and three books by Yves Bonnefoy: *The Curved Planks, Second Simplicity,* and *The Digamma.* With Paul Auster, he published *Openwork,* an André du Bouchet reader (Yale University Press, 2014).

He is translating Bonnefoy's *Rome 1630* and his last poetry collection, *Together Still*, for Seagull Books. He lives in the Dominican Republic and Italy.

Carnegie Mellon just re-published **Ira Sadoff**'s *Palm Reading in Winter* as part of their Contemporary Classics series. Since *True Faith* he has had work in *APR* and *Kenyon Review* and several anthologies. He lives in a converted barn in upstate NY.

Jerome Sala's books include *Corporations Are People, Too!* (forthcoming from NYQ Books), *The Cheapskates* (Lunar Chandelier) and *Look Slimmer Instantly* (Soft Skull Press). His poems and essays have appeared in *The Nation, Pleiades, Ploughshares, The Brooklyn Rail*, and *The Best American Poetry 2005*. His blog—on poetry, pop culture and everyday life—is espressobongo.typepad.com

Sherod Santos is the author of six books of poetry, most recently *The Intricated Soul: New and Selected Poems* (W. W. Norton). A new collection, *The Square Inch Hours*, is forthcoming in 2017. He is the recipient of the Theodore Roethke Memorial Prize and an Award in Literature from the American Academy of Arts and Letters. He lives in Chicago where he works in an outreach program for the homeless.

Lloyd Schwartz teaches in UMass Boston's MFA program. A Pulitzer Prize-winning critic, he writes about classical music, film, and the visual arts for NPR's *Fresh Air*, WBUR's *the ARTery*, and *New York Arts*. A noted Elizabeth Bishop scholar, he has edited three collections of and about her work. His poems have been selected for *Poetry Daily, the Pushcart Prize, Best American Poetry*, and *Best of the Best American Poetry*. His latest book of poems, *Little Kisses*, will be published this spring by the University of Chicago Press.

Born and raised in Boston, **Alan Shapiro** is the author of 13 books of poetry, including *Reel to Reel* and *Night of the Republic*, two memoirs (*The Last Happy Occasion* and *Vigil*), a novel (*Broadway Baby*), a book of critical essays (*In Praise of the Impure: Poetry and the Ethical Imagination*) and two translations (*The Oresteia* by Aeschylus and *The Trojan Women* by Euripides, both from Oxford University Press). His awards include the Kingsley Tufts Award, *LA Times* Book Prize, the O. B. Hardison Award from the Folger Shakespeare Library, the William Carlos Williams Award from the Poetry Society of America, an award in literature from The American Academy of Arts and Letters, 2 NEAs, a Guggenheim, and a Lila Wallace *Reader's Digest* Award. He is a member of the American Academy of Arts and Sciences. His new book of poems, *Life Pig*, was published in 2016 along with a book of essays, *That Self-Forgetful Perfectly Useless Concentration*, both from University of Chicago Press. He has taught at Stanford, Northwestern, Warren Wilson College, and is on the faculty at the U. of North Carolina where he is the William R. Kenan, Jr. Distinguished Professor of English and Creative Writing.

Betsy Sholl served as Poet Laureate of Maine from 2006 to 2011. Her eighth collection of poetry, *Otherwise Unseeable* (University of Wisconsin), won the 2015 Maine Literary Award for poetry. Other awards include the AWP Prize for Poetry, the Felix Pollak Prize, and grants from the National Endowment for the Arts and the Maine Arts Commission. She teaches in the MFA Program of Vermont College of Fine Arts, and lives in Portland, Maine.

Jeffrey Skinner is a Guggenheim Fellow in Poetry, and a recipient of a Literature Award from the American Academy of Arts & Letters. His most recent collection, *Chance Divine*, is a Field Prize winner, and will appear in February 2017. He is co-founder, with Sarah Gorham, of Sarabande Books, and even though born in Buffalo, New York, he is homesick for Switzerland.

Floyd Skloot's recent collections of poetry include *Approaching Winter* (2016), *The Snow's Music* (2008) and *The End of Dreams* (2006), all from LSU Press, which will publish his ninth collection, *Far West*, in 2019. His newest book is a novel, *The Phantom of Thomas Hardy*, published in 2016 by the University of Wisconsin Press.

Tara Skurtu is a Boston-based poet and translator living in Romania, where she is a 2015–2017 Fulbright lecturer at Transilvania University of Braşov. She is the recipient of two Academy of American Poets prizes, a Marcia Keach Poetry Prize, and a Robert Pinsky Global Fellowship. Her recent poems have appeared in *Kenyon Review, Poetry Review, Tahoma Literary Review*, and *Poetry Wales*. Tara is the author of the chapbook *Skurtu, Romania* (Eyewear Publishing 2016), and her debut poetry book *The Amoeba Game* is forthcoming from Eyewear in 2017.

Ron Slate has published two books of poetry, *The Incentive of the Maggot* and *The Great Wave*, both via Houghton Mifflin Harcourt. He reviews poetry and literature at the website On the Seawall and is a board member of Mass Humanities (NEH). He lives in Milton and Aquinnah, Massachusetts.

Tom Sleigh's books include *Army Cats*, winner of the John Updike Award from the American Academy of Arts and Letters, and *Space Walk*, which won the Kingsley Tufts Award. *Far Side of the Earth* won an Academy Award from the American Academy of Arts and Letters. His new book, *Station Zed*, was published by Graywolf in 2015. In 2018, a book of poems, *One War Everywhere*, will be published with a book of essays, *The Land Between Two Rivers: Poetry In an Age of Refugees*. He has also published a book of essays, *Interview With a Ghost*, and a translation of Euripides' *Herakles*. His poems and prose appear in *The New Yorker, Virginia Quarterly Review, Poetry, APR, Yale Review, Threepenny Review* and *The Village Voice*, as well as *The Best of the Best American Poetry, The Best American Poetry, Best American Travel Writing*, and the *Pushcart Anthology*. He has received the Shelley Prize from the Poetry Society of America, fellowships from the American Academy in Berlin and the Civitella Ranieri Foundation, and grants from the Lila Wallace Fund, the Guggenheim Foundation and the NEA, among others. He is a Distinguished Professor in the MFA Program at Hunter College and lives in Brooklyn. He also works as a journalist in Syria, Lebanon, Somalia, Kenya, Jordan, Iraq, and Libya.

Bruce Smith is the author of six books of poems, most recently *Devotions*, a finalist for the National Book Award, the National Book Critics Circle Award, the LA Times Book Award, and the winner of the William Carlos Williams Prize.

Patricia Smith is the author of seven books of poetry, including *Shoulda Been Jimi Savannah*, winner of the 2014 Rebekah Bobbitt Prize from the Library of Congress, the 2013 Lenore Marshall Poetry Prize from the Academy of American Poets and the Phillis Wheatley Award. Other books include *Blood Dazzler, Teahouse of the Almighty*, a National Poetry Series selection, and her most recent book, *Gotta Go Gotta Flow*, a collaboration with the late Chicago photographer Michael Abramson. Her work has appeared in *Poetry, Paris Review, The New York Times, TriQuarterly, Tin House*, the *Washington Post*, and in both *Best American Poetry* and *Best American Essays*. She is a 2014 Guggenheim fellow, a 2012 fellow at both MacDowell and Yaddo, a two-time Pushcart Prize winner, recipient of a Lannan fellowship and a four-time individual champion of the National Poetry Slam, the most successful poet in the competition's history. Her next poetry collection, *Incendiary Art*, will be released in February 2017; she is also working on a volume combining poetic monologues with 19th-century photos of African Americans, and a collaborative novel with her husband Bruce DeSilva, Edgar-Award winning author. She is a professor at the City University of New York/College of Staten Island and an instructor in the MFA program at Sierra Nevada College.

R. T. Smith is Writer-in-Residence at Washington and Lee University, where he has edited *Shenandoah* since 1995. He was previously Alumni Writer-in-Residence at Auburn University, where he assisted with and then edited *Southern Humanities Review*. He took his M.A. at Appalachian State University and founded *Cold Mountain Review*. In 2015 he returned to ASU as Rachel Rivers Coffee Distinguished Professor of Creative Writing. Smith is the author of over a dozen collections of poetry, with *In the Night Orchard: New and Selected Poems* (2014) as the most recent, and *Summoning Shades* forthcoming. His books have twice won the Library of Virginia Annual Poetry Award; in 2014 he received the Weinstein Prize for Poetry from the Library of Virginia. He is the author of five books of stories, with *Doves in Flight* forthcoming in 2017. He has received the Governor's Arts Award from Alabama for his writing and the Virginia Governor's Award for his work with *Shenandoah*. Smith lives on Timber Ridge in Rockbridge County with his wife, the novelist Sarah Kennedy, and their bluetick hound Gypsy, a dedicated student of the whitetail deer.

Ron Smith, Poet Laureate of Virginia from 2014 to 2016, is the author of four books of poems, *The Humility of the Brutes* (forthcoming in 2017 from Louisiana State University Press), *Its Ghostly Workshop* (LSU, 2013), *Moon Road: Poems 1986–2005* (LSU, 2007), and *Running Again in Hollywood Cemetery* (University Presses of Florida,1988). His first book was judged "a close runner-up" for the National Poetry Series Open Competition by Margaret Atwood. Smith has published poems in many magazines and anthologies. His critical prose and poetry columns can be found in *Kenyon Review, Georgia Review, Shenandoah, Blackbird, The Richmond Times-Dispatch*, and elsewhere.

Katherine Soniat's *Bright Stranger* was published in spring 2016 by Louisiana State University Press. Her fifth collection, *The Swing Girl* (LSU), was selected as Best Collection of 2011 by the Poetry Council of North Carolina, and *A Shared Life* won The Iowa Poetry Prize (U. of Iowa Press) and a Virginia Prize for Poetry. Other books include *A Raft, A Boat, A Bridge* (Dream Horse Press, 2012); *Alluvial* (Bucknell University Press); *Cracking Eggs* (University Presses of Florida). *Notes of Departure* received the Camden Poetry Prize. Chapbooks include *The Goodbye Animals*, winner of the *Turtle Island Quarterly* Chapbook Prize (Foothills Press, 2014), *Winter Toys* (Green Tower Press), and *The Fire Setters* (WebDelSol's Chapbook Series). She has won two Virginia Commission for the Arts Grants, a William Faulkner Award, a Jane Kenyon Award, Anne Stanford Award, and fellowships to Yaddo, the MacDowell Colony, and the Bread Loaf Writers Conference. Her work appears in such journals as *TriQuarterly, Poetry, Crazyhorse, Gettysburg*

Review, Antioch Review, New England Review, Kenyon Review, The Nation, New Republic, Georgia Review, and *Southern Review*.

Lisa Russ Spaar's most recent book of poems is *Vanitas, Rough*, and her fifth collection of poems, *Orexia*, is due out from Persea Books in early 2017. Among her edited volumes is the just-released *Monticello in Mind: 50 Contemporary Poems on Jefferson*. Her awards include a Guggenheim Fellowship and a Rona Jaffe Award for Emerging Women Writers. She is professor of English and Creative Writing at the University of Virginia and writes a regular column on second books of poetry for the *Los Angeles Review of Books*.

Born in Lawrenceburg, Tennessee, and raised in several small towns across the South, poet **Jane Springer** earned a PhD at Florida State University. Her debut poetry collection, *Dear Blackbird* (2007), won the Agha Shahid Ali Prize from the University of Utah Press. Her second collection, *Murder Ballad* (2012), received the Beatrice Hawley Award from Alice James Books. Her honors include a Whiting Writers' Award, a NEA grant, the Associated Writing Programs' AWP Intro Award, and the Robert Penn Warren Prize for Poetry. She lives in upstate New York and teaches at Hamilton College.

Page Hill Starzinger lives in New York City. Her first full-length poetry book, *Vestigial*, selected by Lynn Emanuel to win the Barrow Street Book Prize, was published in fall 2013. Her chapbook *Unshelter*, selected by Mary Jo Bang as winner of the Noemi contest, was published in 2009. Her poems have appeared in *Colorado Review, Fence, Kenyon Review, Pleiades, Volt* and many others.

Terese Svoboda's *When The Next Big War Blows Down The Valley: Selected and New Poems* (Anhinga Press) was published in 2015, *Anything that Burns You: A Portrait of Lola Ridge, Radical Poet* (Schaffner Press) in February 2016, *Professor Harriman's Steam Air-Ship* (Eyewear) in October 2016, and *Live Sacrifice*, a book of short stories, in 2017.

Brian Swann's most recent publications are *Companions, Analogies* (Sheep Meadow Press, 2016), poetry; *Dogs on the Roof* (MadHat Press, 2016), prose; *St. Francis and the Flies* (Autumn House Press, 2016), poetry; *Sky Loom: Native American Myth, Story, and Song* (University of Nebraska Press, 2014); and *In Late Light* (Johns Hopkins University Press, 2013), poetry.

Cole Swensen is the author of fifteen volumes of poetry, most recently *Landscapes on a Train* (Nightboat Books, 2015) and *Gravesend* (U. of California Press, 2012), and a volume of essays, *Noise That Stays Noise* (U. of Michigan Press, 2011).

Arthur Sze's books of poetry include *Compass Rose* (Copper Canyon, 2014), *The Ginkgo Light, Quipu,* and *The Redshifting Web*. A professor emeritus at the Institute of American Indian Arts, as well as a chancellor of the Academy of American Poets, he lives in Santa Fe, NM.

Adam Tavel is the author of *Plash & Levitation* (University of Alaska Press, 2015), winner of the Permafrost Book Prize, and *The Fawn Abyss* (Salmon Poetry, 2016). He is the reviews editor for *Plume*. adamtavel.com.

Daniel Tobin is the author of seven books of poems, most recently *Belated Heavens* (winner of the Massachusetts Book Award in Poetry), *The Net,* and *From Nothing,* as well as the critical studies *Passage to the Center* and *Awake in America: On Irish-American Poetry*. He is the editor of *The Book of Irish American Poetry from the Eighteenth Century to the Present, Light in Hand: Selected Early Poems of Lola Ridge, Poet's Work, Poet's Play,* and *The Collected Early Poems of Lola Ridge* (Spring 2017). His awards include fellowships from the National Endowment for the Arts and the John Simon Guggenheim Foundation.

William Trowbridge's graphic chapbook, *Oldguy: Superhero,* was published by Red Hen Press in 2016. A new full collection, *Vanishing Point,* is forthcoming from Red Hen in 2017. His other collections are *Put This On, Please: New and Selected Poems, Ship of Fool, The Complete*

Book of Kong, Flickers, O Paradise, and *Enter Dark Stranger.* He is a faculty mentor in the University of Nebraska–Omaha low-residency MFA in Writing Program and was Poet Laureate of Missouri 2012–2016. wiliamtrowbridge.net.

Chase Twichell's most recent book is *Horses Where the Answers Should Have Been: New & Selected Poems* (Copper Canyon, 2010), which won both the Kingsley Tufts Award from Claremont Graduate University and the Balcones Poetry Prize. A new book, *Now's Dream*, is forthcoming from the same press.

Lee Upton's most recent books are *Bottle the Bottles the Bottles the Bottles* from the Cleveland State University Poetry Center; *The Tao of Humiliation: Stories*, winner of the BOA Short Fiction Award, finalist for the Paterson Prize, and named one of the "best books of 2014" by Kirkus Review. In 2017 *Visitations: Stories* will be published in the Yellow Shoe Fiction Series, Louisiana State University Press. She is the Francis A. March Professor of English and Writer in Residence at Lafayette College.

Michael Van Walleghen is the author of six books of poetry, the most recent of which is *In the Black Window: Poems New and Selected* (2004). He has a Borestone Poetry Award and a Pushcart prize. His second book, *More Trouble with the Obvious* (1981), was the Lamont Poetry Selection of the Academy of American Poets. He has been the recipient of two National Endowment of the Arts fellowships and several grants from the Illinois Arts Council. He is recently retired from the University of Illinois at Urbana–Champaign.

Marc Vincenz is the author of nine books of poetry; his latest are *Becoming the Sound of Bees* (Ampersand Books, 2015) and *Sibylline* (Ampersand, 2016). He is also the translator of Romanian and German-language poets including Herman Hesse Prize winner Klaus Merz, Werner Lutz, Erica Burkart, Ion Monoran, Alexander Xaver Gwerder and Jürg Amman, and has published many books of translations—the latest is *Secret Letter* by

Erica Burkart. His translation of Klaus Merz's *Unexpected Development* is forthcoming from White Pine Press. His novella, *Three Taos of T'ao, or How to Catch a White Elephant,* is forthcoming from Spuyten Duyvil Press in 2017. He has received grants from the Swiss Arts Council and a fellowship from the Literarisches Colloquium Berlin. His own work has been translated into many languages.

Arthur Vogelsang's books of poetry include *A Planet* (Holt, 1983), *Twentieth Century Women* (University of Georgia Press, 1988), which was selected by John Ashbery for the Contemporary Poetry Series, *Cities and Towns* (University of Massachusetts Press, 1996), which received the Juniper Prize, *Expedition: New & Selected Poems* (Ashland Poetry Press, 2011), and *Orbit,* in the Pitt Poetry Series for 2016. He has appeared numerous times in *The Best American Poetry, The New Yorker, Poetry, The Pushcart Prize, Volt,* and *Zocalo Public Square.* He was co-editor of the Norton anthology *The Best Poetry From the* American Poetry Review. arthurvogelsang.com

Diane Vreuls has published a novel, a book of poems, a collection of short stories, and a children's book, as well as work in such magazines as *Commonweal, Paris Review,* and *The New Yorker. After Eden,* a new collection of poems, was released by Pinyon Press in 2015.

Sidney Wade is the author of *Straits & Narrows* (Persea Books, 2013). She teaches at the University of Florida and lives in Gainesville, Florida.

G. C. Waldrep's most recent books are a long poem, *Testament* (BOA Editions, 2015), and a chapbook, *Susquehanna* (Omnidawn, 2013). With Joshua Corey he edited *The Arcadia Project: North American Postmodern Pastoral* (Ahsahta, 2012). He lives in Lewisburg, PA, where he teaches at Bucknell University, edits the journal *West Branch,* and serves as Editor-at-Large for *Kenyon Review.*

Charles Harper Webb's latest book, *Brain Camp,* was published by the University of Pittsburgh Press in 2015. *A Million MFAs Are Not*

Enough, a collection of his essays on contemporary American poetry, is just out from Red Hen Press. Recipient of grants from the Whiting and Guggenheim foundations, Webb teaches Creative Writing at California State University, Long Beach.

Dara Wier's newest book coming in fall 2017 from Wave is *in the still of the night*, a sequence of poems of grief and salvation. Her books have won the San Francisco State Poetry Center's book of the year for *Reverse Rapture*, 2006 and been noted favorably on *The Believer*'s book of the year list, *You Good Thing*, 2014. Guggenheim and NEA grants have supported her work. She teaches workshops and form & theory seminars for the University of Massachusetts Amhert's MFA for poets and writers and co-directs its Juniper Institute and Summer Workshops. She edits and publishes for Factory Hollow Press and *jubilat*.

David Wojahn's ninth collection of poetry, *For the Scribe*, will appear from the University of Pittsburgh Press in early 2017. His previous collections include *World Tree* (Pittsburgh, 2011), which was the winner of the Lenore Marshall Prize from the Academy of American Poets, and *Interrogation Palace: New and Selected Poems* (Pittsburgh, 2006), which was a named finalist for the Pulitzer Prize. He teaches at Virginia Commonwealth University, and in the low-residency MFA in Writing Program of Vermont College of Fine Arts.

Hsia Yü is the author and designer of seven volumes of groundbreaking verse, most recently a book-length bilingual visual poem entitled *First Person*, as in the phrase "first-person narrative". She lives in Taipei, where she co-edits a journal of avant-garde writing known in English as *Poetry Now*.

Cynthia Zarin's most recent books are *The Ada Poems* (Knopf, 2010) and *An Enlarged Heart: A Personal History* (Knopf, 2013). Her new book of poems, *Orbit* (Knopf, 2017) will be published in March. She teaches at Yale.

CPSIA information can be obtained
at www.ICGtesting.com
Printed in the USA
FFHW011635041119
55887696-61768FF